Lloyd and Jennifer Laing

CELTIC BRITAIN AND IRELAND, AD 200-800

Lloyd and Jennifer Laing

CELTIC BRITAIN AND IRELAND, AD 200-800

The Myth of the Dark Ages

St. Martin's Press
New York

First published in the United States of America in 1990

Printed in Great Britain

ISBN 0-312-04767-3

BOMC offers recordings and compact discs, cassettes
and records. For information and catalog write to
BOMR, Camp Hill, PA 17012.

LIBRARY OF CONGRESS CATALOGING-IN-PUBLICATION DATA

Laing, Lloyd Robert.
  Celtic Britain and Ireland, AD 200-800: the myth of the Dark Ages
  Lloyd and Jennifer Laing.
    p.   cm.
  Includes bibliographical references (p.).
  ISBN 0-312-04767-3
    1. Great Britian–Antiquities, Celtic. 2. Great Britain – History – To 1066.
  3. Ireland – Antiquities, Celtic. 4. Ireland – History – To 1172. 5. Celts –
  Great Britain. 6. Celts – Ireland. 7. Britons.
  I. Laing, Jennifer. II. Title.

DA140, L34   199   90-32921
936. 1 – dc20   CIP

PREFACE

In 1975 L. Laing published *The Archaeology of Late Celtic Britain and Ireland c. 400-1200 AD*. This book, which is in a sense a sequel to that one, is not an 'update' of the 1975 study. A glance through the bibliography will show how much has been published in the last ten years or so. Instead, it is a selective book, which questions some of the underlying preconceptions about the Celtic 'Dark Ages'. It is accordingly intended for discussion, not as a statement of total conviction on all issues.

It is a pleasure to acknowledge the help received from others during its production. Professor Wendy Davies, Professor George Jobey and Dr Roger White read sections of it to its advantage, and David Longley offered helpful advice. We are grateful to the British Museum, Scunthorpe Borough Museum, Taunton Museum, Dr Joseph Raftery and particularly Dr Barry Raftery for providing illustrations. The remainder were mostly drawn by Marie Crook and Tasha Guest, sometimes based on originals by Libby Cryer.

We would also like to record our thanks to Dr A. P. Smyth, on whose prompting this book was written, and Irish Academic Press for their patience when it was overdue.

CONTENTS

LIST OF ILLUSTRATIONS

Acknowledgments for illustrations

The publisher and authors would like to thank Marie Crook for drawing figures 4, 12, 17, 28, 35, 37, 39, 40, 49 and 58, Libby Cryer for drawing the originals of figures 34 and 43, Tasha Guest for drawing figures 10, 11b, 13, 18, 23, 25, 27, 29, 33, 34, 36, 38, 42, 43, 45, 53 and 54, David Longley for figures 30 and 52; Barry Raftery for figures 6, 7, 8, 19, 20, 21 and 26, and Joseph Raftery for figure 50. Figures 9, 11a, 16, 22, 24, 31, 32, 41, 46, 47, 48 and 55 were drawn by L. Laing.

1

INTRODUCTION

The British Dark Ages were created as an historical concept because, from the point at which the Roman administration withdrew from Britannia in c.409, the documentary evidence all but ceased. The historical evidence for what happened in the next two centuries or so is limited to a few inscriptions and a random selection of writings, of which those of Gildas and Nennius are prominent, if retrospective.

It is significant to note that the idea that 'a light went out over Europe' was fostered, both at the time and in subsequent centuries, by people who generally had undergone a Classical education or were attempting to re-establish Classical ideals. Thus any cessation of the Roman Classical tradition was necessarily seen as heralding an end of any kind of 'civilized' life. Indeed, nowadays the term 'Dark Ages' is often used as one of abuse.

It is also notable that the departing Roman administration adhered to official Christian beliefs. The re-introduction of written evidence occurred with the coming of St Augustine in 597 on a Christian mission. As in other periods (notably the Viking raids) the descriptions of events are thus inevitably coloured by Christian viewpoints and also by a kind of intellectual snobbery in which phrases are used not for historical accuracy but for their close similarity to those of earlier writers.

The written evidence has been studied and discussed especially in the past twenty years and has been claimed as unreliable. Such are the problems involved in sorting out its accuracy that one prominent historian, Dumville, has argued that there is no reliable 'Celtic' history for the fifth and sixth centuries (1977).

While there is some justification in speaking of the 'Dark Ages' in the former Roman province of Britannia, since it is an ill-documented period following a well-documented one, the term is meaningless for those areas that lay beyond the frontiers of the Roman province, for which documentation had never existed. Indeed, the fifth and sixth century in these areas were not a 'Dark' Age but an historical 'Dawn', since this is precisely the time when documentary evidence starts to become available.

In order to get round this terminological problem, the term 'Early Christian' has often been used to describe many Celtic areas in the fifth-sixth centuries. Even this is inadequate, since many of the people were not necessarily Christians, simply the recipients of certain political/religious missions.

The development of archaeology widened the database considerably, but added new dimensions to the confusion. The material is consistently disobliging — although we are told in the historical sources that, for example, kingdoms developed in the fifth-sixth centuries, the archaeological and art-historical evidence does not often bear any relationship to this fact. Material frequently displays a longer or shorter currency than convenient for our historical presuppositions.

Simply because the archaeological evidence suggests that there is continued used of a type of pottery, no destruction of houses and no mass graves, during a period the historians tell us was cataclysmic, it should not be inferred that either the archaeologist or the historian is wrong. In modern terms, it is clearly impossible to distinguish a person's politics from their car, house, garden, clothes, even their name or title. Whilst these may point us to certain conclusions, they may equally be false conclusions. Nor do we throw out the family teaset and buy new if there is a change of government.

The archaeological evidence frequently insists that society was solid and unpeturbed by the upheavals described in historical sources. However, one might surmise that the vehemence with which the Dark Age writers were able to express themselves was only supported *because* the society in which they operated was relatively stable with roots deep in antiquity. Thus both sources can be regarded as a reasonable reflection of what they record.

The most difficult battle of the Dark Ages must be fought nowadays: against previous scholarly attitudes and approaches. There can be no doubt that the Dark Ages attract their followers partly due to their own view of themselves. Like that of Greece, the British and Irish 'Dark Age' was an Heroic age. Contemporary poems both Celtic and Saxon, speak of heroes, battles, treachery and sorcery that are much at variance with the prosaic finds made in excavation, or the settlement types. The **Gododdin** poem, a seventh-century verse epic by the Welsh poet Aneurin ('the oldest Scottish poem' in the words of Professor K.H. Jackson, 1969) tells of a daring and tragic cavalry raid from Edinburgh to what is now Yorkshire. It conjures up a world that is very difficult to identify in archaeological terms: certainly archaeology has not produced the 'gold torcs' and 'dark-blue armour' Aneurin described. Alas, we cannot dig up heroics and take them home with us.

Not only 'Dark Age' writings but medieval romances cloud the issue: one suspects that concepts from Mallory and Arthurian romance creep in, sometimes simply in order to infuse the text with some 'readability'. Professor Fowler, writing otherwise objectively about reoccupied hillforts showed how this colours thinking when he remarked 'Arthur may not be under every stone, but there were many knights in the Dark Ages' (1971, 212). Professor Alcock has been no less affected by the myth: 'With every justification, we can think of Arthur and his troops feasting and carousing — like the Gododdin army in the hall of Mynynog Mwynfawr — in a hall similar to that at Cadbury; and riding out to battle through a gate-tower like that at the south-west entrance' (1972b, 194). The Laings, of course, frequently use these tactics and terminologies in their writings: 'At the end of the day the warrior could relax in his lord's hall. A sculpture from Invergowrie, Angus, shows a Pict quaffing from a drinking horn with a bird's head terminal mount. Could it be he is celebrating with whisky, which Scottish folklore claims was the invention of a Pict?' (Laing, 1979, 151).

In some measure changes in the outlooks of Celtic society of the period can best be reflected through Celtic art, which illustrates for example the cosmopolitan character of society in a way in which the finds from habitation sites seldom do. It shows the extent to which Roman ideas permeated society, and the extent to which there was a creative cross-fertilization between the various regions of the Celtic world. It also shows the extent to which society was open to influences from abroad, and illustrates how it strove to preserve traditional values. Above all, perhaps, it clearly points to the intellectual sophistication of the Dark Age Celts, focussing attention on subtleties of symbolism that at first sight appear fortuitous.

Indeed, possibly more than in any other period, the art of the Dark Ages can be seen as a reflection of the intellectual, social, technical, creative and occasionally political development of the people who produced it. Although not regarded as essential in mainstream art history, it is worthy of special attention simply because much 'history' is written from the evidence it provides.

Unlike the art of more recent periods, but in common with other areas of ancient art, that of the Dark Ages cannot be evaluated in terms of the psychological or the introverted aims and motives of the artists themselves. It thus can appear to lie outside the chief lines of art historical thought, and has all too frequently been derogated as 'craftsmanship'. Very recent thought is now beginning to question this view, and in a number of areas of ancient art, including the more limited area of Celtic and other Dark Age art, it has been demonstrated that the artists were not working solely as technicians. The imperfect evaluation has been demonstrated to lie in modern perception of the art itself: the symbolism is too obscure to be understood: the use of geometric shapes tends to be equated with the work of artisans rather than artists, and during periods when it has not been fashionable to look at art in terms of religion, all possibility that Dark Age art might be of highly profound religious significance has been shut out.

It is also of significance that the terminology tends to be totally different from that used by art historians of later periods, giving a false impression that ancient art is in some way 'only archaeology'.

The names of the artists are lost: only the objects remain. Thus the scholar is forced to refer to a particular art form as 'Lough Crew-Somerset Style' or 'Monasterevin Disc Style', to take two examples. In more historically-attested times such reference is not necessary: the 'work of Leonardo da Vinci' is the normal term of reference rather than the 'Mona Lisa Style' of painting. Perhaps it is the very cumbersome phraseology that must be employed when discussing Dark Age art, that has led to its comparative non-existence in modern art-historical thinking. The necessity for describing art in almost abstract terms, with reference only to objects rather than personalities, may be partly to blame for Dark Age and other ancient art being commonly regarded as being 'without soul' and difficult, if not impossible, to relate to or to admire.

One feature that all art has in common is the patrons. Clearly only a highly-developed society with an excess of wealth, time and workforce can produce highly sophisticated works of art. Ancient art has however until recently been regarded as generally the product of patrons' taste (almost certainly driven entirely by political rather than artistic motives), fashioned by craftsmen so much under the patron's control that they were unable to put any personal interpretation or creativity into works of art.

Clearly these lines of thought have reached a point where their divergence has produced conflicts and dichotomies, and a re-appraisal of the relationship of ancient art in general to post-Renaissance art, is probably overdue.

A further area, which requires considerably more discussion outside the confines of this book, is the legacy of the seventeenth to nineteenth century views of the Dark Ages.

In particular, the terminologies used and the models adhered to can frequently be demonstrated as having originated in the seventeenth to nineteenth centuries when little historical or archaeological data was available. These were reinforced in the twentieth century by contemporary experience, despite the explosion of data which often contradicted these views. For example, the words 'Saxon' and 'Germanic' are and were generally used for the incomers from the Continent in the late and post-Roman period, and the term 'English' for what were essentially their descendants two hundred years later. This automatically imbued elements of twentieth-century thought with the view that the fourth century 'Saxon/Germans' must be hostile, aggressive invaders, whilst their great grandchildren the 'English' were automatically peace-loving farmers.

In addition, the fact of nineteenth and twentieth century life that has coloured Dark Age studies most greatly is the assumption that a small body of people can wipe out of existence by massacre a very substantially larger body. The view that the Saxons annihilated the Romano-British Celts appears to be founded more on this model than on hard evidence. As is demonstrated in chapter 4, the evidence brought forward for this viewpoint has other intepretations which are more persuasive.

From many viewpoints therefore, questions about the Dark Ages must be phrased carefully, if meaningful answers are to be achieved. The vast majority of questions so far asked demonstrate more about the ignorance of the interrogators than the ability of the material to produce answers.

Despite the difficulties in evaluating the evidence, a picture does emerge. It shows radical (though not necessarily violent) changes that effected Celtic society in Britain and Ireland from the second century AD onwards, with the emergence of new leaders and centres of power. The Roman world had a considerable role to play in some of these changes, acting as a catalyst not only on the peoples within the province of Britannia and on its frontiers but in the more remote regions. This influence continued after the collapse of

Roman control, to be reinforced by Christianity. It was subtly pervasive, and is apparent even in Celtic art.

This kind of problem has complicated the study of Germanic archaeology in the period that we are considering and parallel problems can be observed. For instance, how easy is it to distinguish the different groups of Germanic settlers in England, and is it really possible to define archaeologically Burgundians, Alans, Suebi, Franks or Frisians on the Continent? A similar problem was identified for the medieval period by E.M. Jope, who pointed out that differences in ceramic assemblages or regional variations in house type in medieval England are meaningless in terms of what we know from medieval history (Jope, 1972).

Not only are the finds meagre, the sites themselves do not live up to the descriptions of the mead hall of Aneurin either. The extant hillforts, raths, enclosed hut groups, souterrains, crannogs and post-broch huts have a singularly annoying habit of proving impervious to any 'Dark Age' limitations or terminology. There were crannogs in the bronze age in both Ireland and Scotland, and there were still crannogs in both areas in the sixteenth and seventeenth centuries. Raths in Ireland were still in occupation in the sixteenth century, and some people chose to live windswept existences in hillforts in the middle ages in Scotland, even though re-occupied hillforts cannot be said to be an important feature of the medieval Scottish landscape (Laing, 1969b; Morrison, 1977; Proudfoot, 1977).

In consequence, the reader may reasonably express suspicion over any method of dating that is suggested in the following chapters. Yet without some kind of relative chronology, the study of the archaeology of the 'Dark Age' Celts cannot advance. Fortunately there are some yardsticks, such as Roman pottery and coins, penannular brooches and imported pottery that enable us to set at least some sites within a sequence. The most modest claim of which we can be sure is that these sites have in common that they were occupied in what historians originally called the 'Dark Ages'.

Within a fairly wide scheme, (which spans the period from the second to the seventh centuries AD), a survey of the sites occupied in Celtic Britain and Ireland shows a considerable diversity of form. To some extent these are dictated by regional characteristics. It is rare to be able to point to house-types and assign them to any particular cultural or chronological millieu. This need not surprise us: the political affiliations of modern Britons cannot be infallibly discerned from the house types they inhabit. This has led to a tendency to single out a particular type of monument and consider its implications in social terms. Classic examples of this have been the studies of ringforts in Ireland and hilltop sites in Britain. Such an approach has its obvious merits, but the individual classes of monument can with validity only be viewed against the developing social and economic climate as a whole, set within a regional framework based on the material remains. This framework too is partly artificial since it does not totally reflect the supposed political boundaries of the 'Dark Ages'.

Studies of regional archaeology tend to be introspective: internal factors are sought to explain the particular political developments. It is however misleading to study the Celts of the period from AD 200-700 in a cultural and economic vacuum. Social, economic and political changes are likely to have been profoundly affected by any changes in subsistence economics that might be brought about by climatic change. Improving climate means better food supplies and frequently expanding population. Alongside climatic factors influencing social and economic change must be set other natural population controls, such as plagues and epidemics which may have either a local or a more widespread effect on the population. The wider political scene must also colour regional developments. The problems afflicting the late Roman Empire and the Migrations in Northern Europe inevitably had repercussions for the Celts, though not in the cataclysmic manner suggested by the term 'Dark Ages'.

The book is divided into four sections. The first is concerned with the approaches to the study of Dark Age Celtic archaeology and considers the development of thought on the archaeology of the 'Dark Age' Celts, and how particular standpoints have come to be emphasised. It reviews the chronological framework for study, and discusses the variance between archaeological and documentary evidence.

The next section is concerned with 'Britannia', the former province of the Roman Empire. Chapter 4 discusses what had been the 'Civil Zone' of Roman Britain, the area progressively settled by the Anglo-Saxons. Chapter 5 is concerned with the less Romanized areas which lay beyond in the extreme south-west of England, in Wales and in North Britain as far as the Forth-Clyde line.

The third section is concerned with the Celtic areas outside Britannia — Northern Scotland and Ireland — and discusses social dynamics in the Irish Sea Province.

The final section of the book considers the development of Celtic art.

2

STUDY OF THE
EARLY CHRISTIAN CELTS

T he study of the early Christian Celts began in the late seventeenth century but did not seriously develop until the nineteenth century, when it was coloured by contemporary politics and in some measure by Romanticism.

In Ireland, the study of the topography of the countryside has a creditable tradition stretching back into the medieval period. The most notable early topographical work is the **Dinnschenchas**, a collection of legends in prose and verse connected with Irish place-names. The prose sections date back to the twelfth century, the verse to the tenth or eleventh (for this source, Hughes, 1972, ch. 4). Among the monuments at Tara listed in the **Dinnschenchas** is the **Teach Miodchuarta**, the 'Great Mead Hall'. It is described in the prose version as a 'long house with twelve doors upon it', and the poetry version says it was 700 feet long. Ground plans accompanied the description in the *Book of Leinster* (twelfth century) and in the *Yellow Book of Lecan* (fifteenth century) which show an aisled building with side compartments (*imdai*). These plans and descriptions have no apparent bearing on the earthwork now known by this name at Tara, Co. Meath, the archaeological implications of which have been discussed on several occasions (Richmond,1932; Laing,1969).

The lasting foundations of Celtic linguistic and antiquarian study were laid by a Welshman, **Edward Lhwyd** (1660-1708). Lhwyd's contribution to learning is immense, and he deserves to stand as the founder of serious Celtic studies. Lhwyd was Keeper of the recently-established (1667) Ashmolean Museum in Oxford. He travelled extensively in Wales, in particular in a five-year period following the publication of Gibson's edition of Camden's

1 Early Christian memorial formulae from Wales, after Edward Lhwyd, in Edmund Gibson's edition of Camden's *Britannia*, 1695

Britannia, for which he had provided the supplementary notes on Wales (1695).

It is in Lhwyd's additions to Camden that we can see the beginnings of the study of the Welsh Early Christian memorial stones. He transcribed them, correcting on some occasions earlier readings, and included in Gibson's edition a series of wood-blocks of the actual inscriptions (fig. 1). In Nash-Williams' *Early Christian Monuments of Wales* (1950) can be found constant reference to Lhwyd as a source.

After about 1800 it is convenient to discuss the development of antiquarianism under the regions concerned.

Wales

After Lhwyd, antiquarian research in Wales lapsed. A move towards the study of Welsh archaeology was taken with the foundation of the Cambrian Archaeological Association in 1846. The Association was preceded by its journal, *Archaeologia Cambrensis*, edited by the Revd John Williams (ab Ithel) and the Revd Harry Longueville Jones of Magdalene College, Oxford. The early volumes however did relatively little to further the study of the antiquities of Early Christian Wales.

From 1872 onwards **John Rhys** was a member of the Cambrian Association and contributed to its journal, continuing to contribute on philological matters after his appointment to the chair of Celtic in Oxford in 1877. Rhys also contributed studies of the inscribed stones of Wales, and from 1875 his articles were supplemented by those of John Romilly Allen, who continued to contribute until he died in 1907.

Romilly Allen was a civil engineer and came originally from Pembroke. In the late nineteenth century he was the editor of *Archaeologia Cambrensis*, and was also active in other areas of Celtic art-historical study. Despite his major contribution to Welsh Dark Age archaeology, he is probably best remembered for his monumental corpus of *The Early Christian Monuments of Scotland*, for which Joseph Anderson provided the introductory discussion, published in 1903. But Allen's writings ranged widely, and included a book on *Selsey Bill* and the first comprehensive book on *Celtic Art* (1904). In the field of metalwork, he published a survey of hanging-bowls of the fifth-seventh centuries, in *Archaeologia* for 1898.

Occasional references to the early Christian memorial stones of Wales had previously appeared in *Archaeologia Cambrensis*. The first volume gives Lhwyd's transcript of the text on the Pillar of Eliseg at Llangollen, and a communication on an ogham-inscribed stone. It prompted a comment by the Cork antiquary John Windele, who belonged to a school of amateur enthusiasts who believed in 'the great antiquity of the introduction of ogham writing, an antiquity reaching in all probability to many centuries before the Christian Era' (Macalister, 1946, 123). Ogham inscriptions had been noted before (in for example *Archaeologia*) but had not been understood. Many believed that ogham was 'invented by the Scythian progenitors of the Gaelic race, and was introduced to Ireland by the Tuatha-de-Danaan about thirteen centuries before the birth of Christ' (Wood-Martin, 1895, 34), but Wood-Martin himself assigned the bulk of the ogham inscriptions to the fifth century. Against the fanciful interpretations of ogham current in the mid-nineteenth century the Scottish antiquary Ferguson and the Irish scholars Petrie and O'Donovan spoke out strongly — both Petrie and O'Donovan at first did not accept the inscriptions as genuine.

A large number of the Welsh inscriptions had been discovered and published by 1850. Amid the serious notices, there were others of a more fanciful kind. In 1855 *Archaeologia Cambrensis* reports the discovery of 'a large number of inscribed stones, some with marks of an early alphabet alleged to be 'cuneiform' at Bryn Eglwys. Around this time Longueville Jones published an 'Ogham Rosetta Stone' from St Dogmael's (Macalister, 1946, 125).

In 1876 the first survey of Welsh stones, *Lapidarium Walliae*, was published, priced at ten shillings, the work of J.O. Westwood, who had regularly contributed to the Association's journal.

Much of the concern in the late nineteenth century was with the inscriptions. Romilly Allen focussed attention again on the art of the sculptured crosses with his 1893 paper in *Archaeologia Cambrensis* on Celtic art in Wales and Ireland, in which he set out his methods of analysis of Celtic ornament.

During the early decades of the twentieth century, Celtic antiquarian studies did not progress much in Wales. The possible exceptions to this was the work done by Harold Hughes at Ynys Seirol (Puffin Island) off Anglesey and the comparable work done at Penmon on Anglesey itself.

Excavations at the Dark Age fort of Dinas Emrys, Gwynedd, by Major C.E. Breese in 1910 posed more problems than they solved. Not published until 1930, the object of the excavation was to find Dark Age remains, and in particular the legendary tower built by Vortigern. Breese indeed found a tower which fitted the bill — a medieval castle. His finds were given to the landowner and were lost, except for one terret which managed to survive in a school in Caernarvon. As is so often the way of these things, Breese probably *did* find the Dark Age occupation of Dinas Emrys, but it was left to the excavators of 1954-6 to prove it.

With the arrival of **R.E.M. Wheeler** as Keeper of Archaeology in the National Museum, Welsh archaeology lurched into the twentieth century, but the trail blazoned by Wheeler and subsequently by Nash-Williams was initially in the field of iron age and Roman studies. Prehistory too fared well with Cyril Fox and W.F. Grimes, but the Dark Ages were to remain Dark a while longer.

A new phase in Welsh Dark Age archaeology began in 1950 with the publication of **V.E. Nash-Williams'** *Early Christian Monuments of Wales.* This dealt not only with inscribed stones but the uninscribed as well, and set out a scheme for their classification and dating. He defined four groups, which remain valid. The stones were illustrated with photos and line drawings, and it was a model of what such a survey should be.

Soon after Nash-Williams' work was being published, the first professional excavation of a 'Dark Age' Celtic site was being carried on as a training exercise for Cardiff University students as Cwrt-Yr-Ala Park, Glamorgan, later better known as Dinas Powys.

The excavator of Dinas Powys was **Leslie Alcock**, who began the excavation in 1953, and went on until 1958. As a young man Alcock had travelled to India to become Wheeler's assistant at Mohenjo-daro, having 'served a while in the Indian army, worked his way out to Karachi and presented himself as a volunteer. He had energy and a modicum of archaeolgical experience' (Wheeler, 1958, 200). The ensuing report on *Dinas Powys* (1963) was, and remains, a landmark in Celtic Dark Age archaeology. It is still the only extensively published excavation on a Dark Age Celtic site outside Ireland, and its discussion of the site in its wider context broke important new ground.

While Dinas Powys was being investigated, other archaeological work was in progress. **H.N. Savory** published a useful study of zoomorphic penannular brooches in Wales in the volume on *Dark Age Britain* (1956) edited by Harden, and also re-excavated Dinas Emrys with rather better results than Breese. Alcock too was publishing a series of short papers and some survey articles reviewing the state of knowledge on Dark Age Welsh archaeology.

Isle of Man

Until the late nineteenth century no serious archaeological work was done in the Isle of Man. That was to change with **P.M.C. Kermode** (1855-1932), who though a lawyer devoted much of his life to the study of Manx archaeology. His major achievement was the publication of *Manx Crosses* (1907), and the writing of *Manks Antiquities* with William Herdman. He is also known for the field survey of keeills (early chapel sites) under the title of the *Manx Archaeological Survey 1909-1918*, published at intervals until 1935. A Sixth Report, completing the survey, was added in 1968.

Kermode founded, and was the first curator of, the Manx Museum in 1922. His devotion to archaeology took a financial toll: the local law society is reported as having had to buy his library three times to save him from financial embarrassment, which each time resulted in Kermode working with zeal at his legal duties to earn enough to buy it back (Selkirk, 1971, 98).

Some very inadequate work was done at the beginning of World War II at Ronaldsway, where a complex of secular and ecclesiastical remains were investigated. Since the War the main figure active in the Isle of Man was Peter Gelling, who carried out a number of useful excavations.

South-west England

In Cornwall a similar survey to Kermode's had been carried out by A.G. Langdon of *Old Cornish Crosses* (1896) which had been first surveyed in 1856.

The next main landmark in Cornish archaeology was the excavation of Tintagel by **C.A.R. Radford**, published in 1935. It was at Tintagel that imported Mediterranean pottery was first recognized (though not published till 1956), and the remains on this site were interpreted as those of a monastery.

Ralegh Radford's contribution to Celtic studies has been immense, being mainly concerned with aspects of the early church and relating documentary sources to surviving remains. Other sites that he has excavated include Glastonbury Abbey, Somerset and Whithorn, Wigtowns.

Since World War II **Charles Thomas** has carried on work in Cornwall. His excavations at Gwithian remain virtually unpublished after over thirty years, but he was responsible for major developments in the study of imported Mediterranean pottery (which he first defined in a paper in *Medieval Archaeology* in 1959) and for wider studies of the church in Celtic lands, of which the most important studies have been *The Early Christian Archaeology of North Britain* (1972) and *Christianity in Roman Britain to AD 500* (1981).

Elsewhere in south-west England, considerable interest was prompted by Leslie Alcock's excavations at South Cadbury, Somerset, claimed to be Camelot (popular account published 1972). On this site he was able to demonstrate very extensive refortification in the post-Roman period. Also notable have been the as yet unpublished excavations by Philip Rahtz at Cadbury Congresbury, Somerset. These gave rise to a wider survey of re-occupied hillforts in southern Britain in the late- and post-Roman periods, most notably by Ian Burrow.

Other important landmarks in Celtic archaeology in Britain as a whole this century have been Elizabeth Fowler's study of fifth and sixth century metalwork (published in *Archaeological Journal*, 1963) and Leslie Alcock's general survey *Arthur's Britain* (1971).

Scotland

Scottish archaeology may be said to begin with the formation, in 1780, of the **Society of Antiquaries of Scotland**, under the leadership of David Steuart Erskine, eleventh Earl of Buchan. The new society saw itself as directly comparable to the Society of Antiquaries of London. The early days of the Society of Antiquaries of Scotland have been admirably chronicled (Cant, 1981; Stevenson, 1981). It is sufficient to note here that a museum was an important adjunct of the emergent society, as indeed was a regular volume of *Transactions* (later *Proceedings*).

There are signs of early nineteenth century interest in vitrified forts and in souterrains: **John Stuart**, the professor of Greek in Aberdeen, reported on examples near Kildrummy, Aberdeens., and was concerned by the need 'to prevent the total loss and destruction of our remaining monuments of antiquity'. He thought money ought to be collected for 'two or three active young men who might perambulate the whole of Scotland in the course of one or two summers, and make out correct drawings and descriptions of them, to be afterwards either published or deposited in their archives' (Stevenson, 1981, 61). Stuart was subsequently to pioneer the study of Pictish stones with his two volumes of *Sculptured Stones of Scotland* (1856-67), a major achievement of lucid description and detailed illustration.

The early nineteenth century also saw the discovery of the **Norrie's Law**, Fife, hoard, which was written up by George Buist in 1838. Buist did his best to be objective (though the drawings were abysmal): 'In the preceding pages it has been desired to propound no theory. . . . The subject is most interesting but obscure referring as it does to a period of our national history, in which reference to the voice of written annals and of tradition are alike silent, which, if it ever be cleared up, must be through the medium of existing monuments' (Buist, 1838, 4) (fig. 2). It was the beginning of a serious interest in Pictish monuments, which though long recognized as curiosities (they figure in eighteenth-century works such as Pennant) were not seriously discussed. Pictish stones, and casts of them, were being regularly added to the Society's collection in the early years of the nineteenth century.

In 1831 the recently-discovered Hunterston Brooch was exhibited to the Society, along with some of the Lewis chessmen (subsequently bought along with other pieces, 98 in all, by the British Museum for £84) (Stevenson, 1981, 72).

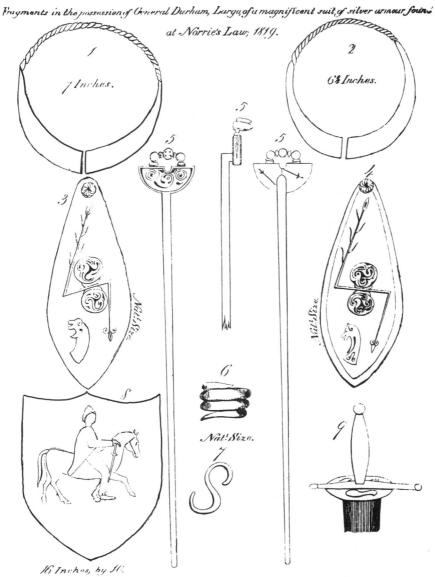

Fragments in the possession of General Durham, Largo, of a magnificent suit of silver armour found at Norrie's Law, 1819.

2 The Norrie's Law, Fife, hoard of Pictish silver,
from Buist's account, 1838 (the illustration is approx. half the original size).

From 1851 onwards, with the publication of the *Proceedings of the Society of Antiquaries of Scotland*, it is possible to monitor the developing concern in Scottish archaeology with its Early Christian period remains.

The 1860s saw rather fuller publication of Norrie's Law and a series of papers on artefacts, including the Hunterston brooch and its runic inscription.

During the 1870s Dark Age finds were recovered from the Broch of Burrian, in Orkney. Pictish silver chains, 'Celtic' bells, the Monymusk reliquary and St Fillan's crozier were all discussed in the decade (Graham, 1973, 260), but no real progress had been made in Dark Age archaeology. The opening of the 1880s however saw several important landmarks. In 1881 the first volume of Joseph Anderson's Rhind lectures on *Scotland in Early Christian Times* was published. The same year saw the second volume, and in 1882 came the publication of Robert Munro's *Ancient Scottish Lake-dwellings or Crannogs*.

Gordon Childe pronounced in his opening to *The Prehistory of Scotland* that by 1886 **Joseph Anderson** 'had sketched the essential outlines of Scottish prehistory in a comprehensive and scientific survey such as then existed in no other country' (1935, xi), and he might have said the same for Anderson's contribution to Early Christian Celtic archaeology.

Born at Arbroath in 1832, the son of a weaver, Joseph Anderson became a teacher, first in Scotland then in Constantinople. Returning to Scotland he began his archaeological career in 1860 (Graham, 1978, 281).

In 1872 and 1876 he published papers on the survival of pagan elements in Christian burial practice, discussing *inter alia* the iconography of Daniel in the lion's den and Jonah and the whale. In the latter of these papers he wrote that 'there are no breaks, no well-marked lines of separation between the successive formations (if I may call them so) of the periods of archaeology' (1876, 363). He saw the need to set the local material in a wider perspective 'In order to understand the phenomena of early burial in any country of Europe, at any period, it is necessary to study the phenomena of all neighbouring countries, if possible, in all European countries' (1876, 365).

Anderson's achievement has been fully discussed by Graham (1978), and a few points only need be made here. First, Anderson was a dedicated patriot, but one who believed that a true appreciation of the achievements of his land could only lie through critical appraisal set in as wide a perspective as possible. For his time, his standards were meticulous. It is characteristic that he begins his Rhind lecture on early Christian metalwork with a factual account of the discovery of the Hunterston brooch and its description. In his lecture on the symbolism of the early Christian stones of Scotland he sets the Pictish iconography in the context of comparative studies of Irish and continental sculpture and manuscript sources. *Scotland in Early Christian Times* is a classic, still used by those who work in the field (fig. 3).

3 Ruined monastic beehive cells at Eileach an Naoimh, Garvellachs, Argyll, after Joseph Anderson, *Scotland in Early Christian Times*, 1881

Anderson's greatest achievement however remains the volume he wrote with Romilly Allen on *The Early Christian Monuments of Scotland* (1903). The book was the outcome of a decision by the Society of Antiquaries of Scotland to allocate a three-year fellowship and £100 to Allen for fieldwork, the conclusions from which were to be drawn by Anderson in the Rhind lectures for 1892.

Just before the outbreak of World War I, **Alexander Curle** carried out excavations at the Mote of Mark, Kirkcudbright. Curle was employed as secretary of the Royal Commission on Ancient and Historic Monuments for Scotland, an appointment he had held since 1908, and adopted a vigorous approach to his field surveys. Curle conducted the surveys for the county *Inventories* in the summers, writing up his surveys in the winter. The excavation at Mote of Mark was prompted by a curiosity about the vitrified forts encountered in field survey in Galloway, and their relationship, if any, to those of the north.

Of Curle and his first survey of Berwickshire, Angus Graham has written that he was 'a tall and powerful man of splendid physique, (who) succeeded in recording, single-handed, a total of two hundred and fifty monuments, of which seventy were new discoveries. There used to be preserved in the office a small-scale Ordnance Survey map on which he had marked his daily bicycle-journeys, with lines of red-ink dots. Again a passage in the Commissioner's Third Report, which accompanied the Caithness Inventory, records that the Secretary 'conducted the survey of the county of Caithness (whereof the greater part is desolate moorland, involving prolonged physical exertion) with indefatigable zeal . . .'. Perfectly in character was the fact that, at the age of seventy-nine, he climbed Rubers Law to show me some Roman stonework, re-used in a dyke at a spot known only to himself' (Graham, 1981, 217-18).

Curle's excavation at Mote of Mark brought to light a metal-working site of some importance. His excavation was thoroughly reported in the *Proceedings* for 1913-14, and re-excavation in the 1970s in the main confirmed his description. Curle believed the Mote of Mark was an iron age fort that was re-occupied at the time of the Viking arrival in Galloway: 'Who were these Celtic craftsmen making brooches, crosses, pins, carding combs etc in this secure retreat, at a time when the Viking, in his long black galley, was infesting the creeks and estuaries of Western Scotland?' he asked in the report (1914,167).

In his discussion of the finds, Curle was able to draw upon the discoveries made by Christison at **Dunadd**, which had been turned over like a field of potatoes in 1904-5. Writing in 1930 of Christison's excavations, Hewat Craw felt obliged to say, 'The extent of the work done at that time at Dunadd is not quite clear. The lines of all the walls were certainly followed, and enough of the interior was turned over to warrant the statement that no foundations or buildings existed there. . . . I have little doubt that the soil of a large part of the interior was turned over' (Craw, 1930, 112-13).

Dunadd was believed to be the capital of the Dalriadic Scots, but Christison had effectively destoyed all hope of finally disentangling its sequence. No wonder Curle is reported as having said, 'We've had enough of old Christison, going round the forts and measuring them up with his umbrella' (Graham, 1981, 216).

The years prior to World War I also saw the publication of excavation, to varying standards, of a number of other sites,

30

notably the Viking mound with Celtic metalwork at Kiloran Bay, Colonsay, discovered 1882-3 and published by Anderson in the *Proceedings* for 1906-7.

The Inter-War years saw a series of important contributions to the subject. In Orkney a series of excavations were carried out by **James Richardson**, Inspector of Ancient Monuments for Scotland, notably at the Broch of Gurness, Aikerness and at the Brough of Birsay. The Brough of Birsay was a Pictish site with later Norse occupation of major importance. Richardson was nominally in charge of the opening stages of the excavation, but work was taken over by Miss Cecil Mowbray (later Mrs Curle) in 1936-7. Mrs Curle published the finds from her excavations (and subsequent excavations by Radford and Cruden) in a monograph which appeared nearly fifty years later (Curle,1982).

Meanwhile, **Hewat Craw**, who died suddenly in 1933 having begun the supervision of the excavations at Aikerness for Richardson, had gone back to Dunadd to try to solve some of the problems posed by Christison. Craw was a farmer who turned to archaeology after retiring. He was unable to make much of Dunadd through no fault of his own, but his report on the disturbed material that he recovered along with some stratified finds was extremely useful for later workers.

Another figure active in the inter-war years was **H.E. Kilbride-Jones**. Kilbride-Jones was active in both Ireland and Scotland, and published a survey of zoomorphic penannular brooches in Ireland (1937) and in Scotland (1936) as well as a survey of hanging bowls illustrated as usual with his meticulous drawings. The latter had been prompted by the discovery of the Castle Tioram bowl, and his list of bowls was a useful addition to the literature (1937 b).

The outbreak of World War II saw a major publication from the standpoint of Pictish studies — Cecil Mowbray's 'The Chronology of the Early Christian Monuments of Scotland' in the *Proceedings* for 1939-40. Using comparative material from a wide range of sources, she provided a framework for the future study of the Class II and Class III stones, the first real advance since Anderson and Romilly Allen nearly forty years previously.

After World War II Dark Age Scottish archaeology moved ahead in the 1950s through the work of one or two dedicated scholars. The major landmark was the publication in 1955 of *Problem of the Picts*, edited by **F.T. Wainwright** who was one of those rare scholars who worked with equal ease with documentary and archaeological sources. He founded the Scottish Summer School in Archaeology, and was head of the department of History in University College, Dundee. He died in 1961 at the early age of 43, robbing Dark Age studies of one of their most original thinkers.

In retrospect, *Problem of the Picts* in many ways was a disservice to Pictish studies because of its title. Henceforth Picts were considered a problem, and the dismissal in a few brief pages of 'Fortifications' and 'Houses and Graves' put the emphasis in Pictish studies firmly in the fields of documentary and art historical research.

Apart from Wainwright's own paper, 'The Picts and the Problem', the most important contributions to the volume were the discussions of language, by Kenneth Jackson, and of Pictish art by R.B.K. Stevenson, which carried on from where Cecil Mowbray left off.

R.B.K. Stevenson has led the field in Scottish Dark Age studies in the period from 1949 onwards. Many of his contributions have concerned artistic problems, but his study of 'Dalmahoy and other Dark Age Capitals' (*Proceedings*, 1948-9) first defined the character of Dark Age fortifications and distinguished the 'nuclear fort' which had considerable impact on later thinking. Among his other studies mention may be made in particular of 'The Inchyra stone and other unpublished Early Christian monuments' (*Proceedings*, 1958-9), 'The Gaulcross hoard of Pictish silver' (with Emery, *Proceedings*, 1963-4) and 'The Hunterston brooch and its significance' (*Medieval Archaeology*, 1974).

In the field, **Leslie Alcock's** campaign of excavations on Scottish 'royal' sites, notably Dundurn, Dunollie, and Dumbarton Rock in the 70s and early 80s, though limited in scale, have been useful contributions to Dark Age archaeology, as have Alan Lane's further investigations at Dunadd.

Among other landmarks in Scottish Dark Age archaeology, special mention must be made of the discovery of the St Ninian's Isle Treasure in a tiny church on a tidal island off the coast of Shetland in 1958, and its publication in 1973. The most important part of this was the discussion of the metalwork by Sir David Wilson, which put Pictish silverwork firmly on the map as a distinct tradition.

Also important have been Isabel Henderson's book on *The Picts* (1967), and three papers by Charles Thomas, two on Pictish symbols (in *Archaeological Journal* for 1961 and 1963) and one on his excavations at Ardwall Isle, Kirkcudbright (in *Medieval Archaeology* for 1967). The conclusions of the two Pictish papers have not been widely accepted, but have stimulated useful further discussion, as has the same author's controversial 'Evidence from North Britain' on the diocesan organization of the church in southern Scotland, in Barley & Hanson's *Christianity in Britain 300-700*.

Ireland

Ireland has long been concerned with its early Christian antiquities. In the seventeenth century Sir James Ware, although primarily a historian, wrote about antiquarian subjects (Macalister, 1928, viii). The Royal Irish Academy began publishing its *Transactions* in 1786, this journal being replaced by the *Proceedings* in 1836. In 1846 the Kilkenny Antiquarian Society was founded: it became the *Royal Historical and Archaeological Association of Ireland* in 1869 and, in 1890, the *Royal Society of Antiquaries of Ireland*. The *Ulster Journal of Archaeology* was first issued in 1853.

The Royal Irish Academy began a collection of antiquities around 1840 which subsequently became the basis of the collection of the National Museum in Dublin.

In the early nineteenth century the leading figure was **Sir George Petrie** (1790-1866), whose study of *The Ecclesiastical Architecture of Ireland* (1845) was a classic in the tradition of Rickman's *Styles of Architecture* of 1842. Round towers had long been a subject of idle speculation in Ireland: theories abounded about them, and included the views 'that the towers were temples for the holy fire of the Arch Druids, of Phoenician construction, or built by the African sea-champions; sorcerers' towers, pillars for celestial observation; towers for dancing round after the manner of the Canaanites in honour of the heavens; towers for the proclamation of anniversaries; towers for the Persian or Chaldean Magi; temples of Vesta; astronomical gnomons; phallic temples; Danish watctowers; sepulchral monuments' (Sheehy, 1980, 22). Petrie rejected all this by 'the constant exercise of a calm and philosophic spirit' (Stokes,1868). His conclusions are acceptable today.

Petrie was a distinguished painter and collector, and his efforts resulted in the acquisition for the nation (his collection went to the Royal Irish Academy after his death) of such treasures as the iron age Petrie Crown which bears his name and the crozier of St Dympna, bought by him from the hereditary keepers in 1835. Other notable acquisitions around the time of Petrie were the Tara Brooch and Ardagh Chalice (1868) and the Cross of Cong (1839). Petrie also was responsible for two volumes of *Christian Inscriptions in the Irish Language*, edited posthumously by Margaret Stokes (1872, 1878).

Petrie was also partly instrumental in the founding of the historical department of the Ordnance Survey of Ireland, with the assistance of O'Curry and O'Donovan. So successful was the enterprise that the government suppressed it on financial grounds, though more probably they were actually afraid it was fuelling interest in national antiquities and therefore nationalism (MacSweeney, 1913, 50).

Petrie, O'Curry and O'Donovan also contributed to the *Dublin Penny Journal*, founded by Caesar Otway to foster a national identity, and concerned *inter alia* with antiquities, history, legends, biography and literature.

Petrie, as has been noted, was a painter, the son of a distinguished miniaturist. Apart from his own topographical drawings, he collaborated with other artists including Henry O'Neil (1798-1880), who separately published in 1857 *The Most Interesting of the Sculptured High Crosses of Ancient Ireland* (Sheehy, 1980, 23).

These antiquaries and painters brought about a major upsurge of interest in Irish antiquities. It was to give rise to the 'Celtic Revival' which reached its peak at the end of the century with W.B. Yeats and the 'Celtic Twilight'. Already by 1861 we can see Early Christian Celtic ornament being used in book decoration, for example in Samuel Ferguson's edition of his poem 'The Cromlech on Howth'. The ornament, based on the books of Kells and Durrow, was the work of another antiquary, Margaret Stokes (1832-1900), the daughter of a Dublin physician, and sister of Whitley Stokes, the Celtic linguist.

It is not improbable that the considerable upsurge of interest in Early Christian Ireland in the mid-nineteenth century was the outcome of two trends — a growing national feeling and an interest in medieval antiquities, which in England was seen in the Gothic Revival. This trend led to the copying in all media of objects and motifs from early Christian Ireland: the classic examples are the copies of the Tara Brooch and Ballyspellan Brooch made by Waterhouse & Co. Copies of early Christian brooches were even made in bog-oak. Waterhouse had bought the Tara Brooch from a watchmaker in Drogheda who had acquired it from a poor woman whose children had found it. Waterhouse called it the Tara Brooch (despite the fact it had been found at Bettystown), and showed it to Queen Victoria and Albert at Windsor in 1850. Delighted by it,

4 Bedouin girl wearing a penannular brooch. Ethnographic illustration to show how penannular brooches were used in early Ireland, from Wood-Martin, *Pagan Ireland*, 1895

the Queen bought two copies, and thus prompted a brisk trade for Waterhouse (Sheehy,1980, 87).

It has already been noted that there is a long tradition of interest in topography in Ireland. This may explain why Petrie's pupil, William Wakeman, published in 1848 *Archaeologia Hibernica, a Hand-book of Irish Antiquities Pagan and Christian*. Wakeman's little volume is a forerunner of similar monument guides published in the last twenty years it is divided up into chapters dealing with cromlechs, sepulchral mounds, raths or duns and stone circles (all in Part I, prehistoric), and oratories, churches, crosses and round towers under early Christian in Part II. A third section deals with Anglo-Irish monuments. It was a sensible work, full of good illustrations and drawing heavily on Petrie. Wakeman also published a field survey entitled *A Survey of the Antiquarian Remains on the Island of Inishmurray* (1867), still a key to the understanding of this major site.

Wakeman's contribution to Irish archaeology was considerable, but it was matched by the work of others. W.G. Wood-Martin published numerous papers and several books, of which the most notable are *The Lake Dwellings of Ireland* (1886) and *Pagan Ireland* (1895) (fig. 4).

In the late nineteenth century the Keeper of the National Museum was **George Coffey,** who produced a *Guide to the Celtic Antiquities of the Christian Period* in 1909. Drawing upon the earlier catalogue of the Royal Irish Academy, this dealt with the portable counterpart to Wakeman's sites. The chapters covered penannular brooches, the Ardagh Chalice, shrines, croziers, bells, miscellaneous, 'The End of Interlaced Style' and ogam-inscribed stones, with some discussion of Celtic ornament including possible Roman models for interlace, a subject also dealt with around the same time by Romilly Allen. Coffey's work is the Irish counterpart of Joseph Anderson's *Scotland in early Christian Times.* It is cool and objective, and shows Coffey's breadth of knowledge and perception. In its compilation he was aided by E.C.R. Armstrong, then the assistant keeper, whose subsequent contribution to Dark Age studies included a paper on stick pins published in *Archaeologia* in 1927.

The later nineteenth century also saw the publication of the first major survey of Irish art, **Margaret Stokes'** *Early Christian Art in Ireland,* the first part of which on *Early Christian Architecture,* had appeared in 1878. The unified volume came out in 1894, to be reprinted as late as 1932. It is a seminal study, still of use for its perceptive comments (fig. 5).

The progress of studies on early Christian Ireland in the twentieth century has been so rapid and so extensive, only a few landmarks can be singled out here. In the field of excavation, the real landmarks were the investigations between the Wars by the Harvard Expedition, led by **H. O'Neill Hencken**. The project involved the excavation of Cahercommaun, Lagore, Ballinderry 1 and Ballinderry 2 crannogs. The Lagore report has become the main reference work of all later researchers, and this has probably obscured some at least of the report's weaknesses, though attempts to overthrow the chronology set out by Hencken have not been very successful. Hencken (who had worked in Cornwall and produced *The Archaeology of Cornwall and Scilly*, 1932, and who went on to work on the definitive catalogue of the material from La Tène), is a polymath who was able to cite parallels for the Lagore material from museums all over Europe. All too frequently, his studies of individual categories of artefact were the outcome of his own pioneering investigations. Despite the intervention of World War II, the reports were produced rapidly. Lagore, the last of the series, appeared in 1950.

Contemporary with the Harvard expedition were a series of excavations carried out by **S.P. Ó Riordáin**, working sometimes alone (as at Garranes, published 1942 or Lough Gur, published 1952) or sometimes with others (with Foy at Leacanabuaile, published 1943, and with Hartnett at Ballycatteen, published 1943, or with MacDermott (Mrs de Paor) at Letterkeen, published 1952). Ó Riordáin's excavations leave something to be desired by modern standards, but for their time they were exemplary, and along with the Harvard reports formed the basis of all subsequent writing and thought on early Christian period secular sites.

In Northern Ireland progress has been similarly rapid. Among the names to be singled out are Dudley Waterman and A.E.P. Collins, whose excavations included those at Lough Faughan crannog, Co. Down, and V.B. Proudfoot, whose excavations at Downpatrick and elsewhere combined with his studies of raths have been of singular importance.

In the field of ecclesiastical archaeology, **H.C. Lawlor's** investigations at the monastic site of Nendrum was important, though the publication, *The Monastery of St Mochaoi at Nendrum* (1925) is hardly what is recognizable today as an excavation report. The same cannot be said for **M.J. O'Kelly's** excavations at Church Island, Co. Kerry (published 1958), which introduced scholarship to the idea of timber oratories preceding later stone chapels. O'Kelly mainly made his name for his masterly excavations of the neolithic chambered tomb at Newgrange, but this should not obscure his other important contributions to Early Christian archaeology, notably his excavation at Garryduff (published 1962) and his technical studies of metalwork in papers on the Moylough Shrine (1965) and the Cork Horns and related pieces (1961). More recently, T. Fanning's excavations at Reask (published 1981) continues the tradition.

Of studies of art, the main landmarks are the two volumes of **A. Mahr** and **J. Raftery**'s *Christian Art in Ancient Ireland* (1932 and 1941), which was a Corpus illustrated with photos of all the key pieces. Raftery, who was Keeper of Archaeology in the National Museum in Dublin, has continued to write important studies of metalwork and early Christian topics subsequently. The main contribution however has been that of **Françoise Henry**, a French art historian who devoted much of her life to Irish art. Her pioneer study was *Irish Art* (1940). This was expanded into the three volumes of *Irish Art* published between 1965 and 1970, in translation from the French. Apart from these books she also wrote *Irish High Crosses* (1964) and a short volume on *Irish Art* (1965). Her other important contributions to Irish art history include a seminal paper on hanging bowls (published 1936) and a study of enamel work (published 1956) as well as an edition of the *Book of Kells* and various papers on manuscripts. Formerly on the staff of the museum at Saint Germain-en-laye, she became director of studies in archaeology and history of painting at University College, Dublin.

3

RECENT DEVELOPMENTS
IN CELTIC STUDIES

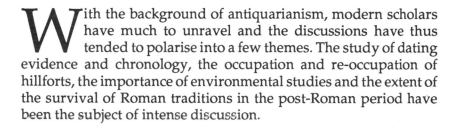

With the background of antiquarianism, modern scholars
have much to unravel and the discussions have thus
tended to polarise into a few themes. The study of dating
evidence and chronology, the occupation and re-occupation of
hillforts, the importance of environmental studies and the extent of
the survival of Roman traditions in the post-Roman period have
been the subject of intense discussion.

Dating evidence

Clearly the type of material available for dating evidence and the
specific arguments relating to key sites are of vital importance to
an understanding of Dark Age Celtic Britain and Ireland.

The chief problem that beset the early antiquaries was that dating
evidence was very shaky. Modern scholars, however, have to
overcome not only the preconceptions of their forebears but the fact
that recent technology has still not managed to provide a meaningful chronological framework for the period.

Many of the academic arguments have hinged on the dating of
particular sites — especially examples in Ireland. These have then
been used to date other Irish sites and also the key sites in Britain.
In a surprising number of cases insubstantial or circumstantial
evidence has been afforded disproportionate validity. The surviving evidence is highly complex and the arguments centring
upon it tend to become difficult to unravel.

Dating evidence in Dark Age Celtic Britain and Ireland consists
chiefly of pottery, documentary sources, artistic styles (especially
metalwork, sculpture and manuscripts), architecture (mostly

ecclesiastical) and to a lesser extent coinage and radiocarbon calculations.

Not all these categories of evidence are available in all areas and frequently the lines of argument cross geographical and material boundaries, using the most subtle and delicate links. Certainly the tightrope walked by the scholar is often like thin elastic over a choppy sea of speculation.

POTTERY

The evidence of pottery is illustrative of the general problems in dating. Although there is a native pottery sequence for the 'Atlantic province' of Scotland (i.e. the north Scottish mainland and Northern and Western Isles) and for Cornwall, and although in north-east Ireland there is a vernacular tradition of coarse pottery known as 'souterrain ware', elsewhere in the Celtic areas the early post-Roman centuries are effectively aceramic, though a few high-status sites have produced imported pottery of Mediterranean origin.

Native coarse wares had simple forms and had a very long currency, and it is extremely difficult to try to provide a date range. The problems of **'grass marked ware'** in Cornwall and on Iona are dealt with elsewhere in this book (p. 169). In northern Ireland Ryan's study of grass-marked pottery has shown that it has a currency from the sixth to the seventh century until the second half of the twelfth century, and possibly later (Ryan, 1973, 626). In view of the presumed iron age ancestry of souterrain ware, however, there is no inherent reason for supposing it was not also current in the fourth or fifth century also.

The imports are more closely datable; but not perhaps always as closely as archaeologists like to pretend to themselves. Additionally, since they are found on 'high status' sites their currency may be slightly different in the Celtic world than in the Late Antique Mediterranean whence they came.

Enormous emphasis has been put on the dating of Mediterranean imported pottery in the Celtic West, because it has long been believed to be very closely attributable.

Imported pottery was first recognized at Tintagel, Cornwall, by C.A.R. Radford (1956), and subsequently studied by A.C. Thomas in greater detail (1959) in a survey which defined a series of imports which he termed classes A-G. In the years that followed detailed study was made of these wares, both in Britain and Ireland and in their homelands, and closer dating and identification of provenance was carried out. The key studies in this connection have been Peacock and Thomas, 1967, Rigoir, 1968, Warner,1979, Peacock 1977 and 1977b, Hayes 1972 and 1980 and Thomas 1981.

It is now possible to define the imported wares as Phocaean Red Slip, African Red Slip (these two grouped together under the British labels Ai and Aii), various types of East Mediterranean amphorae (in Britain labelled Bi and Bii), handled jars (British B iv), Byzacena (North African) amphorae (British Bv), Gaza amphorae (British Bvi), grey mortaria known variously as 'Visigothic' grey ware and Gaulish *terre sigillée paléochrétienne grise* (British D ware) and a variety of vessels in gritty grey/brown wares known as E ware.

F and G wares are now generally grouped with various other miscellaneous potsherds of uncertain provenance and date.

Of these categories of import, some flanged bowls can now be seen to begin earlier than was once supposed, before AD 400 (Hayes, 1977). The main types of A ware however that were current in the Celtic West are attributable to the period *c.* AD 475-550.

The same date range still seems generally applicable to the B wares, though some B amphorae and jars have been assigned to the fourth century, or, in the case of B iv, even earlier (Fulford, 1979, 126-7; Peacock, 1977; 1977b). B iv is not however represented in either Scotland or Ireland (Thomas, 1981, 14-15 for list), and therefore has not been used widely as a chronological indicator.

Despite the possibility of a longer chronology for some wares, the fact remains that *all* the imported Mediterranean vessels (nearly 400 recorded) in the Celtic areas of Britain could have been brought to these shores between about AD 480 and 500 (Thomas,1981, 27 for chronological summary). Class D remains effectively undated, but the 'early fifth century' date assigned to it now seems invalid. Its presence at Mote of Mark and Dunadd in Scotland, neither of which site has produced any A and B wares or other material which could confidently be assigned to the fifth century, suggests its currency lies in the sixth century or later, a view endorsed by Thomas (1981, 27).

E ware presents some problems, since it is the commonest form of 'imported' pottery in Celtic Britain. That it was generally imported after A and B wares is shown from the evidence of the Clogher 'Yellow Layer', where the A and B wares were separated from the E by a sterile layer (Warner,1979). There is no reason to suppose however that the E ware at Clogher is as late as the seventh century as Warner supposed: there is nothing that is conclusively seventh-century about its context. At Mote of Mark it was associated with Germanic glass and metalworking of the late sixth century, and this would seem to be a reasonable date for its arrival in the Celtic world. It certainly now appears to continue in use into the seventh century, possibly as late as AD 700 (Thomas, 1981, 27). Campbell however has sounded caution for the dating and significance, pointing out that although a late sixth century date is now generally accepted for its appearance, its identification as southwest French is extremely dubious (Campbell, 1984; Campbell, 1988, 155). He has also argued that the distribution of E ware suggests secondary redistribution from major coastal centres around the Irish Sea, and that E ware vessels may well have been an element in gift exchange: its association, particularly form E4, is with high status sites (Campbell, 1988, 156).

If Campbell is right, then E ware is of little chronological value, and may have had a very long currency as a status commodity. By extension, the same observation can probably be seen to apply to the earlier imports, which may well have survived rather longer in Celtic realms than would regular domestic vessels. This is suggested by the evidence of Dinas Powys (see below, p. 56)

All in all, pottery is only useful for dating within very broad brackets, preferably when there is other supporting evidence available.

DOCUMENTARY SOURCES

Historical dates are often used for archaeological dating. Usually this takes the form of a reference to the site at some fixed point in time in a documentary source. This at once raises three problems: (1) Is the date contained in the documentary source 'historical' and valid (i.e. is it a genuine reference not invented for some other purpose, and is the date likely to be correct)? (2) Does the reference actually refer to the site being considered, and not to somewhere else entirely? (3) Does the reference relate to the occupational phase represented in the excavations, and not to some previous (or later) occupation on the same site?

Even if there is no doubt that the date is 'real' and relates to the site under consideration, it has only the same validity as a single radiocarbon date, in that it only points to occupation at that time, and tells us nothing about how much before or afterwards occupation continued.

42

In some cases attempts are made to equate the 'historical' reference with a particular event in the site's history. A reference to a siege and a destruction for example may be associated with a burnt deposit on site. This is immediately translated in the literature as a firm fact, and becomes **'the fire** of 689'. There can be numerous explanations for a fire (or even a destruction level) on a site which have nothing to do with an historical siege.

Our main historical sources for Ireland are the **Irish Annals**. Professor Kelleher has argued that every entry in the Irish Annals up to 590 is unreliable, most of those up to 735 and even later are equally suspect and it will be 'a long time before we shall be able to say with confidence what is reliable and what has been tampered with or falsified' (Kelleher, 1963).

Of the fifth century, Binchy has written, 'I do not believe that there is a single "genuine entry" throughout the whole of the fifth century' (1962, 77). The same conclusions were drawn by Kathleen Hughes discussing the Irish Annals: 'I would hesitate to attach any importance to the dating even of the common entries before 585, for I think that the separate copyists after 913 fitted those entries in where they thought best. . . . There were probably no contemporary annals until late in the seventh century, but there must have been earlier material to draw on. . . . I think that between 740 and 775 a set of Uí Neill annals becomes contemporary, and that from about 780 or 790 they were kept at Armagh' (Hughes, 1972, 145). Or again 'I am afraid that there is no short cut to estimating the historical reliability of the annals. The method stated by Professor Kelleher and Professor Byrne, i.e. putting them alongside other contemporary material, is the only one. The trouble is that these scholars have both come to different conclusions' (Hughes, 1972, 146).

What applies to annals applies, of course, with equal validity to other documentary sources. None of this is to say that modern historical scholarship is unable to extract reliable information about pre-eighth century Ireland, merely that 'absolute' dates are rarely if ever absolute and documentary sources for particular sites cannot be taken at face value.

A similar caution can be expressed regarding fifth- and sixth-century dates in British history. On some of the problems Dumville has sounded a suitable note of caution — writing of the fifth and sixth centuries: '. . . most of the available written "evidence" is more apparent than real. Critical assessment of the earliest of these sources, which date only from the end of the eighth and the earlier ninth centuries, is still in its infancy, and writers who invite us to swallow the testimony of these sources offer only large doses of "tradition" as the sweetener of this Celtic pill' (1977, 173-4).

Two examples of historically-dated sites underline the problem. The issue of historical dating and Lagore has been examined by J. Raftery (1981, 88-9), and similar points could be made about Garranes, which has been identified as Rath Raithleann, the seat of the rulers of the Uí Eachach, one of the branches of the Eoganacht dynasty (Ó Riordáin, 1942, 7). Although there is a serious possibility the equation is a correct one, it cannot be proved.

In short, history can provide few certain dates for the fifth and sixth centuries, and little reliable information for the seventh. Only with the eighth and ninth centuries do we move into a more dependable period.

ARTISTIC STYLES

The chief categories of art surviving are ornamental metalwork and manuscripts, around which a considerable amount of scholarship centres. This type of material brings its own limitations when used for dating.

Ornamental metalwork Metalwork consists largely of penannular brooches, pins, reliquaries, hanging bowls and mounts, not all of which have been subject to the same amount of scrutiny. Penannular brooches have enjoyed considerable attention, and outstanding objects such as the Tara Brooch and the Ardagh Chalice or Moylough Belt Shrine have been the centre of spectacular amounts of scholarship. Hanging bowls are discussed briefly in chapter 10.

It is frustrating that the most important pieces of ornamental metalwork are either without any association, or without association with other potentially diagnostic material.

A few items of metalwork however do come from archaeological contexts, notably various types of brooches and pins. But even here there are problems. The hand-pins from the Norrie's Law hoard have been dated variously from the fourth century to the late seventh, while penannular brooches of class F have been dated to the late second century (Kilbride-Jones, 1936, 133), the third century (Raftery, 1941, 59), the fourth century (Wheeler and Wheeler, 1932, 137),the fifth century (Smith, 1913, 223) and continuing through fifth into sixth century (Fowler, 1963, 103-5).

The general situation can be usefully represented by discussion of three objects, the Tara Brooch, the Ardagh Chalice and the Moylough Belt Shrine.

The Ardagh Chalice It is a common jest that the 'Tara' brooch is dated by the Ardagh Chalice, which is dated from the 'Tara' brooch. The 'Tara' brooch, from Bettystown, Co. Meath, was found in the nineteenth century, reputedly by some children, and is without context. The Ardagh Chalice was found with a smaller, undecorated chalice and some penannular brooches, probably of the tenth century. In the latest discussion of the Ardagh Chalice, Etienne Rynne has pointed out that the dates suggested for it since its discovery in 1868 'range from about AD 700 to the eleventh century, the majority, however, falling some time within the eighth century' (1987, 85). Rynne's own date is *c.* 710-735. Michael Ryan, writing in the same decade, has said that 'it clearly belongs to a mature phase of the development of style perhaps the later part of the eighth century' (1981, 125). There are features however of the Ardagh Chalice that might point to a later date: the slender filigree with plant-like terminals are not readily matched in eighth-century Ireland, but have their counterparts in Anglo-Saxon England on objects such as the King's School, Canterbury, disc brooch, the Windsor sword pommel and the Kirkoswald trefoil brooch, all of the late ninth or early tenth century.

The Tara Brooch The dating of the Tara brooch is similarly wide — Ryan has suggested that 'a generalized 8th century date for the 'Tara' Brooch is probably indicated because its ornaments are so clearly amongst the finest work of the Golden Age but reference to a precise bracket within that period would be questionable' (1981, 121).

The Moylough Belt Shrine was found without association in a peat bog in 1943. Many commentators would favour a date around AD 700 for this object (de Paor, 1979, 30; Haseloff, 1979, 238). But Harbison has argued that it shows features in common with the Adelhausen Altar and the Tall Cross at Monasterboice, suggesting that it was made between 750 and 850, coming down in favour of a date in the late eighth or early ninth century (Harbison, 1981, 237). In his discussion of this object, Harbison accepts its close relationship with the Ardagh Chalice and 'Tara' brooch, but believes these too should be much later than usually supposed. In particular, he has seen certain animals on the 'Tara' brooch as being similar to those on the Steeple Bumpstead boss, which has other creatures related to some in the St Ninian's Isle hoard, dated to around 800 (Harbison, 1981, 236). This type of argument, which suggests that

A must be contemporary with C because B has ornamental devices found on both A and C though is not in itself datable, has led to complex and often very ill-founded dating sequences.

Manuscripts While a few manuscripts appear fairly securely dated by historical references in them, others, including the two most famous, the Book of Durrow and the Book of Kells, are less so.

The Book of Durrow has attracted a wide spectrum of dates. Uta Roth has recently listed the attributions by the foremost art historians, and has shown that 11 authorities in the period 1904-1980 favoured various dates between AD 600 and 650; 14 authorities between 1940 and 1979 came out in favour of a date in the period 650-700, and 5 authorities between 1916 and 1956 favoured a date in the eighth century (Roth, 1987, 25). Many of these authors claimed different dates within these date brackets!

The Book of Kells has not fared much better. Early nineteenth century commentators thought a sixth century date possible; Stokes and Sullivan favoured an early to mid-ninth century date; Baldwin Brown opted for the mid-eighth century and Brunius suggested it was as late as the tenth (Harbison, 1985, 190). Most arguments seem now to favour a date around AD 800: Henry suggested *c.* 760/70-815/20 (1940,149). The most recent date canvassed is 'in the later 820s' (Harbison, 1985, 7).

Many of the arguments advanced in the dating of manuscripts rest on citing parallels for ornamental devices in metalwork, which, as has already been seen, is not the least hazardous approach.

Sculpture Sculpture is dated to some extent from manuscripts and metalwork. Although there is a greater consensus of opinion on the dating of some groups, others remain very diversely attributed. Thus the class I Pictish symbol stones, discussed on pp. 230-5, have been seen at various times as originating between the fourth and the seventh centuries.

The problems are well exemplified in a series of very important sculptures from Co. Donegal, which bear interlace decoration and have been seen as ancestral to the Irish High Crosses. Particularly important is a cross from Fahan Mura, with a Greek inscription, and that from Carndonagh. The Fahan slab was dated to the seventh century by Henry (1930, 16, 96 and 194), to the tenth century by Stevenson (1956, 94-6), and to the ninth century by Harbison (1986, 59).

Architecture Celtic architecture (standing ecclesiastical buildings and house remains from excavation) contains no innate clues with regard to date. Archaeology has for example failed to date any early Irish church or secular building indisputably. We will discuss a number of important examples below.

The **Gallarus Oratory**, a 'classic' Early Christian oratory in Co. Kerry, has been studied by Harbison. This small rectangular stone-built edifice is 10ft 2in by 15ft 3in internally, with a single window and door, with sloping walls which rise to a profile not unlike that of a pointed vault. It is usually taken as being of the eighth century (but dates as early as the sixth have been claimed for it). Harbison has shown however that it 'cannot be proved to date from the eighth century, and could even be as late as the twelfth' (1970, 58). The Gallarus oratory has been seen as a stone skeuomorph of a cruck-built timber structure, and this fact, along with the use of stone butterfly gable finials and projecting **antae**, has been used to argue for a native translation in stone of timber buildings (Leask, 1955, 43-7).

St Columba's House at Kells, a stone built chapel with stone roof and relieving vault, is dated because of a reference in documentary sources to a church being completed at Kells in 814, the first church there having been destroyed in 807. Now it is true that it is recorded that in 819 the 'doimliac' (i.e. stone church) of Cennanus (Kells) was 'broken' by the 'Gentiles' (Vikings) (Leask,1955, 33) — but can we be sure it was this church? There are features of the building (triangular-headed window, for example) that betray an Anglo-Saxon connection. If the reference relates to this church, then it might be that stone church building developed in Ireland in response to Anglo-Saxon building traditions. This was the case in Pictland: Restenneth church tower and the round towers at Abernethy and Brechin have Anglo-Saxon architectural features. Indeed Harbison has suggested this; his view was that Gallarus and the related monuments represent a 'last outpost' of a spread of stone building from east to west (1970, 58). In this connection, it it noteworthy that the earliest reference to a stone church in the Irish Annals is in 788 when an **oratorium lapideum** is recorded at Armagh (Macdonald, 1981, 306), though references to stone churches do not become common until the ninth century (Macdonald, 1981, 307).

Skellig Michael is the classic 'Early Christian' monastic site, occupying a craggy rock off the coast of Co. Kerry. The remains comprise two stone oratories and some beehive corbelled huts. The buildings on Skellig Michael have been dated from a cross-slab there, but the face cross-slab (of the seventh-eighth century, see Thomas, 1972 129-30) need not actually be contemporaneous with the beehive cells on the rock, and indeed need not be dated as early as it usually is: it is not an actual face cross. The fact remains, there is no date historical or otherwise for Skellig Michael, for the beehive cells of the Dingle peninsula studied by Henry (1957) or for the stone churches at Church Island (O'Kelly, 1958).

At **Church Island**, another ecclesiastical site on an island off the coast of Co. Kerry, with a stone chapel, a cell and a stone graveslab within an enclosure, we are back to the circular argument: 'If we accept him (H.G. Leask), Gallarus was in existence by 750. Now except that our oratory is larger by about 1m (3' 3") in length and by 66cm (2' 2") in width, and that its stonework does not reach such technical perfection, the buildings are much the same. . . . But the presence of the additional window in the south wall at Church Island might be used to argue that it is slightly later than Gallarus! Thus there is no basis for argument — if the one could have been in existence by 750, so also could the other, and there is no reason to think that the Church Island oratory is markedly later than this date' (O'Kelly, 1958, 128).

SCIENTIFIC DATING

Although dendrochronology, thermoluminescence and other scientific methods of dating are used, radiocarbon is the most frequently employed method of 'scientific' dating, due to the material available. Dates provided by it are too few to provide a reliable framework. In the period with which we are concerned when taken to two standard deviations they usually provide too wide a time-span. The most recent evaluation of radiocarbon dates has pointed out that they are of limited value for the 'Dark Ages' as they are only accurate within a span of 200 years.

The problems of radiocarbon dating are underlined by the fort of Raheennamadra (Stenberger, 1966) which produced no fewer than nine radiocarbon determinations: one date was 'early' and explained away as pre-dating the main occupation of the site; the others appeared to lie within a span of 170 years. Re-appraisal however has shown that duplicate estimates on the same sample in one case varied by more than a century and a half, and the standard error is large for all the samples, so that the 'consistency' implied by the report is not as great as might be supposed.

Caulfield, in re-appraising this, has suggested that the 'early' date actually indicates the first occupation of the site (Caulfield,1981, 207-8).

There was no native coinage in Celtic Britain in the period under review, although Roman coins filtered beyond the frontiers during the period of their currency in Roman Britain. The last coins to come into Britain were issues of silver of *c.*420, the latest bronze coins being the SALVS REIPUBLICAE issues struck at Rome and Aquileia after 395 but before 404 (Kent, 1961; Kent, 1979, 21). Few of these late coins penetrated the Celtic areas, where Roman coinage had in any case never been in regular use for trade purposes. Apart from two Byzantine coins from Caerwent in South Wales, which George Boon claims are not ancient losses (Boon, 1958; Whitting, 1961, 27), and finds from Ireland and Scotland of equal dubiousness, there is no coinage in Wales until the tenth-century penny of Hwyel Dda (which was hardly currency in any case: for the issue, see North, 1963, 20), or in Ireland until the Vikings. Scotland had to wait till the Normans for her coinage.

The problems of using coins for dating in Celtic Britain and Ireland are underlined by the way in which a Byzantine bronze coin was supposedly associated with the Pictish silver hoard from Norrie's Law, Fife, and then used to date the hoard (see p. 134) — recent research has suggested that the coin had no association with the hoard at all, and in any case was incorrectly identified (Laing, forthcoming).

The crannog at Buston, Ayrshire, has always been dated to the seventh century on account of a gold 'forgery' of an Anglo-Saxon coin associated with it. The coin however was not found during the excavation of the crannog, but by a visitor later (Munro, 1882, 230). The coin itself need not be a forgery: it seems to be a 'London derivative' issue of gold plated copper. It is of a type only current in the south-east of England (Sutherland, 1948 for these coins). The circumstances whereby it reached Ayrshire are difficult to imagine, and it is extremely likely that there is some time-lag in its arrival at the site, if indeed it belongs with the crannog. The hoard from Crondall, Oxfordshire, of similar gold coins, also contained a forgery, and its deposition has been dated to around 670 (Dolley, 1976b, 352). The coin could have reached Buston as late as 700.

The chronology of key sites

The first time that the traditionally accepted chronology for Celtic 'Dark Age' archaeology was seriously questioned was in a study by Barry Raftery of Irish forts, in which he suggested that one of the classic 'Early Christian' stone forts, **Cahercommaun, Co. Clare** (1972, 51-3) belonged to a pre-Christian iron age. In what can now be seen as a prophetic statement, Raftery commented, 'There can be no doubt that the whole chronological structure of the period known loosely in Ireland as the Early Christian Period needs to be reassessed' (*loc. cit.*, 53). Cahercommaun is therefore central to any discussion of site chronology in Ireland.

In 1981 Joseph Raftery endorsed Barry Raftery's argument that the only datable find from Cahercommaun was a silver brooch which came from a souterrain and therefore although quite probably secondary had coloured all the dating on the site (1981, 85). This was disputed (Laing, 1975, 147-9), and subsequently Barry Raftery (at the sixth International Congress in Galway in 1979) has said he considers Cahercommaun to be no earlier than 500 (quoted in Caulfield, 1981). But the arguments over the date of Cahercommaun still rage, Caulfield pressing for a constructional phase for the fort in the iron age, on the grounds that it produced saddle querns and no rotary querns, which replaced the saddle quern at the end of the bronze age: 'Cahercommaun . . . could potentially have a BC rather than an AD date for its construction and initial occupation' (Caulfield, 1981, 211).

Against this, Lynn has argued that the main occupation of Cahercommaun belongs in the early Christian period (1983, 49-50) and his arguments seem valid. They do not however detract from the possibility that the first constructional phase of Cahercommaun was much earlier than the excavator, Hugh Hencken, supposed.

Carraig Aille, Co. Cork, was excavated by Ó Riordáin (1949). The site comprised two adjacent ringforts which were dated to the eighth and the tenth centuries. Caulfield has argued that a large stone house was built at Carraig Aille 2 when the ringfort 'had virtually ceased to exist as a fort', and that the ibex-headed pin from the site is in keeping with a much earlier date for the ringfort than the bulk of the finds would suggest (Caulfield, 1981, 208-9). Caulfield also singles out as 'early' a barbarous 'Fel Temp Reparatio' coin, a 'Roman' toilet article and a hand-pin which on account of the similarity of its plate to a Romano-British pelta brooch should be seen as earlier than the 'seventh or eighth century' date assigned to it (Caulfield, 1981, 209).

Caulfield is correct is saying the coin was of a type not in circulation in Britain later than the mid-fourth century, and may well be right with the hand-pin, which could belong to a fourth-century horizon. The ibex pin need not be as early however as he and Ó Riordáin before him suggested — ibex pins seem to belong to the fourth century (Stevenson, 1955, 291), and the possibility of their later survival at Lydney now seems less certain since Lydney has a longer chronology than was originally believed.

Carraig Aille 1 could equally belong to the fourth century in its initial occupation. Here there are two finds that are helpful. The first is a three-fingered iron handpin of a type that seems related to those from Norrie's Law, Fife, and Castletown, Kilpatrick, Co. Meath, which elsewhere we argue are of fourth or early fifth century date (p. 204). The second object (Ó Riordáin, 1949, fig. 21, 159) appears closely related to the series of knobbed terrets found in North Britain, which were mainly fashionable in the second century (MacGregor, 1976, 46). Caulfield has suggested an early dating for the querns from both sites (1981, 209).

Two other sites for which the dating has been questioned by Caulfield are **Raheennamadra**, Co. Limerick, where he has doubted the interpretation of the radiocarbon dates to suggest a longer chronology (1981, 207) and the complex of ringforts at **Cush**, Co. Limerick. The excavator, Ó Riordáin, believed the complex to be bronze age (1940), but later commentators have seen the ring-forts as post-dating a bronze age cemetery on the site. Caulfield has seen the complex as early iron age (1981, 209), pointing to a bone slip from one of the barrows that, on his own arguments, need have nothing to do with the ringfort complex.

It remains that a composite bone comb from the site is unlikely to pre-date the fourth century, a ringed pin is unlikely to pre-date the eighth century, and the overall character of the finds is in keeping with a date somewhere between the fourth and eighth centuries (for brief discussion, Laing, 1988, 264).

Also questioned has been the date of the royal crannog at **Lagore, Co. Meath**. This site was originally dated to the seventh to tenth centuries AD on the basis of documentary references (Hencken, 1950, 3-7). In a fairly detailed analysis, Raftery has questioned the traditional dating. He has argued that the crannog may have a much longer life than Hencken supposed, and that the 'historical evidence, such as it is, is taken to provide the initial date for the site and that anything in the archaeological record likely to conflict with this tends to be explained away' (Raftery, 1981, 84; Warner, 1988). All Raftery's arguments about the original dating for Lagore are valid, but he offers no alternative chronology (though he implies it may have begun in use in 'late Roman' times and continued in use until 'late medieval' times (Raftery, 1981, *loc. cit.*).

The fact is, however, that Lagore has not produced any of the diagnostic types of F penannular brooch current in the sixth century, nor any of the other fifth-sixth century brooches discussed below, nor has it produced any imported pottery of classes A, B or D, the earliest imports being E ware, which as is argued above, is not likely to pre-date the late sixth century, and is more likely to be of the seventh. Yet E ware was present in Hencken's periods Ia and Ib (1950, 126) and also from Ia comes an H penannular of plain type which is unlikely to pre-date the late sixth or early seventh century either. In view of this, Hencken's dating of the end of Ia to the seventh century on the evidence of a filigree object with Anglo-Saxon affinities probably still is valid (Hencken, 1950, 6; Raftery, 1981, 84; Warner, 1986).

Ballinderry 2 Crannog, Co. Offaly, was identified by the excavator as having a 'late bronze age' occupation and then an 'early Christian' phase which was assigned to the seventh or eighth century AD (Hencken, 1942, 29). The finds included a sherd of Arretine ware, discovered under the timber floor of the 'Early Christian' crannog.

Hencken regarded the Arretine as of 'no significance as to dating' (1942, 49). The question is whether this statement is justifiable? Arretine is very rarely found in Britain, being mostly imported in the pre-Roman iron age, with a few instances of residual survival on Claudian sites. It is not like the later types of samian, which might well have been used as a pigment or for some other function in the post-Roman period. Arretine is unlikely to have reached Ireland later than the first century AD, and its survival down to the 'seventh or eighth' stretches all credibility.

There are other finds from Ballinderry 2 which might point to an earlier occupation phase. There is, for instance, a Roman melon bead of the late first or second century (Hencken, 1942, fig. 21, no. 12), a piece of glass which may be Roman (Hencken, 1942, fig. no. 21, 787) and a twisted bronze bracelet that has its counterparts in late Roman contexts (bracelet — Hencken, 1942, fig. 18, no. 609; fourth century hoard with similar bracelets — Bush-Fox, 1949, pl.

XLIX, from Richborough; or Wheeler & Wheeler, 1932, fig. 17, no. 56, and N for the type of fastening as well).

There are other objects with an 'iron age' look about them, such as a tubular bronze bracelet (Hencken, 1942, fig. 18, no. 565 and discussion p. 45, where Hencken says 'it is surprising to find so late an example'). To continue to spread the chronology, a fragmentary bone comb (fig. 22, no. 383) might fit in with a fifth-century Germanic millieu, while, despite the ogham numbers combined with Roman, the 'parallelopiped dice' (fig. 22, nos. 17 and 45) have a distinctly 'iron age' look about them, with closest parallels in secondary contexts in Scottish brochs. E ware and an enamelled F brooch (Hencken, 1942, fig. 12) take the sequence to the end of the sixth century or early in the seventh, as does the binding with affinities to the Sutton Hoo 1 hanging bowl escutcheon bindings (Hencken, 1942, no. 641), while a Pictish brooch (Hencken, 1942, fig. 15, no. 716) and some Viking-style pins take the occupation down to at least the end of the eighth century.

It is of course possible from their context (under the floor of the later crannog) that the Arretine and tubular bracelet belong to the 'bronze age' occupation, as does the twisted armlet, which was found outside the crannog. In which case, the 'bronze age' occupation may belong to the first or second centuries AD, and occupation thenceforward continued, perhaps with breaks, until the eighth or ninth.

The finds from the crannog of **Ballinderry 1, Co. Westmeath**, are mostly compatible with a Viking-period date, perhaps in the tenth century, but one penannular brooch (Hencken, 1936, fig. 24, D) is of a type now classed as Fc and is likely to be of the sixth century if not the fifth.

One further 'classic' site requires reconsideration. This is **Garranes, Co. Cork**. Here dating is provided by Mediterranean imported pottery of classes A and B, indicating an occupation in the later fifth-early sixth centuries. A harness pendant from the site (Ó Riordáin, 1942, fig. 3, no. 167) is similar in character to a knobbed terret of the North British iron age, fashionable around the second century AD, and a repousse bronze plate (*loc. cit.*, fig. 3, no. 276), again has similarities to North British metalwork of that period (Mac Gregor, 1976, 338-9 etc). A metal knob Ó Riordáin suggested might be the terminal of a cross-bow brooch (1942, 98). A projecting disc- headed pin (1942, no. 352), though without precise parallels, is like some Scottish iron age projecting ring headed pins, which may have provided the inspiration, while the 'unfinished' penannular brooch of class H (Ó Riordáin, 1942, no. 265) is unlikely to be much earlier than the seventh century, if at all. There is also E ware from the site, carrying its occupation to the end of the sixth, if not the seventh century.

Ó Riordáin makes it clear that the bulk of the pottery at Garranes came from a 'black habitation layer' on site D, and says it 'extended over a distance of 112' along the inner rampart'. At one point under the layer he found a pit with crucible fragments and a flint (Ó Riordáin, 1942, 87) which he pointed out pre-dated the black layer with the imported pottery. From these clues, it would appear that the imported pottery is not primary to the site, though how much earlier the construction of the rath took place can only be guessed. His section (his plate XVI) suggests that the rampart was already slightly eroded when the black deposit ran over its tail.

BRITAIN

The chronological problems that are paramount in Ireland are echoed in Britain, where through a 'knock-on' effect finds, and therefore occupation phases, have frequently been dated by reference to Irish finds. In a recent paper (Laing, 1988b) a rapid survey suggested that there was evidence for the re-occupation of hillforts in the third and fourth centuries, even though the construction of defences may not pre-date the fifth. This is true in Wales for example at Dinorben, Clwyd (Gardner & Savory, 1964, 205-7), Coygan Camp, Glamorgan (albeit usage by forgers! — Wainwright, 1967, 70-1; 157-8), and a number of other sites, including the classic site of Dinas Emrys (Gwynedd), where a case for fourth century occupation has recently been advanced by us (Laing & Laing, 1988, 213). In south-west England Burrow has argued that 'a substantial proportion of hillforts have produced Roman material' (1979, 212). This is discussed below (p. 103).

Relatively few sites have been extensively excavated in recent times, and **Dinas Powys, Glamorgan**, is therefore of particular importance in any chronological discussion. In his revised publication of the site, Alcock (1987, 7) put forward the sequence of occupation on this hilltop as:

(1)   Iron age pottery, but no structures
(2)   An incompleted hill-slope fort
(3)   Rare Romano-British material, introduced in phase 4

(4) Occupation and earthworks datable to the fifth to eighth centuries AD

(5) Lengthy abandonment, followed by Norman ringwork

(6) Additions to the Norman ringwork.

Alcock has been at pains to emphasise that Dinas Powys is not a re-occupied iron age fort (Alcock, 1980) and to suggest that all the Roman material on the site was introduced between the fifth and the eighth century (1987, 20-3).

The list of Roman material is impressive — five fragments of glass vessels, one fragment of window glass, one fragment of a glass counter, eighteen sherds of samian pottery from a minimum of six vessels, ten sherds of coarse pottery from a minimum of six vessels, one lump of Roman brick, one fragmentary brooch, one coin of the third century and a waste-core from a Kimmeridge shale armlet with a flint lathe tool 'typical of those used in armlet manufacture' (Alcock, 1987, 22).

In addition there are other objects from the site which could be Roman, of which the most convincing are a bone plaque with ring-and-dot (Alcock, 1987, fig. 7.1 no. 11), an enamelled chevron-decorated bronze strip (Alcock, 1987, fig. 5.1 no. 7), a silver bronzed strip with bosses and scrolls (*ibid.*, fig. 5.1 no. 12) and possibly a strap end (*ibid.*, fig. 5.1 no. 5) as well as some beads (*ibid.*, 148-9 *passim*).

Alcock has argued that the pottery and glass are for the most part datable to the first and second centuries AD, and indeed this date could apply to all the Roman finds from Dinas Powys apart from the third-century coin. As Alcock has commented on the subject of the Kimmeridge shale armlet, 'it is difficult to imagine any purpose, whether utility or luxury, which could have brought it to the site' (1987, 23).

If Alcock is correct in believing that all these Roman finds were brought to the site in the fifth century, why were these useless fragments brought? The glass could have been used as cullet in Dark Age glassworking, the brooch fragment and the coin could have been, as Alcock has suggested 'sentimental mementoes, perhaps, of the happier days of Roman rule'. But waste material from the manufacture of a Kimmeridge shale armlet and the tool used in the manufacture? That must surely have reached the site at a time when Kimmeridge shale was being actively worked. Indeed, if the 'mementoes' theory is valid, it is likely that the souvenirs would date for the most part to the fourth century. Yet there is nothing of the fourth-century in this finds list. The whole assemblage is compatible with some kind of occupation on the site in the first-second century AD. The Kimmeridge shale is still anomalous, since it comes from Dorset, but much less so in a contemporary context than one centuries later. In the fifth century it is arguable that Roman rubbish of the fourth century was relatively easy to find, but first and second century rubbish (as opposed, perhaps, to luxury items with some function, such as brooches or coins, which could have been heirlooms) is unlikely to have been littering the countryside in Wales.

The possibility of an occupation of the site in the Roman period raises the question of the date of the earthworks. Bank II and Ditch II Alcock has suggested belong to his fourth (Dark Age) phase (1987, 24-5). The other earthworks on the site he has considered to be Norman. Recently however it has been argued that all the earthworks belong to the early Christian period, not to the Norman period at all (Campbell in Edwards & Lane, 1988, 60-1). Alcock has himself cast doubt on the 'Norman' date of Bank I (1987, 12).

If there is a case for suggesting the 'later' banks (I, III and IV) in fact belong to the Dark Ages, there is also a case for dating Bank II earlier. Bank II is slight, and quite different in character from the later more substantial and stone-revetted banks. Bank II post-dates the early iron age occupation on the site, as it overlay a number of iron age potsherds (Alcock, 1987, 25), but the only find which actually suggested a Dark Age date for it was a sherd of red ware assignable to the fifth-sixth centuries, seemingly under it. But Alcock has sounded a caution: 'since the sherd was very small and came from an area much disturbed by burrows not much weight should be given to it' (1987, 25). The only reason for not considering a Roman date for the bank appears to have been the rejection of the 'Roman period occupation' model for Dinas Powys. Bank II could, though need not, date therefore from the first or second century AD.

The chronology of Dinas Powys is further complicated by the apparent association of imported pottery of classes A and B and D with E. The evidence from Clogher suggests that there A and B wares were out of use by the time E was imported (Warner, 1979). If E and A ware were in use together, it is likely that the A ware is among the latest imported to Britain, perhaps in the mid-sixth century (with the possible exception of the Phocaean red-slip of the late fifth), and that after a Roman iron-age occupation the site was abandoned until some time in the sixth century, a date which best accords with the glass and penannular brooch from the site.

Dinas Emrys, Gwynedd, is a hilltop site, excavated by Breese in 1910 (1930) and again by Savory in the 1950s (1960).

Dinas Emrys has a series of indeterminate earthworks linking outcrops of rock. Breese was concerned with discovering the legendary tower of Vortigern, and thought he had found it when he discovered a Norman castle. Savory investigated a 'Pool' with associated structures, and worked out a sequence for the site. He believed initial occupation was in the first century AD, and was associated by him with 'iron age' pottery, first-century samian, two Caledonian 'massive' or 'Donside' terrets (rein-rings from a chariot) and a pit. Savory distinguished between this presumed first century occupation and another in the fourth-fifth century, which was associated with late Roman pottery and glass, a smelting furnace and what was probably a circular hut (Savory, 1960, 39). A third 'Dark Age' phase was believed connected with the construction of a cistern and a platform over a wet hollow, called 'the Pool'.

It has been suggested that the 'iron age pottery' should be more accurately described as fragments of furnace linings and other industrial waste (Edwards & Lane,1988, 56). We have argued that there is now no reason to believe there was any first-century occupation at Dinas Emrys, and that the material ascribed to that phase actually reached the site in Phase II, when there was late Roman occupation of the hilltop (Laing & Laing, 1988, 213). This does not seem to be contradicted by other earlier Roman material identified by J.L. Davies (cited in Edwards & Lane, 1988)

The 'Pool' has a radiocarbon date which when calibrated suggests construction c. AD 1265-1410 (Williams & Johnson, 1976), and upcast from the digging of the associated cistern included a medieval sherd, suggesting that the 'Dark Age' date originally suggested for this feature is erroneous.

The archaeological evidence for 'Dark Age' occupation comprises a sherd impressed with a Chi-Rho between alpha and omega, from a pot imported from the Mediterranean, and 44 sherds all from the same Biv amphora (Edwards & Lane, 1988, 55), suggesting occupation in the fourth-sixth century. The middle and main rampart on the site are built on a layer containing late Roman material, but there is no firm evidence for dating them later than the fourth century.

Dinas Emrys, then, would appear to be an important site occupied first in the late Roman period, with possibly some re-occupation in the fifth-sixth century, though this date rests on the single sherd with the Chi-Rho.

The **Mote of Mark, Kirkcudbright**, was first excavated by A.O. Curle in 1913, then re-excavated by the present writers in 1973 and by David Longley in 1979. Curle believed that he was excavating a vitrified fort of the iron age which had been re-occupied in the eighth century (1914). The subsequent identification of the pottery and glass as being imports of the fifth-sixth centuries (Harden, 1956; Radford, 1956) led to the site being re-interpreted as having an iron age occupation followed by two phases in the Dark Ages, one centred on the fifth-sixth century, one on the later seventh-eighth. The excavation in 1973 showed that there was no iron age occupation, the rampart being a 'Dark Age' construction, as shown by radiocarbon (Laing, 1975d; Laing, 1975b; Longley, 1982).

In 1973 L. Laing suggested that the first occupation of the site was in the fifth century (without fortification), to be followed in the sixth by the construction of the rampart at a time when ornamental metalworking was being carried on at the site and E ware and Teutonic glass was being imported. This was seen as coming to an end with the arrival of the Angles who were seen as slighting the site in the early seventh century. Points in the provisional inter-pretation were modified by Longley's excavation (the supposed 'emergency blocking of the rampart gateway' was seen as simply disturbance caused by the 1913 excavation).

Most of the debate concerning the Mote of Mark has centred on the dating of a series or interlace-decorated moulds, which L. Laing suggested in 1973 were of the sixth century. The opponents of this dating argued that the interlace showed in certain instances evidence of being zoomorphic, and belonged to a later seventh-century Anglian occupation of the site (Graham Campbell *et. al.*, 1976). Alcock has summed up one school of thought by suggesting that the fort was constructed by the Britons sometime shortly before 600, who began metalworking but who were taken over by the Angles under whom a hybrid tradition of metalworking con-tinued in the seventh century (1987, 241).

Alcock was correct to highlight the fact that the radiocarbon dates for the Mote of Mark fall within a period for which recali-bration is particularly problematic (1987, 241). There does not seem however to be any incontrovertible evidence for assigning the moulds to an Anglian phase of occupation. For reasons that are set out elsewhere in this book, the interlace on the moulds is quite in keeping with late-sixth century interlace in England and on the Continent (p. 208), and it is also clear that the metalworking belongs to a single phase contemporary with the import of Teutonic glass and E ware. That this metalworking was in process when the rampart was erected is suggested by the stratification of a glass fragment from the levelled rock surface under the rampart.

As Alcock has argued, the defending of hilltops with timber-laced ramparts is unknown in Anglo-Saxon England, and thus the rampart and with it the metalworking, predate the arrival of the Angles. There are no objects decorated in a comparable style to the Mote of Mark pieces in Northumbria (though there is a disc in a related style from Cumbria), and the penannular brooches and pins made at the same time as the interlace-decorated pieces are purely British in style. There is no evidence for an Anglian occupation at the Mote.

Close-Brooks has suggested that the ramparts of the Pictish fort at **Clatchard Craig, Fife**, were built in the sixth or seventh century on the basis of radiocarbon determinations. Here the finds included a piece of East Gaulish samian of the later second or third century AD from the core of rampart 2 (Close-Brooks, 1988, 155), a **trompetenmuster** mount of similar date (Close-Brooks, 1988, 169 no. 123), a penannular brooch pin for a brooch with knobbed ends of a type current in the second century (Close-Brooks, 1988, 180 no. 124 and discussion) and an enamelled disc with interlocked pelta scrolls which would be quite in keeping with a fourth (or even third) century date (Close-Brooks, 1988, no. 122 and discussion 168-9). Some of the 'iron age' pottery would be compatible with occupation in this period. Thus, even if the ramparts were later, there is good reason to suppose the hilltop was in occupation around the second or third century AD.

Perhaps the most famous site in British Dark Age archaeology is **Dunadd, Argyll**, often assumed to be the capital of the Dalriadic Scots. Dating has followed this assumption, and it is generally held that Dunadd was first occupied by the Scots in the late fifth century AD.

Feachem suggested that Dunadd was an iron age fortification, re-used in the Dark Ages (1967). This was refuted by Laing (1975b, 3-5) in some detail, where it was argued that Dunadd was entirely of Dark Age date. This seems to have been followed by later commentators on the site, notably Lane (1984, 44). Lane has also shown there is no documentary evidence for Dunadd being the capital of the Scots, and that the earliest documentation than can be directly related to it is a reference to a siege 'obsessio Duin Att' in 683 (Lane, 1984, 43).

Lane's recent excavations at Dunadd have produced an assemblage of metalworking debris including moulds for objects with Pictish affinities that must centre around AD 800, and there is other material from Dunadd that belongs to an eighth-ninth century horizon. Apart from the reference to the late seventh century siege, there are finds of seventh century date from Dunadd, including from the recent excavations. The total absence of imported pottery of class A and B might suggest there was no occupation in the late fifth-early sixth century. To argue that these imports did not reach this part of Scotland seems invalid, since they reached Dumbarton slightly to the south. This might suggest the earliest occupation at Dunadd lay somewhere in the sixth century, and a date nearer 600 than 500 is quite probable on the evidence of the finds-list. Indeed, there is nothing from Dunadd that need pre-date 600.

Hillforts

The problems of trying to draw conclusions about social and political institutions from the archaeological evidence has been the focus of recent attention. By definition, archaeology, which is concerned with material remains, sheds very little direct light on institutions, social or political. Any conclusions that are drawn tend to be coloured by the evidence of documentary sources. The problems have been particularly apparent in the study of the occupation of hillforts in the late Roman and post-Roman periods, which have been explained in various different terms over the past twenty years.

In the 1970s the attention of scholars was firmly focussed on the subject of 're-occupied hillforts' in Western Britain. It was argued that long-abandoned iron age forts were re-occupied in a period of strife towards the end of the Roman occupation and more particularly in the fifth and sixth centuries. This re-occupation was explained in terms of the need to fortify sites against barbarian raids and as elements in the offensive against the Anglo-Saxons. In the words of Professor Fowler, 'It may be that they should be thought of more as elements of communal defence, organized either on a local or a wider basis as strongpoints in times of crisis, by confederacies of local peasants or aristocrats' (1971, 212). Fowler felt inclined to dismiss the Roman material as survival in the fifth century.

The 'Dark Age fortification' view of late-Roman and post-Roman hillfort occupation in western Britain was canvassed by Alcock in his preliminary views on his excavations at South Cadbury, Somerset (e.g. 1972, 182-94), but he has since modified this view and now sees South Cadbury and similar sites as administrative centres and royal villas.

Alcock, like Fowler, believed the re-use (or in a few cases the construction) of hillforts was a phenomenon of the later fifth century. While accepting that a number of hill-top sites in western Britain have produced evidence of late Roman usage, he has argued that 'Congresbury . . . is, on present evidence, the only major fortification in Wales and Dumnonia to have produced acceptable evidence for continuous occupation from the third through into the sixth century AD' (1987, 165).

Alcock's model is firmly based on his interpretation of the documentary sources, which are concerned with the emergence of new administrations and kingdoms in the fifth and sixth centuries.

On the politics of fourth-century Celtic Britain and Ireland the documents are, effectively, silent: the chieftains of the third- and fourth century were all (or nearly all?) pagans, and their political struggles were of very little interest to Christian writers in later centuries, except perhaps occasionally embroidered as folk-tales or when they came to the attention of the Roman authorities. It is extremely unlikely that the political climate that led to the re-occupation of hillforts in the later fifth century was entirely a product of new political aspirations. What we are much more probably seeing is a phase in a prolonged process that was only documented in its last stages.

In tracing the slender clues for political changes in Celtic Britain and Ireland in the early centuries AD, we are again confronted with chronological obstacles. It is noteworthy that Alcock's chronology is based on the dating of imported pottery. In consequence, because there is no imported pottery before the mid-fifth century, there is no datable hillfort occupation either. As we have seen, (p. 54), Alcock has interpreted the site he excavated at Dinas Powys as being first occupied in the fifth century (450 is the date he has suggested), but there is a case for projecting its occupation back to the fourth century.

The break in hillfort occupation that is seen as lying between some meagre fourth century usage of the site and the establishment of a princely centre in the late fifth is quite probably in many cases more apparent than real. It is notoriously difficult to recognize early fifth-century occupation even in Romano-British towns, so we should not dismiss the array of late Roman finds in hillforts simply because it seems paltry. Our models for what constitutes a fourth-century Romano-British assemblage come for the most part from rich contexts in towns and villas. That there *are* any Roman finds of the fourth century from hillforts is a mark of the status and wealth of the occupants rather than their poverty. The analogy can be made with native farmsteads in North Britain in the second century AD, which, for example, tend to produce a sherd of Roman pottery, a melon bead and a piece of a glass armlet as proof of contact with the Roman world. Even in the civil zone of Roman Britain, native farmsteads yield remarkably sparse finds.

This fact however should not tempt us to go to the opposite extreme of trying to find the courts of Celtic leaders of the third and fourth centuries within every enclosure. There is a diversity of possible explanations for the re-use or use of hillforts in the fourth century in Britain, only one of which is that they were the centres of local leaders.

In some cases the re-use is clearly connected with a revival of local cults. In western Britain, for instance, late Roman temples are known from the hillforts at Maiden Castle, South Cadbury, Blaise Castle, Congresbury and Lydney, and from hilltops at Lamyatt Beacon, Pagans Hill, West Hill, Uley and Cannington (discussion in Rahtz and Watts, 1979, where continuity into the fifth century and later is considered).

In other cases they may well have been the retreats of outlaws, either local or immigrant. Dinas Powys could have been, as Gresham suggested (1965) the stronghold of Irish raiders, who subsequently settled down to establish a local dynasty. The distribution of fortified sites in Wales and Dumnonia known to have been occupied in the period 400-800 is notably coastal: all are within twenty miles of the sea with the exception of South Cadbury, Somerset (in itself a unique site for the scale of its refortification), and New Pieces, adjacent to the Breiddin, Montgomery. The only reason for believing there was 'Dark Age' occupation at New Pieces was a solitary fragment of Teutonic glass of the fifth-sixth centuries — all the other material from the site belongs to the later second to fourth centuries (Edwards and Lane, 1988, 97-8).

In the question of re-occupied hillforts the weight that should be attached to particular pieces of evidence is especially difficult to estimate as a result of these factors outlined.

Climate and subsistence

Climatic improvement can lead to better harvests and an increasing population, just as deteriorating climatic conditions can lead to bad harvests, the flooding and abandonment of farmland and a fall in population. Alongside this must be set evidence for improvement in farming methods, the appearance of new crops, and so on. Any expansion in population may produce internal strife and the emergence of new leaders and tribal groupings, and might be equated with climatic factors.

In general terms in Britain and Ireland there was climatic deterioration from around the beginning of the first millennium BC, which continued until the middle of the second century BC to be followed by climatic improvement reaching an optimum somewhere between AD 250 and 400.

Particularly strong evidence for this comes from **Wales** (Lamb, 1977, II, 424-9; 1981, 55-6). At Tregaron Bog in the period from the second to fifth century AD there was a marked rise in the ratio of herb to shrub pollen, indicating an increase in farming sometime during the Roman occupation (Hogg, 1979, 288-9). Later still, in the 500s, the climate was colder and wetter again (Barber, 1981, 132).

In **North Britain** the pattern is repeated, and there are signs that 'the Roman occupation coincided with a population expansion which continued over several centuries, but which was rooted in improving environmental conditions beginning before the invasion occurred' (Higham, 1986,198). The situation prevailed until after the withdrawal of the Roman legions. Study of pollen diagrams shows there was no recession in population during the fifth and sixth centuries: at Hallowell Moss, Durham, tree pollen declined to below five per cent of the total in a clearance phase that began in the Roman period but reached its peak after 400 (Donaldson & Turner, 1977). In the Northumbrian pollen diagrams economic stablity in the fifth and probably also the sixth century is the norm (Davies & Turner, 1979).

In **Ireland**, the climatic deterioration seems to have set in a little later than in Britain: the classic pollen diagram from Red Bog, Co. Louth, shows that this happened between 700 and 600 BC (radiocarbon dating). Rising water level may have flooded lake settlements, such as Knocknalappa, Ballinderry 2 and Rathtinaun, Lough Gara, Co. Sligo (Mitchell, 1976, 158-9). Following the decline, the Red Bog sequence shows the disappearance of weeds of cultivation followed by cereal pollens. This was succeeded by a rise in pollens of hazel, ash, elm and oak. In chronological terms, this decline must have taken place in the last centuries BC and early centuries AD. Radiocarbon provides evidence for the recovery at Red Bog, with the reappearance of cereals and weeds of cultivation around AD 225 (Mitchell, 1976, 159). Pollen diagrams from Limerick, Tipperary, Meath, Antrim and Tyrone date the recovery in these areas slightly later — to around AD 300 (Mitchell, 1976, 160). In south-west Ireland pollen diagrams show less signs of recovery in the later centuries AD (Lynch, 1981, 125-7).

Mitchell has equated the recovery of *c.* AD 300 with the introduction from Roman Britain of the coulter plough (1976, 166). In Roman Britain however there is no evidence for the use of the coulter plough outside the south-east at this time, though here there is also evidence for the appearance of the mould-board plough, attested by assymetrical coulters (Evans, 1975, 157). Long balanced sickles, a new type of scythe and tribulum flints, set in a sledge to facilitate threshing, all improved fourth-century Romano-British agriculture in south-east England (Rees, 1979).

The first evidence for the mould-board plough in Ireland dates from the sixth century AD. In the pollen charts around the sixth century AD the weed of cultivation **artemisia** appears, and this Mitchell has equated with the introduction of the new type of plough (1976, 173). It may also have been attendant on the arrival of open-field strip farming, and possibly even ridge-and-furrow cultivation. The evidence is mainly documentary, and is sufficiently convincing to support the suggestion that some of the strip cultivation apparent from aerial photography in Ireland pre-dates the arrival of the English (Hughes, 1972, 51-2).

Ridge-and-furrow is apparent in Wales before the Norman conquest, as shown by the fields underlying the Norman motte and bailey castle at Hen Domen, Montgomery (Barker & Lawson, 1971).

In Cornwall the evidence from the fields at Gwithian suggests that the mould-board plough was in use here in the sixth century, though ridge-and-furrow is not attested before the ninth or tenth (Fowler & Thomas, 1962).

These changes in farming methods in the fifth-sixth centuries may have contributed to a gradual transition from enclosed to open settlements.

Against this must also be set the evidence for plague. The majority of the documentation for this dates from the sixth century, when plagues seem to have afflicted the Celtic rather than Anglo-Saxon areas. An outbreak of bubonic plague spread from Egypt in

541 or 542, reaching Constantinople the following year then sweeping across to Gaul by 544. The Irish Annals record an outbreak in that year, but the main epidemic, the 'Yellow Plague', swept through Ireland and Wales in 550-1 and seems to have killed Maelgwyn about 550 (Morris, 1973, 222). In Wales, plagues are documented for the fifth and seventh centuries as well (Davies, 1982, 31). Despite this, the population in Ireland does not seem to have appreciably declined in numbers in the fifth to seventh centuries, though the plague may have had a greater impact on the population in Britain.

Contact with the Roman Empire

In recent research there has also been a growing awareness of the importance of setting Celtic Britain and Ireland in a wider context of contemporary trends. A major factor common to Celtic and non-Celtic lands in the first century AD is the impact of the Roman Empire on the barbarians beyond it. The constant threat from Rome might well be seen as a unifying force between groups of people previously disunited. Roman intervention in the affairs of the peoples on the frontiers could similarly upset the traditional political balance. Rome could provide a new model for political aspirations, and Rome could upset the traditional economic balance by providing a new market for merchandise and a source for new consumer goods. This has been considered by L. Laing elsewhere (1988 b).

Developing from this, a further concern in recent years is the question of Romano-British survival and its possible contribution to Anglo-Saxon England. For some time it has been fairly clear that the traditional picture of waves of Anglo-Saxon incomers exterminating the Britons (ex-Romans) or driving them into the Celtic West is probably a facile model born of nineteenth-century ideas about imperialism and the processes of culture change. It continued into this century in the writings of the influential historian G.M. Trevelyan, who wrote in 1926 in his classic *History of England* of Anglo-Saxon warriors 'storming the earthwork camps and stone girt cities, burning the towns and villas, slaughtering and driving away the Romanized Britons'.

Alongside the 'fire and sword' approach to English history, racism attempted to argue for the disappearance of the Britons by pointing to nigrescence in the British population (Whittock, 1986,

86 on this subject). The Britons *v.* Saxons image was not helped by the political climate of two world wars. The 1930s produced a spate of propaganda which equated Anglo-Saxons with Germans and which tried to either paint a picture of them as violent barbarians or as vigorous conquering heroes sweeping away a decadent society, depending on the political affiliations of the writers. As late as 1948, in a survey of ancient monuments compiled by the Council for British Archaeology, it was felt reasonable to assert that 'The invaders were for the most part in a culturally primitive condition — their habitations were so wretchedly flimsy — a rectangular scraping in the ground with wattle walls and thatched roof seems to have been the limit of their known architectural competence. . .'. An anxiety to redress the balance may have resulted in archaeologists stretching meagre evidence for Romano-British survival to its limits.

4

THE ROMANIZED ZONE
OF BRITANNIA

The degree to which the Romano-British population was 'Celtic' or 'Roman' has never been properly resolved. To an extent many of us are guilty of using a shorthand convenience and dubbing the population 'Roman' if we find sherds of samian and inscriptions on a site, and 'Native British' if we do not. It has only been in fairly recent years that there has been either interest or ability to identify rural sites in the Roman period.

As a result it has not been possible to evaluate the relationship between rural inhabitants of Britannia, after the withdrawal of the legions, and the Anglo-Saxons. This relationship is a key to understanding the situation in the fifth and sixth centuries.

The evidence of the towns that has come to light in the past two decades has drastically changed and sometimes reversed ideas of their fate. It seems possible that the data from the countryside will do the same. Certainly both areas are confusing to discuss through the problems of terminology alone, and by assumptions left over from early scholarship.

Relations between Saxons and Romano-Britons

The tendency has been to argue that because the diagnostically Roman finds diminish, and the diagnostically Saxon increase, then so did those elements of the population, correspondingly. This argument is surely hazardous. By this analogy, I am German if I run a car imported from Germany, but my son is Japanese because he listens to popular music on a walkman made near Tokyo.

The twentieth and nineteenth centuries in particular have proved to us that a numerically small force can annihilate a larger popu-

PROBABLE ●

POSSIBLE ○

Carlisle

York

Lincoln

Chester

Wall
Wroxeter

Leicester

Colchester

Dorchester (Oxon.) St Albans
Gloucester

Caerwent ● Cirencester
London

Bath
Silchester
Winchester
Chichester

Exeter

Map 1 Civitates of fifth-century Britain

lation in a terrifyingly short time. This is undoubtedly true, but in such cases the oppressors were in possession of war machines of considerable strength.

In point of fact, it was the traditional 'victims' — the urban Romano-British — who had substantial advantages with their high walls and organized defences. The Anglo-Saxon settlements are notable for being undefended. This is in contrast to other invaders, such as the Romans, with their forts, fortresses and camps, or the Normans, with their motte and bailey castles. There is no evidence whatsoever for the widespread massacre of the Romano-British population in either towns or countryside. Conversely, there is proof of close juxtaposition in both the towns and the countryside of Anglo-Saxon and Romano-British lifestyles and for Saxons living in Britain before the fifth century, clearly tolerated by officialdom, and in some cases actually invited.

The late Roman evidence shows the countryside to be thickly scattered with people. Statistics point to a massive Roman-period population of possibly as much as four million with, in addition, a drift into the countryside in late Roman Britain. The figure normally quoted across the board for rural Roman populations is about ninety per cent : the late Roman rural figures were thus probably considerably in excess of this.

Against this can be placed the population figures for fifth-century Saxon England — which one estimate puts at 10,000 individuals. Even the most conservative estimate of the population of Roman Britain puts it at over a million, and the most extreme claim for the population of Anglo-Saxon incomers is not more that 25,000 (both figures inclusive of women, children and the infirm).

In view of these figures, it defies explanation how a series of disorganised bands set about entering the area unwelcomed. Indeed to suggest that the Saxons were simply 'very dominant and good fighters' — able to cross the Channel and then persuade the local population to give up their lands, or to accept them as 'squatters' nearby — sounds too like the twentieth century fantasy of aliens from outer space who mesmerize the population into acquiescence.

Much of the Roman administration was removed in 409 — and it has long been agreed that the military force by this time had been radically reduced over a prolonged period. The area in which the loss of capable administrators was probably most strongly felt may have been not in the depopulated towns, but in the countryside: in the management of the large estates. It is therefore quite probable that Saxons found there were opportunities for advancement as bailiffs on the rural estates and through these means that control was established. The situation is paralleled in Gaul, where the late Roman writer Sidonius Apollinaris commented in his letters on the billeting of barbarians on Roman estates.

Furthermore, the Romano-British depended on mass-produced goods, and there was little domestic production. With the breakdown of markets and trade, the Romano-British population would have been less well-equipped to make their own goods than the immigrant Anglo-Saxons, and thus a 'pure' Roman-British settlement in the depths of the countryside would have had little option but to buy Saxon goods. It is therefore likely (though as yet unprovable) that Anglo-Saxon became the language of trade, much as French did in the Norman period. From an archaeological standpoint, the material culture of fifth-century Britain would under such circumstances appear to be Anglo-Saxon, regardless of the ethnic origins of the population.

One of the overriding arguments used to suggest that the Anglo-Saxon population increased to the detriment of the Romano-British is the fact that there are many Anglo-Saxon cemeteries for the period whereas, (apart from those known from an urban context), we have relatively little information about what happened in the Romano-British countryside. Yet this is a pattern familiar in Celtic Britain: there is a comparable dearth of pre-Roman iron age graves. An absence of burials does not necessarily indicate an absence of population. There are many possible, though as yet unprovable, reasons why this should be. In fact, there is considerable evidence of both peoples living together.

Urban life

Urban life in the fifth and sixth centuries has been the subject of massive interest recently and scholarship has been much coloured by, in particular, the historical evidence. The archaeological remains have often seemed at variance with the history, yet, as observed in the Introduction (p. 14) this does not necessarily mean that they are therefore incompatible.

BRITISH KINGDOMS

The Dark Age literature abounds with tales of kings and kingdoms: yet there were no kingdoms under the Romans in Britain. Therefore any kingdoms known from literature in the fifth-sixth centuries must have evolved after the Roman period and must represent a modification of the administrative and political arrangements of later Roman Britain.

Cirencester, Gloucester and Bath are recorded as having survived as entities until the later sixth century. This is attested by the *Anglo-Saxon Chronicle*, which records the names of their kings, Coindail, Farinmail and Condidan, who died at the hands of the Anglo-Saxon leader Ceawlin at Dyrham in 577 (or 578).

This record seems to have been accepted by historians as valid, and it is quite possible that men claiming the titles of kings were living in these settlements. The word is emotive, however, suggestive of a court, an administration, even sceptres and crowns. At the very least, it suggests a courtesy title echoing those of Roman emperors, such as that apparently bestowed in the first century AD on the local leader in Sussex, Cogidubnus. The word 'city' too in this context must be regarded with circumspection for its various connotations. Here it probably meant the continuation of a **civitas**, which, as demonstrated below, was less a focus for culture, economics and sophistication than an agriculturally-based unit.

In his reference to 'cities' Gildas writing in the 540s clarifies the picture. He says, 'The cities of our country are still not inhabited as they were; even today they are squalid deserted ruins.' John Morris pointed out that he was using similar words to those employed by St Jerome writing about fourth-century Italy; he meant that they were 'shrunken, decayed, dying, but not that they were grassgrown archaeological sites without human inhabitants' (1975, 137).

The archaeological evidence for these 'cities' is meagre, and it coincides more with Gildas' claim than Morris's in this instance. Instead of courts and crowns, we find for example that areas of the 'cities' were turned over to fields. We must bear in mind that Romano-British cities were not large: the largest averaged around 100 acres (40 ha) with the majority between 10 acres (4 ha) (Ancaster) and 45 acres (18 ha) (Water Newton). Population estimates have suggested that small towns ranged from 150-300 inhabitants, civitas capitals from 2-3,000 inhabitants: Silchester was slightly larger, being estimated as having about 4,000 residents — but this was in the heyday of Roman Britain (Frere, 1974, 296-7). In the fifth century we are probably speaking of a few families only. The fifth-century king's domain begins to look more like the large, well-enclosed estate of an eighteenth century nobleman or a medieval manor.

A review of the fortunes of Romano-British towns at the turn of the fourth century shows that many continued in occupation well into the 'Dark Ages'. Others died earlier and the essential message is that urban Britannia clung to its values rather than reverting to an 'Iron age' Celtic way of life.

LATE ROMAN TOWNS

The fortunes of the Roman towns in the fifth century are inextricably bound up with their previous development. By AD 314 there were four provinces in Roman Britain — the Britannias. Each province had a governor with a bureaucracy and was composed of civitates, which in the early days after the conquest had been some twenty tribal areas, administered from a Roman-style town. By the fourth century there seem to have been about 28 such civitates, the name having come to mean the town itself. The territory of each was an administrative area controlled by the town, the larger tribes now being broken down for administrative purposes into smaller units (Johnson, 1980, 9).

It is not clear to what extent the towns were purely administrative centres or to what extent they functioned economically in the fourth century as centres of markets and industry. In this context Reece has advanced the thesis that towns were declining in Roman Britain in the fourth century, with a drift into the countryside (1980). He has pointed out that at Verulamium, a town for which continuity of town life into the fifth century has been argued (see below), there is evidence that extensive areas of the town fell out of use.

At Cirencester fourth century pottery is rare in construction layers, rubbish pits or as casual losses, but occurs occasionally in rubbish dumps. At Lincoln roadside ditches were clogged with rubbish (Reece, 1980, 78-9). This list can be extended: the temple precinct at Bath was flooded early in the fourth century and not restored, the basilica in Silchester went out of use as a public building (Fulford, 1982a and b) and at Exeter the forum was maintained only to the middle of the fourth century. By 380 'grass and weeds were apparently growing in the palaestra of the baths' (Wacher, 1974, 373). In London the Roman wharf silted up in the third and fourth centuries, and the Roman waterfront on the Ouse at York was in use until the fourth century but no later (Arnold, 1984, 34).

Against this catalogue of decay and abandonment can be set the evidence for building and restoration in the later fourth century: '. . . a number of towns received some form of additional defensive provision, new walls or bastions, during the middle quarters of the fourth century. . . . The latest known case of such building work is in London, where the walls were strengthened after AD 390' (Arnold, 1984, 34). There is also evidence for the refubishing of public buildings in some towns, for example Cirencester, where the forum complex was altered (Wacher, 1974, 313) (see below).

Salway has suggested that the troubles of the mid-fourth century had a 'catastrophic' effect on the towns, and has suggested that the strengthening of town walls in the mid to later fourth century was to provide secure places of refuge for a population mainly resident in the countryside, though this would seem to be negated by Ammianus' account of the restoration of the cities of Britain (1981, 411-2).

There can be no simple explanation for a decline or floruit of towns in the fourth century. Depending on local circumstances, some continued to exist primarily as administrative centres, employing existing buildings where they were suitable, or refurbishing or rebuilding them where they were not. Some may have continued to serve an economic function, with the provision of local markets. This process could be expected to continue into the fifth century, some towns dying completely, others surviving in one form or other.

TOWNS IN THE FIFTH CENTURY AND BEYOND

Given that the administrative groupings centred on the civitates, it seems logical to try to trace their fate in the fifth century. Can we, for example, discover to what extent they survived as 'British' enclaves in a population that was either Anglo-Saxon by birth or adoption of lifestyle?

There are several methods open to us in our researches. We can for example map out Anglo-Saxon material. We can claim that where none exists in an area surrounding a town, then this must demarcate the town's territory, within an otherwise foreign culture. We can analyse the dates at which Saxon material becomes common in the territory or the town itself, to postulate at which point in time the town became dominated by an Anglo-Saxon way of life. We can use placenames to discover whether the inhabitants of a region were 'Saxon' or 'British', and sometimes we can make historical intepretations from these, in much the same way that interpretations are made from material evidence. We can also use datable finds, of which coins are the most definitive example, and from the worn condition in which they might survive, can postulate that they were in use long after the supposed 'end of civilised life'. Layers of black soil (Arnold, 1984, 30-1), have frequently been found on late Roman sites, and have been put forward as evidence for occupation after the Roman period in which mostly perishable material was in use. A review of the archaeological evidence demonstrates clearly that in at least some settlements, a semblance of urban-style life continued well into the fifth century.

In 1934 R.E.M. Wheeler argued that a British population survived in the south-east, essentially the **Chiltern Zone**. This has subsequently been discussed in some detail by Davis, who has pointed out that the Chiltern region could represent a civitas centred on Verulamium which remained relatively intact from Anglo-Saxon settlement during the pagan period. Here place-names of British origin are unusually frequent. This **civitas** seems to have survived until the time of the battle of Bedcanford, in 571 (Davis, 1982, 42).

Similar arguments have been advanced for enclaves of Romano-British in the Ouse-Thame basin, about which Jackson commented 'the story of the battle of Bedcanford in 571 seems to point to the survival of British inhabitants as late as the third quarter of the sixth century, strong enough to have prevented much Saxon settlement in central and northern Buckinghamshire' (1953, 236). Davis' thesis is that the few indications of fifth-century Anglo-Saxon settlement in the Chilterns are to be accounted for by controlled settlement of **foederati** (1984, 42).

The evidence for **Verulamium**'s survival is impressive, coming mainly from Professor Frere's excavations on Insula XXVII. Here in a house built after AD 370 a major series of alterations included the laying-down of high-quality mosaic floors, one of which had seen so much use that it had to be patched. Into this was cut a corn-drying oven, the stoke hole of which had to be replaced. No coins or pottery were found in its filling, from which Frere deduced that its usage probably extended into a period when both coins and pottery were no longer available, i.e. after 430 (Frere, 1975, 319). The house was then demolished, and the site used for a stone barn or hall, which Frere reckoned continued in use until 460 at the earliest (1975, 319). One of the butresses of this building was destroyed when a wooden water pipe was laid down, suggesting continued provision of running water (though whether this was for a a single dwelling, for a fountain or part of a more ambitious system, cannot of course be judged).

Alongside this should be set the evidence provided by the *Life of Germanus*, which reported that the saint visited the shrine of St Alban in 428, and met some of the well-dressed inhabitants (Johnson, 1980, 154). Reviewing all this, Frere stated 'If life there survived until the Anglo-Saxon tide was halted late in the fifth century by the British recovery signalized for us by the battle of Mt Badon there was nothing to prevent it continuing peacefully until the Saxon victories of 571' (1966, 98).

A memory of the Verulamium **civitas'** survival is perhaps preserved in a medieval Welsh tradition of **Argoed Calchvynydd rhwng Trenn ag Afon Tain** — the 'land of the chalk (or limestone) hills between Trent and Thames' that was listed then as one of the principal territories of Britain (Morris, 1965, 172). One of its rulers, Cadrawd or Cadrod, seems to be listed among the 'Men of the North' in Welsh tradition (Davis, 1984, 43).

If it is allowed that Verulamium does represent the centre of one surviving (Romano) British region, then we can claim evidence of similar non-Saxon territories surviving into the later fifth and sixth century.

The most outstanding site in this connection is **Silchester**, where a series of dykes demarcate an area round the Roman town (Boon, 1974, 78-9). The main dyke is Grim's Bank, lying approximately two miles north-west of the town (O'Neil, 1943). O'Neil argued that the earthworks were put up after the battle of Mons Badonicus (perhaps 518) at a time when the Saxon advance was halted (1944). However, they need not be as late.

The later material from Silchester was studied by Boon (1959). The list comprises mostly metalwork of a type that can now be seen to span the period from the late fourth to early fifth century, two penannular brooch pins which could as easily be fourth century as fifth, a Saxon button brooch, a very dubious Byzantine bronze coin and the round terminal of an H3 brooch which again could be fourth-century. One of the pins (from an F penannular brooch) was extremely worn when lost, tempting Boon to suggest that it had survived into the fifth century. More interesting perhaps is the glass, which include fragments assigned to the fifth century (Boon, 1959, 81). Furthermore, the coin sequence from Silchester implies occupation into the fifth century. Since the few Anglo-Saxon finds from Silchester belong to the seventh century or later, the archaeological record as a whole suggests strongly that Silchester survived as a **civitas**-based entity into the fifth or sixth century.

Gloucester demonstrates a confusing picture. There is some direct evidence for ornamental metalworking continuing in the Bristol Channel region from the New Market Hall, Gloucester. Here were found a fragment of an enamelled bowl with geometric cloisons, a penannular brooch pin and various pieces of scrap, as well as sherds of a later fifth-century North African red slip bowl. A coin hoard concluding with 12 pieces of Honorius and 29 of Arcadius seems to have collapsed on to the debris from a hiding place in the rafters (Hassall & Rhodes, 1974, 30, 89 and fig. 34). There is evidence that the Forum area was in continuous use after the Forum itself had been dismantled (Hurst, 1972, 58). Two or three occupational phases postdate the deposition of late fourth century **Fel Temp Rep** imitation coins at 13-17 Berkeley St (Hurst, 1974, 23), and there was a late- or post-Roman cemetery at Kingsholm (Hurst, 1975, 272).

At **Cirencester** there is evidence that the forum was used into the fifth century: the topmost layer of paving 'revealed the straight edges of slabs that must once have been a splendid floor but worn to a state beyond recognition' (Wacher, 1976, 15). The absence of coins suggested that cleaning of the area continued until all coins were out of circulation (Wacher, 1974, 313). Against this, there is the evidence of unburied bodies, seemingly left to rot in roadside ditches (Wacher, 1974, 313). The evidence for these bodies is not strong, however. One was found associated with medieval pottery, and the circumstances of discovery of the other have never been properly published.

In **Bath** the brooch which Cunliffe has suggested was a votive offering of the post-Roman centuries need not have been, but there is some evidence for a very late (post-Roman) repaving of the temple precinct floor, after the flooding which effectively brought an end to Bath's prosperity in the late Roman period (Cunliffe, 1980, 201).

At **Lincoln**, it may be possible to define the surrounding territory. There is no early Anglo-Saxon settlement attested near the town: on the north side, the nearest site is Hackthorn, two miles beyond the present city boundary. There is pagan Saxon pottery from Middle Carlton, three miles north-west, and from Cherry Willingham, again three miles away. Six miles away a cruciform brooch has been found. In south-west Lindsey there are no early Anglian sites, but four villas (Eagles, 1979, 183). Excavations in the city have shown street surfaces were repaired into the fifth century, and a spiral-headed pin (without context) might suggest continuing occupation into the sixth or later (Eagles, 1979, 157).

The king-list for Lindsey is revealing — Caedbaed, who ruled the area in the sixth century, had a British name. The first king after Woden was called Uinta, which has been pointed out as looking suspiciously like the Roman placename Venta (Whittock, 1986, 178). The name Lindsey itself is formed by adding the Old English **eg** (island) to the British **lindon**, while Kesteven, a district of Lindsey, also has a British root, from **ceto**, a wood.

Exeter shows signs of decay in the later fourth century. Alterations were made to the east end of the basilica in the fifth century, and there seems to have been some occupation in the town until the arrival of the Anglo-Saxons in the late seventh century. There is a well-known reference to a sixth-century grain ship from Alexandria arriving at Exeter and returning with tin, though whether this refers to the town itself has been questioned (Wacher, 1974, 334-5).

In **London** the evidence of 'black soil' has been taken to imply abandonment, as analysis has shown it to be a mixture of local and imported soils with human waste dumped on built-up areas during the fourth century (Macphail, 1981). This need only demonstrate that London, like many other places, had areas of dereliction and ploughing; the description does not necessarily apply to the entirety of the city. Excavations in Lower Thames St showed that one house was occupied after 395 (Hobley & Schofield, 1977, 55-6; Marsden, 1980, 180-1). Imported pottery from London is represented by a Byzacena amphora sherd, from Tunisia. Similar sherds are recorded from the New Market Hall, Gloucester, from Exeter and from Dorchester, Dorset. All the towns are possible candidates as surviving fifth-century **civitates**. Imported pottery could imply that Carlisle and Ilchester were also surviving civitates.

Imported pottery comparable to that found in London has been found at the Anglo-Saxon site at Mucking, Essex (Peacock, 1977). The **Mucking** vessel is somewhat surprising, but it could have been traded from a neighbouring British centre. In this context, Myres has noted the continuity at Mucking from Roman to Saxon in both the settlement and cemetery. He has suggested that the site may have been a look-out patrolling the Thames estuary, on the eastern borders of the **territorium** of London. In which case, the earliest Saxon settlers there could have been taking over from an initially Roman signal post (Myres, 1986, 131).

The evidence for **Colchester's** survival beyond the fifth century is not strong, but the distribution map of early Anglo-Saxon material shows no find within about a fifteen-mile radius of the city (Dunnett, 1975, fig. 44), though a solitary fifth-century Saxon sunken-floor hut has been found within the city itself (Dunnett, 1975, 144).

In Sussex, **Chichester** continued to be occupied into the fifth century: the evidence comprises two houses in Chapel Street, a gold solidus of Valentinian III, and the usual 'black earth'. In addition, there are signs that in the neighbourhood some villas (such as Bignor) and settlements (such as Rookery Hill, Bishopstone) continued to be occupied in the fifth century (Welch, 1983, 14-15). Welch has suggested that Anglo-Saxon settlement in the vicinity of Chichester was under control in the fifth century (1971; 1983, 278). He has pointed out that there is a density of fifth-century settlements between the Ouse and the Cuckmere, which he has seen as the result of a fifth-century treaty (Welch, 1983, 278).

At **Winchester** there is no evidence for Anglo-Saxon settlement in the vicinity of the town before the beginning of the sixth century, the date of the earliest graves in the cemetery at Worthy Park (Meaney, 1964, 102). The other cemeteries near the city, Winnall I and St Giles, are of probably similar date to Worthy Park. Writing of the latter, Sonia Hawkes has said that it provides 'the best and earliest information about Germanic settlement history in the Winchester area' (Meaney & Hawkes, 1970, 1). From Winchester itself, the earliest Anglo-Saxon material comprises a series of finds of the sixth century from Lower Brook Street (Biddle, 1975, 303). As far as the present authors are aware, there is no certain fifth-century Anglo-Saxon material within a five-mile radius of the city.

Dorchester-on-Thames, Oxon., is often regarded as a Roman town occupied at an early date by the Anglo-Saxons. Yet at Dorchester in the early fifth century a rectangular Roman building was erected on one of the town streets, with mortared stone footings. Its cobbled yard was laid on a very worn coin dated to 394-5, and it was thus unlikely the building was erected before the first quarter of the fifth century. The yard is likely to have survived to the end of the century or even later and was still in use when an Anglo-Saxon style building was constructed on top of it. To the north of it a sixth-century Anglo-Saxon sunken-floor hut was built. It lay alongside the Roman street, which seems to have still been in use as the hut was approached from it by some steps (Frere, 1962, 131). Elsewhere in the city, coins of Honorius and Arcadius show that occupation continued into the fifth century (Alcock, 1987, 272).

78

Whether Dorchester, (which was not a **civitas** as such in the Roman period), aspired to such status in the fifth century cannot be surmised. The town itself certainly survived until the sixth century.

Wall, Staffs., was one of the twenty-eight cities listed by Nennius. As it is the only town in Nennius' list that was not a cantonial capital, it is assumed that Nennius must have had special knowledge to prompt him to include it. There is an account of a pagan raid on Wall in an early Welsh poem called 'The Lament of Cynyddlan', which may have been known to Nennius (Webster, 1958, 8).

Other Roman towns apparently without any fifth-century Anglo-Saxon occupation in their vicinity include **Ancaster**, Lincs. (where there is a Christian(?) Romano-British cemetery of the fourth- fifth century (Wilson, 1968; Thomas, 1981, 236-7) and **Water Newton**, Cambs.

The fullest evidence for the survival of a **civitas** comes from **Wroxeter**, Shropshire. Excavations on the Baths Basilica site have suggested that the building was refloored in the late third century, was repaired, then refloored up to three times, coins providing a **terminus post quem** of AD 375. The roof of the basilica was then removed along with the columns of the nave and porticos leaving a walled open space. Again this can be coin-dated as happening sometime after 388-92. Major timber framed buildings were next built, which show signs of at least three successive phases, some with domestic occupation. The adjacent gravel street now had booths on its south side and a timber boardwalk on its north. A coin showed this phase to post-date 402. These timber buildings were next deliberately dismantled and removed, and two smaller structures put up on the western part of the site. Finally a burial (with Romano-British characteristics?) was dug just to the south of one of the buildings. A radiocarbon date showed this to have happened around AD 600 (Barker *et. al.*, unpublished interim, 1988). The whole sequence, then, seems to span a period down to the later sixth century, and Wroxeter could not have been unique.

ANGLO-SAXONS IN TOWNS

Against this record of purely Romano-British survival, the occurrence of the Saxon-style sunken-floor huts within the town walls at Canterbury and Dorchester serve to underline the possibility of communities of Anglo-Saxons living alongside Britons in some towns of the fifth century. This is the likeliest explanation for the situation at **Heybridge**, Essex, for example. Here in the first half of the fifth century within the limits of the Roman town, a small Anglo-Saxon settlement was established. The inhabitants used Romano-British Oxford colour-coated pottery in their huts, and it would seem that both the Roman town and the Saxon settlement dwindled to nothing together in the later fifth century (Drury & Wickenden, 1982, 33-4). In the same study, attention was drawn to the presence of Anglo-Saxon pots (at least one, probably three) in the late Romano-British cemetery at Heybridge, and to comparable late Roman inhumation cemeteries at Kelvedon and Magdalen Laver.

It is of exceptional interest that Drury and Wickenden have noted that where Anglo-Saxon burials seem to be made in Romano-British cemeteries, the cemeteries favoured are those used by the upper ranks of Romano-British society. At Lankhills, Winchester, where there were Anglo-Saxon burials in the late Roman cemetery, it was noted that these were interred in the 'best' part of the cemetery (Drury & Wickenden, 1982, 35; Lankhills in Clarke, 1979, 389-402).

CHRISTIAN INFLUENCE IN TOWNS

Roman towns certainly housed Christian communities. Thomas has argued the evidence for intra-mural churches in the late Roman period at Caerwent, Canterbury, Colchester, Exeter, Lincoln, Silchester, and Verulamium, all towns which have been suggested above as surviving as civitates (Thomas, 1981b, 166-70). He has also argued for extra-mural churches at Colchester and London (1981b, 170-80). In addition he has postulated for churches at a few sites where there is no evidence for a post-Roman **civitas**, namely Dorchester (Dorset), Richborough, Icklingham and Canterbury. Of these Richborough is exceptional, being a Roman fort. It should not however be discounted as a possible **civitas** simply on these grounds: it is notable for its wealth of post-Roman finds, a full analysis of which has never been properly carried out. Ausonius, the fifth-century Gallic writer, wrote of Rutupiae (Richborough), under which name he seems to refer to Britain (Chadwick, 1958, 232). For Dorchester there is no evidence to either prove or disprove continuity: the coin list from the town 'is not so very different from towns with attested fifth-century occupation' (Wacher, 1974, 326), though again there are sunken-floor huts from the town (Wacher, loc. cit.), and the Byzacena amphora cited above.

Country life

Outside the urban limits, the situation was undoubtedly different, both sociologically and economically, though equally rooted in the Roman and pre-Roman traditions. It seems premature at the time of writing this book, to try to draw conclusions (beyond the tentative suggestions made at the beginning of this chapter), from the material which will undoubtedly be seen in new perspectives in the near future.

The evidence available for gauging the relationship between 'Saxon' and 'Briton' in the countryside is very limited. Cemeteries, rural settlements, place-names and personal names, and certain types of artefact and technology are considered below.

CEMETERIES AND POPULATION

A study by M. Faull of orientation in Anglo-Saxon cemeteries led her to believe that native Romano-British burial rite tended towards contracted skeletons with the head oriented between north and north-east, sometimes tending towards the east, but not towards the west.

Having studied 5,293 inhumation burials of the pagan Saxon period south of Northumbria, Faull found that the commonest burial form was extended or loosely flexed, with the majority of heads pointing to the west (1977, 5). In analysing burials in Northumbria, she has noted that the majority of Romano-British burials were oriented between north and north-east, and were usually extended, following native tradition, but that Anglo-Saxon burials in the area conform to the pattern found in the rest of England (1977, 7). Some Saxon burials conforming to the Romano-British custom are discernible in Anglo-Saxon cemeteries — these are usually female, and sometimes accompanied by penannular brooches, a Romano-British artefact type (see below). They are more likely to be Romano-British burials in a predominanly Anglo-Saxon graveyard.

Studies of the physical anthropology of Anglo-Saxon burials are still in their infancy. However, a study made of skeletal material from Romano-British and Anglo-Saxon cemeteries in Hampshire very notably suggested that the majority of burials with Anglo-Saxon-style goods (which made up a small proportion of the total), in the later fifth and sixth centuries were of Romano-British stock (Arnold, 1984). A similar pattern is observable at a slightly later date in the cemetery at Eccles, Kent (Thomas, 1981b).

There are other clues in burial ritual to the survival of Romano-British customs. Whether this was a general fashion, taken up by Anglo-Saxons as well as Britons, cannot be resolved, but at face value it is probably best to regard them as burials of Romano-British people. Perhaps the most diagnostic of Romano-British rituals are the customs of decapitation, the placing of hob-nailed boots by the feet, prone burial and the placing of a coin in the mouth or hand to pay Charon's fee. These customs are apparent in the late Romano-British cemetery at Lankhills, Winchester (Clarke, 1979, 347-76). The evidence for the survival of these customs has been reviewed by White (1988, chapter 9).

Only about fifteen burials from Anglo-Saxon England can be shown to have been decapitated.

There are a number of alternative explanations for prone burial apart from a survival of Romano-British custom: execution is one. In a burial from Collingbourne Ducis, Wilts, the body was wearing a Romano-British brooch at the shoulder and an inlaid buckle at his waist, perhaps pointing to a British burial (White, 1988, 154).

Hob-nailed boots are extremely rare in Anglo-Saxon graves, but have been attested at Stretton-on-Fosse, Warwickshire (Ford, 1971, 22).

There are no instances of coins in the mouth from Anglo-Saxon England, though seven instances of coins in the hand have been recorded (White, 1988, 156).

The position of objects in graves is also suggestive of Romano-British tradition. Bracelets, often laid on the wrist rather than round it, are a feature of late Romano-British burials, and the survival of these into Anglo-Saxon times has been suggested by Dickinson to be a Romano-British trait (cited in White, 1988, 154).

A single brooch worn at the shoulder is a feature of late Roman dress, particularly that of men (Welch, 1983, 60) and its survival is therefore perhaps significant. Sometimes Romano-British brooches were re-used in this manner, sometimes Anglo-Saxon brooches were so employed (White, 1988, 155).

The study of grave-goods might be expected to produce evidence of surviving Romano-British lifestyle, and until recently it was assumed that Romano-British residual material in Anglo-Saxon graves should be regarded in terms of the heirlooms of Britons who had adopted an Anglo-Saxon way of life. Other interpretations of Roman material in Anglo-Saxon graves accounted for it in terms of 'small change' for trading in the absence of a money economy, or as scrap.

Brown has suggested that many of the miscellaneous Romano-British accessory objects found in Anglo-Saxon graves could have been suspended, and indeed often turn up in female graves along with objects suspended from girdles. From this he has deduced that they had an amuletic significance (1977). While accepting this, White has suggested that certain of these objects, namely spoons and keys, were used when the usual status objects of Anglo-Saxon society, girdle hangers and sieve spoons, were unavailable (White, 1988, 164-5).

In assessing the occurrence of Roman material in Anglo-Saxon graves, White has come to the conclusion that the 'scrap metal' and 'small change' theories are not tenable, but that Romano-British material turns up in 'bag collections' in female graves (where it can be seen to be amuletic) and more particularly as substitutes for more costly Anglo-Saxon objects of similar shape. This seems to have been the case particularly in the later sixth and seventh centuries, when there was growing stratification in Anglo-Saxon society, but also occurs earlier (White, 1988).

The material, collectively, does little to prove or disprove a survival of Romano-British population or customs on any significant scale. Why Romano-British material was used in bag collections of the later pagan period is another issue, and raises the entire question of the nature of susperstition in Anglo-Saxon England, discussed extensively by Meaney (1981). In reviewing the Anglo-Saxon attitude to the Roman past, Hunter has been able to show that there was considerable reverence for it, though undoubtedly due to the influence of the Church (1974). For the pagan period he has seen no such reverence for a Roman past, though he has followed Myres in believing the Anglo-Saxon incomers showed a reverence for the Roman site at Abingdon (1974, 50; Myres, 1969, 121-2). Elsewehere, they also seem to have favoured the sites of bronze age barrows.

To calculate British survival, population sizes (refered to briefly at the beginning of this chapter), become important. The estimates for the size of the population of Roman Britain has varied considerably over recent years, the latest estimate for the fourth century suggesting a figure in the order of more than two million; 'at its peak Romano-British population numbered between three and four million people' (Jones, 1979, 245).

Against this, estimates of the incoming Anglo-Saxon population seem remarkably small. Calculations for the pagan period are based on the number of known graves. Yet we cannot be certain what proportion of the population buried in Anglo-saxon cemeteries was in fact of immigrant stock, and not of Romano- British stock that had married into Anglo-Saxon families or adopted an Anglo-Saxon life (and/or burial) style. We also do not know what proportion of the cemeteries of pagan Saxon England have been discovered. The matter is complicated by the fact that apart from urban cemeteries, the occasional mausoleum and a few other groups of burials we have no graves for the rural inhabitants of Roman Britain, at a time when most of the population lived in the countryside. A similar comment may be made for the pre-Roman iron age. Clearly the Britons were buried individually rather than collectively probably on their farms, and their remains have been scattered and possibly even ploughed out. However, given that the number of excavated graves amounts to 25,000, taken at face-value it suggests an incoming population in the fifth century of no more than a few thousand individuals. But here again we have a problem: how many of the graves are of incomers and not of Britons who had adopted an Anglo-Saxon burial style? If the conclusions drawn above from anthropology are correct, only some of these burials were in fact of immigrants. Even allowing that most of those in fifth-century graves had been immigrants, we may still be only considering two thousand or so incomers.

Alcock has argued that the size of Anglo-Saxon cemeteries is small compared with those on the Continent. Abingdon and Long Wittenham had 203 and 234 burials, and most cemeteries have a tenth of these. Even the large cremation cemeteries seldom have more than 300 or so urns, though Spong Hill, Norfolk and Loveden, Lincs are exceptional. On the Continent, in contrast, cemeteries have between one and two-thousand urn burials (Alcock, 1971, 291). On this evidence Alcock has suggested an Anglo-Saxon population in the sixth century amounting to between 50,000 and 100,000 (Alcock, 1971, 311). Working on a population estimate of Roman Britain at a million, and allowing for a fourth-century decline from that, Alcock has pointed out that 'It would require at least a ten-fold decline to bring the British figure down to the most optimistic estimate for the English' (1971, 311). Given the more recent population estimates, it is probably more reasonable to suggest the British outnumbered the Saxons in the order of 20:1, or even 50:1.

Twenty years ago such large estimates for the population of Roman Britain would have seemed absurd, but intensive field survey in recent years has shown just how densely settled Roman

Britain was. 'In eastern Northamptonshire . . . there was a minimum of one settlement every 0.4 to 0.5 km. . . . In some areas of Bedfordshire, Roman settlements turn up with almost monotonous regularity, 500 metres apart, regardless of soil or situation. . . . Most remarkably, on the silt Fenlands of south Lincolnshire and north Cambridgeshire, Roman occupation sites were only a few hundred metres apart' (Taylor, 1983, 83). Present evidence however, does not show whether these settlements were concurrent.

These settlements were of great variety, ranging from villas and single native farmsteads to hamlets and villages, sometimes with evidence for deliberate planning. Again to quote Taylor: 'The multitude of rural settlements . . . were thus not set in an unorganized limbo of fields, but were each associated with a clearly defined estate or land unit, which perhaps approximated very closely to the later parish or township arrangement' (1983, 104).

There is good reason to suppose that some at least of the land units found in Roman Britain had already become established in the pre-Roman iron age. There is also some reason to suppose that they survived into the fifth century. Work by Bonney in Wiltshire has shown that early Anglo-Saxon burials there all lie on or are close to medieval parish or estate boundaries, indicating that these boundaries must have been in existence at the time of the Anglo-Saxon arrival and were taken over by them (Bonney, 1960).

Study of charter evidence in Dorset again suggests that land boundaries adopted by the Anglo-Saxons were of Romano-British origin (Bonney, 1972; Bonney, 1976). Similar deductions were arrived at in Humberside (Eagles, 1979, 177-8). This continuity of boundaries (which can also be seen in south Wales, see p. 112), implies that there was a take-over of existing land units by the Anglo-Saxons, though as Arnold and Wardle have argued, not necessarily without a shift in settlement location (1981).

This continuity of territorial units does not of course necessarily imply any kind of continuity of tenurial arrangements, merely that, as field and farm boundaries were already established, linked no doubt to a system of trackways and ditches, the new arrivals found it easiest to operate the farms much as they had been run before.

By this reasoning, the Anglo-Saxon incomers might be seen as a new minority, controlling from the top, very similar in fact to the Norman immigrant aristocracy who in the eleventh century brought about no significant changes in the pattern of rural life. The dearth of settlement sites of the fifth century might well be explained by this inbalance in the population. Just as it can now be seen that many of the 'villages' of Domesday were not in fact villages but manors (Taylor, 1983, ch. 8), so the surviving place-names from the early stages of the Anglo-Saxon settlement may not have been the names of villages or even hamlets, but simply the halls of the dominant families.

LATE ROMAN VILLAS AND ESTATES

Far too little has yet been done on the dating of rural settlements of the Romano-British period, but there are some indications that they became denser in the fourth century. In some measure this was due to the fact that the corn tax for the army, (the **annona militaris**), and the general increased burden of taxation fell for the most part on the food producers — the tenant farmers — rather than the large land-owners. This led to a growing gulf between rich and poor: estates increased in size, absorbing smaller farms, and progressively, free small-landowners found themselves either the tenants of the big landowners or **coloni**, little better than serfs tied to the land (Arnold, 1984, 58-9).

The growth of villas from the late third century may be connected with the growth of big landowners, an increasing number of whom built their homes nearer towns to exploit urban labour. It was a pattern found elsewhere in the Roman Empire, as A.H.M. Jones noted (1966, 366). Smaller villas, unable to compete, went into decline in the later fourth century (see below).

With the end of central Roman authority, the situation which had enabled the rich landowners to get richer came to an end. Villa-owning magnates could only prosper while protected by the super-structure of the Empire. It is not therefore surprising that the large villas followed the small and rapidly fell out of use. It is possible that those which were built within the hinterland of the surviving **civitates**, lasted longest.

Given this, we might reasonably expect growing impoverishment would result in villa buildings being allowed to decline and become progressively ruinous until the estates eventually came under the control of Anglo-Saxons. Such a rural population would have been ripe for takeover from the top. This is the situation that the archaeological evidence appears to reflect.

The villa at **Latimer** (Bucks.) shows signs of dilapidation in the mid-fourth century. The main villa building saw reduced occupation and four occupational phases followed, with new timber structures erected inside and outside the old villa courtyard. The first of these phases was assigned to the end of the fourth century, the last was 'very late in the fifth century if not later' (Branigan, 1967, 149-50).

At **Llantwit Major** (Glamorgan), the main villa building was abandoned, but occupation continued in the farm buildings. Prior to this the bathing facilities had been reduced in size and subsequently demolished, the area sealed off from the rest of the house by blocking up the only door (Webster, 1969, 231-2). A similar demolition of bath houses, presumably in the interests of economy, is recorded from **Atworth** (Wilts.), **Lullingstone** (Kent) and **Barnsley Park** (Cirencester Glos.) (Webster, 1969, 232). Such signs of declining prosperity start in the fourth century. There are few signs of constructional phases in villas of the late fourth or fifth centuries. One rare example of this is **Great Casterton** (Rutland), a villa which may have been protected by belonging to a **civitas**.

At **Rivenhall** (Essex), an aisled barn was put up in the fourth century, associated with a small amount of Roman pottery and a great deal more 'Anglo-Saxon' hand-made ware. Following the collapse of the side of a well, the hollow was used as a hearth, which produced some Saxon pottery and an Anglo-Saxon cone beaker of the fifth century. The villa itself produced late wheel-thrown native pottery notably different from the Saxon (Rodwell & Rodwell, 1973). The aisled hall could be seen as the residence of the Anglo-Saxon chief who had taken over the estate.

At **Orton Hall Farm** (Northants) a villa went into decline in the later fourth century, and timber buildings with associated rubbish pits were set up around the court. The finds included a barred Frisian comb, characteristic of the fifth century (Mackreth, 1978).

At **Barton Court Farm** (Oxon.), where there was a long occupation from iron age through Roman times, the late Roman farmhouse was occupied to the end of the fourth century and probably into the fifth. It was then demolished and replaced by a series of timber huts, that were still in use in the sixth century. Handmade pottery, some with carinations, indicated an Anglo-Saxon presence from early in the fifth century. In the sixth century the inhabitants moved to a new site, and dug two burials into the ruins of the villa (Selkirk, 1978).

At **Orton Longueville** (Cambs.), a fifth-sixth century farmstead was built alongside the villa, utilizing one of the Roman paddocks (Taylor, 1983, 112).

There is similar evidence from village sites, though it is often extremely difficult to demonstrate whether there is any connexion between the late Roman occupation and the Anglo-Saxon over-lying it. In some cases the Anglo-Saxon settlement was adjacent to the Roman: this was the case at Catholme (Staffs.) (Losco-Bradley, 1977). In other cases, such as Great Doddington, a Saxon village appears to be the direct successor of a large Roman settlement (Taylor, 1983, 116).

Recent work at **Alington Avenue, Dorchester** (Oxon.) has re-vealed a late Roman farmyard with associated cemetery, which extends from the second to the fourth century. The settlement 'appears to lead on imperceptibly into the Early medieval (= Saxon?) period. Three timber halls were excavated, similar to those at Chalton and Cowdery's Down' (Selkirk, 1988, 172).

It is worth noting here that the large numbers of rural sites were not necessarily concurrent, and might be the result of settlement drift which is known to have taken place in later periods (and earlier?). This would also explain both the difficulty of distin-guishing Saxon or Roman style rural sites, and the 'sudden' appearance of settlements, usually near Roman sites, which are predominantly 'Saxon' : they were merely another stage in a long process of moving settlement sites, and their appearance as new entities is thus fortuitous.

ANGLO-SAXON SITES

If we attack the problem from another angle, we can scrutinise Anglo-Saxon sites for evidence of Romano-British material. This would incontrovertibly suggest a close and peaceable link between the two cultures if it were to be found. In fact, such material is not uncommon. At **Chalton** (Hants.), apart from a British hanging bowl escutcheon of developed trumpet pattern type, there were Roman coins, pieces of Roman tile and Romano-British pottery (Addyman & Leigh, 1973, 19-20; Addyman, Leigh & Hughes, 1972, 28). There were also numbers of oyster shells, traded probably from Portsmouth harbour, possibly a taste acquired from Romano-Britons. Similarly, the Saxon village at **West Stow** (Suffolk) pro-duced an appreciable amount of Romano-British material. This included bracelets, finger rings, five brooches or fragments, seven spoons, several pins, toilet articles, a balance beam, a votive axe, an iron stylus (West, 1985, 122), and Romano-British pottery (West, *op. cit.*). West has argued that as the site was in a location without previous Romano-British occupation, the objects arrived as 'salvage' from nearby Romano-British sites, most notably Icklingham (1985, 167). However, this might more easily be interpreted as a foundation comprising Romano-British stock but organised on Anglo-Saxon lines.

There are some hints that Romano-British buildings served as models for Anglo-Saxon architects. This was first proposed by Philip Dixon (1982), who suggested that Anglo-Saxon immigrants adopted Romano-British building types from their neighbours, but used their own constructional techniques. This suggestion has also been made for the earliest buildings in the Northumbrian palace complex at Yeavering (Hope-Taylor, 1977, 140). An alternative view has been advanced by James, Marshall and Millett, who have suggested that the type of building represented at **Cowdery's Down**, Basingstoke, in fact represents the home of Romano-Britons who had adopted an Anglo-Saxon way of life (1984, 206).

All in all, the evidence points to there being no break in the general settlement pattern with the arrival of the Anglo-Saxons. The old estates continued to be farmed, but with the gradual demise of villa buildings and replacement by less grandiose farm-steads — a process that had begun within the fourth century.

Much of the foregoing evidence can be interpreted most easily as showing a smooth assimilation of the two cultures — 'Saxon' and 'Romano-British'. As would be expected of such a dis-organised phenomenon, the variety in depth, style and quality of the results is convincingly what would be expected.

Placenames Recent evidence has suggested that the traditional picture of Anglo-Saxon settlement provided by placenames is not as secure as was once thought. To begin with, we have to remember that we have very few early forms for Anglo-Saxon placenames. The pagan Saxons were illiterate, and very few names survive in a seventh-, eighth- or even ninth-century form. Most of them survive in a form set down by the Normans (Myres, 1986, 30).

Secondly, -**inga** placenames, which are folk names meaning 'the settlement of X's people', do not, as was originally supposed, relate to the very earliest settlement. One reason for being suspicious of the **inga** names is the fact that their distribution does not seem to coincide with that of early Anglo-Saxon cemeteries. It is also clear that **inga** names were still being formed after the spread of Christianity in the seventh century, and to thus belong to another phase in the evolution of placenames (Dodgson, 1966). It could well be that they represent political configurations of the seventh century rather than the spread of settlement.

The same kind of strictures apply to other 'early' Anglo-Saxon placenames. There are problems for example over -ham names, which seem to have a distribution related to Roman roads and settlements, and which are often found associated with inga names, in the form -ingaham. As it is now clear that inga names are frequently late, it is assumed they are preceded first by -ham names and then by -ingaham names (Myres, 1986, 40).

The -ham element however can have another origin in some placenames originating in -hamm, which has a variety of meanings and survives quite late. Dodgson in discussing -ham names has suggested that their appearance in south-east England relates to the expansion of Anglo-Saxon settlement from Thanet into the south Downs of Sussex and the East Surrey Downs, in the fifth — sixth century (Dodgson, 1973). However, Dodgson's survey of ham names also drew attention to a major series in Cheshire, which he saw as relating to a phase of colonization in the seventh century. If it is accepted that the Cheshire placenames belong to the seventh century, then so may those in south-east England. The placename element itself, which just means 'a settlement' contains no pointers to an 'expansion of settlement' theory. We cannot take this and other placename evidence as proving that a large number of Saxons entered Britain and established brand new villages populated entirely by newcomers.

To take the argument one stage further, there is no real evidence to prove that any of the Anglo-Saxon placenames actually belong to the fifth century rather than later. They could all relate to a stage at which Anglo-Saxon was becoming widely assimilated by the predominantly British population, in the sixth or seventh century.

Whilst placenames certainly reflect the presence of Anglo-Saxons, (even if the extent or style of this is debatable), they can also be used to demonstrate Romano-British survival. This is found to be relatively abundant. Anglo-Saxon placenames with ceaster are derived from Latin castra, a fort, and were used to describe man-made fortifications. The word was borrowed from the Latin-speaking Britons, as it is found in no other Germanic language (Jackson, 1953, 252). Some caesters retained elements of their original Roman name (e.g. Winchester, Gloucester, Cirencester), others had new names added to the ceaster element. Only Canterbury retained its civitas name.

Three further Latin placenames survived into the Saxon period

— Cataracta (Catterick), Calcaria (Kaelcacastir in Bede), and Spinae (Speen, Berks.) (Whittock,1986,78).

Three other elements also survived. **Wic**, from Latin **vicus**, a Roman settlement, has a variety of meanings in English. In its earliest compound, however, combined with **-ham** (as in Wickham), it has been shown to coincide with Roman settlements (Gelling, 1967). **Eccles**, from Latin **ecclesia**, a church (Cameron, 1968), is another, but this may have been mostly borrowed indirectly from Primitive Welsh. Where it is found in the south-east however — Eccles, near Rochester, Kent for example — it seems to originate before 500, and may owe its name to a villa church (Henig, 1984, 227). **Funta**, from Latin **fontana**, a fountain, may be an indirect borrowing from Old Welsh (Myres, 1986, 32-3).

A placename element found on the Continent as well as in England contains the element 'camp', from **campus**, a field. In England it seems to mean 'an enclosed piece of land', and it has been suggested that it meant uncultivated land round a town or villa — peripheral land perhaps given to the earliest Anglo-Saxon settlers in return for military service (Gelling, 1978, 77).

More problematical are names with **port**, a harbour (from **porta**), **cort(e)**, a piece of land cut off, and 'faefer' (as in Faversham, Kent) from the Latin for a metalworking yard. (Gelling, 1977, for these and the other elements).

Also useful are **Wala** placenames, from **Walh**, the English term for a Briton (Faull, 1975). As Faull has pointed out, the placenames are found in areas where British communities still surviving are to be distinguished from those round about, and are thus absent from predominantly British areas such as Cumbria, but occur occasionally in Yorkshire (1977,12). They imply that enclaves, deliberately resisting an Anglo-Saxon lifestyle or control, survived quite late. **Bret-** placenames also indicate the presence of Britons (from OE **Brettas**). These however tend to be later. As Faull has shown from her study of Northumbria, 'The absence of Celtic place-names in the primary settlement areas can no longer be taken to prove the extermination of the British population. . . . The **Walh/Brettas** placenames point to scattered examples of British communities surviving for a time as recognizable entities on the less attractive sites' (1977, 20). One might postulate that this simply shows that the Anglo-Saxon controllers simply did not bother to gain influence over unattractive areas, as opposed to the view that they were unable to gain such control.

Some placenames indicate pockets of British speakers survived very late: Pensax, near Hereford, is an Old Welsh name meaning 'hill of the Saxons', and employs a grammatical arrangement, noun first, used in Welsh from the sixth century onwards. Similar clues suggest that there were Welsh speakers round Lichfield (Staffs.) until the 670s and at Hints, in the same county, until at least the late sixth century (Whittock, 1986, 92).

It has frequently been pointed out that despite all the cited examples, there are relatively few Celtic names in Anglo-Saxon England. However, as a result of a study of east Dorset placenames, where only about one per cent of the names are of Celtic origin, despite the late arrival of the English, Whittock has suggested that some English placenames contain unrecognized Celtic or Latin elements, and has pointed out that etymologies of names have often been misleading (1986, 93-4).

Personal names Personal names also indicate a surviving British population element. The **wealh** element, found in placenames, also appears in personal names in Anglo-Saxon England, such as Cenwealh, king of Wessex in the seventh century, or Ethelwealh, king of Sussex. Merewalh, a Mercian king of the seventh-century, had a name which meant 'famous Briton' (Whittock, 1986, 86). Caedwalla, king of Wessex, seems to have been British in origin — his brother was Mul, 'mule', or 'half-breed' (Whittock, 1986, 86). Cerdic, founder of the West Saxons, had a British name, as did Caedbaed, a king of Lindsey. Cynric, who conquered the west, had a name of Irish origin, as did Ceawlin (Morris, 1973, 225-6).

There is no reason to assume that these rulers with Celtic-derived names were Britons, or even of British origin, but their usage shows the extent to which British names had been assimilated by the Anglo-Saxon population. Indeed, it would defy logic unless there was a high degree of interplay between the two cultures based on mutual respect. The above list of names alone suggest far more strongly that 'Saxon' was by this time a term refering to a socio-political or even economic situation (basically to distinguish the rural from the urban) rather than a genetic background.

Technology It is extremely difficult to identify many Romano-British objects from those of pagan Saxon England, since some elements derived from the Roman world, and could just as easily have been acquired by the Anglo-Saxon peoples in their original homelands.

The problem is underlined by the issues raised by Romano-

Saxon pottery (Anglo-Saxon in style but using Roman fabrics). This was first defined by Myres (1956), and further studied by him (1969, 66-71) when he also defined Saxo-Roman pottery (Roman in style but 'Saxon' in fabric). Myres interpreted such pots as the products of Anglo-Saxon settlers within Roman Britain. Subsequent studies have shown that the pots were part of a widespread late Roman style, and were produced in orthodox Romano-British kilns (Gillam, 1979; Roberts, 1982).

Myres accepts these findings and drew attention (1986, 89-93) to the fact that their distribution lies in the major areas of Anglo-Saxon settlement: the Saxon Shore forts; the principal Roman east coast ports; major towns in the hinterland; and in some villas and vici (Myres, 1986, 89-93). He has highlighted two particularly interesting pots. The first (from Billericay, Essex), is in a local Romano-British fabric but was decorated in typically Saxon form and contained a partial cremation. A Romano-British colour-coated jar was used as a lid (Weller, Westley & Myres, 1974). As inhumation was universal in the Roman world at this period, this burial is likely to be of a Saxon.

A second urn, from Chelmsford, Essex, is also Saxon in decoration but carries an inscription in good quality Roman lettering DISETE, which Myres has seen as 'of (or for) Diseta', (a girl's name). Although the circumstances of its discovery make it uncertain, Myres has suggested it was used as a cremation urn for Diseta, presumably a Romano-Briton (1986, 96).

The incidence of millefiori and the significance of the hanging bowls in the Sutton Hoo ship burial are noted on p. 213. The ceremonial whetstone or sceptre from Sutton Hoo has also been seen as a 'Celtic' object, as has its counterpart from Hough-on-the-Hill, Lincs. In Sutton Hoo, too, the technology of the wrought-iron cauldron chain has been seen as a legacy from Roman Britain. The use of niello, a black paste of silver sulphide, in the decoration of some Kentish disc brooches, has been seen as a surviving Romano-British technique.

Enamelling may be another skill borrowed by the Anglo-Saxons from the Britons, although there is very little enamelwork in Anglo-Saxon England. A disc brooch from Ebrington, Glos, has a arrangement of concentric rings and pellets in a 'British' style, inlaid with what appears to be white enamel (I am indebted to Dr John Hines for drawing my attention to this), and there is a small group of enamelled objects from the west Midlands and East Anglia, mostly dating from the sixth century (Evison, 1977; Brown,

1981; Scull, 1985). Cyril Fox was the first to suggest that the use of enamel was a Romano-British survival (1923, 283). Skull (1985) has drawn attention to a possible example of a fifth-century Anglo-Saxon enamelled saucer brooch from Bury in East Anglia, and if his date is accepted, it goes some way to bridge the chronological hiatus between the Roman material and the Anglo-Saxon.

Considerable debate has surrounded the intepretation of 'Quoit Brooch Style' metalwork. This style of work is named after a superb parcel- gilt brooch from the Anglo-Saxon cemetery at Sarre, Kent, and was used mainly, though not exclusively, in the decoration of brooches with a flat annular ring and central element similar to a penannular brooch. The decoration is typified by realistic animals, frequently crouched or backward-looking, with hatched fur and double outlines. The group was first identified by Hawkes (1961) who believed the ornament 'Jutish'. Evison (1965) favoured a Frankish interpretation.

Debate has surrounded the extent of the Romano-British contribution to the evolution of Quoit brooches. Hirst (1985) sees them as evolving from a Romano-British quoit brooch, taken up by the Anglo-Saxon incomers. Ager (1985) has pointed to Continental quoits, and suggests they evolved in Scandinavia. However, whether developed in Britain or on the Continent the quoit brooch stems from Roman prototypes, and the influence of Romano-British penannulars on them seems undoubted. The ornament too owes its origin to late Roman styles, whether in Britain or on the Continent. A Romano-British plate brooch from Lydney has a creature clearly ancestral to those of the Quoit brooch style (Wheeler & Wheeler, 1932, fig. 16, no. 46). The general picture from this type of evidence once more favours the theory of widespread intermingling of the two rural cultures rather than polarisation.

Metal-inlaid work is another possible Roman legacy in Anglo-Saxon England. Evison (1965) assumed it was all imported and evidence for Frankish settlement in south-east England. More recently Welch has suggested that some at least of this type of metalwork was produced in England in the fifth century, and that the technique of silver-wire inlay was a Romano-British one (1983, 94-7).

Dickinson has argued that disc brooches, which she had dated to the fifth century, continuing in use into the sixth, were produced first by Saxons in the Thames Valley and to its south, and were developed out of Romano-British metalworking traditions (Dickinson, 1979, 53). She has pointed out that the use of 'bull's eyes', stamps, nicked edges and rough casting are all features of late Roman military belt equipment (1979, 51).

Finally, the use of penannular brooches in pagan Saxon England has been taken as evidence for Romano-British metalworking techniques still in use. Penannulars in Anglo-Saxon graves may be re-used Roman ones, and thus provide no direct evidence for British survival, or Anglo-Saxon copies: some of the brooches from Anglo-Saxon graves, particularly the iron versions, have no close counterparts in the Celtic world. White (1988) has shown that penannulars are frequently found in pairs in graves, that is, worn in a Anglo-Saxon as opposed to Romano-British manner, suggesting that the use of penannulars was something taken over by the Anglo-Saxons from the Romans, rather than the property of surviving Britons.

In conclusion, if we accept that these material pieces of evidence reflect not merely movements of objects (through looting, chance finds, for amuletic purposes, for superstition or whatever), but actions of people currently using them, the overwhelming evidence is for a peaceful and nearly wholesale assimilation of Romano-British and Anglo-Saxon cultures which, eventually by the seventh century took on the umbrella term of 'Saxon' or 'English'. Where the present authors would see the polarisation is between the cities (still attempting to retain at least a semblance of civilised Roman traditions, and to cling to a lost heritage of the empire and citizenship) and the rural population. It is notable that in the late sixth century, an Anglo-Saxon king (Ceawlin) bearing a Celtic name resoundingly defeated the last of the towns on behalf of a rural population.

5

THE NON-ROMANIZED ZONE OF BRITANNIA

Outside the civil zone of Roman Britain, Roman control was effected by a network of forts. There were Roman towns at Caerwent and Carmarthen, but elsewhere in Wales was a military zone with little Romanization. In North Britain south of Hadrian's Wall the situation was generally similar to that in Wales and the South-West, the outposts of urban life being Carlisle and Corbridge. North of Hadrian's Wall the Roman presence was confined to the army, and after the second century the land north of Hadrian's Wall was abandoned to the native population, after only perhaps a century of minimal Romanization. Somerset and Dorset, on the edge of Romanized Britannia, boasted a few Roman towns, some of which are discussed in the previous chapter. The most westerly Romano-British town was Exeter, which lay in Dumnonia (now roughly Devon and Cornwall), an area in which both military control and Romanization can be said to have been of minimal importance.

These areas share in common that the effect of Roman civilization on the iron age Celtic way of life was small in a cultural sense. The impact of Anglo-Saxon settlement was not felt until much later than in the rest of England, where it was felt at all. We can therefore observe the process of 'Dark Age' state formation through two centuries, unhampered by external factors.

In our search for what befell the Celts during the post-Roman 'Dark Ages', we can use historical, linguistic and archaeological evidence. Unfortunately none of these are satisfactory or conclusive. The historical evidence consists of clues contained in king-lists and Annals, and less reliably poetry and saints' lives, as well as references in writers such as Gildas and 'Nennius'. The linguistic evidence is stronger. Throughout south-west England, Wales and south Scotland a form of P-Celtic (Brythonic) speech was employed, and it was during the early centuries after the withdrawal of the Roman forces from Britain that Old Welsh and the other dialects evolved out of a common tongue. This fact gave something of a common identity to all these peoples. For the inhabitants of Wales, their fellow Celts in Northern Britain were simply the 'Gŵyr y Gogledd', the 'Men of the North', whose land extended as far as the Forth-Clyde line.

The history of the Celts who are the subject of this chapter is to be found scattered through a variety of sources — the **Historia Britonnum**, epic poems such as the **Gododdin** of Aneurin, references in Anglo-Saxon sources, such as Bede, the writings of Gildas, a series of genealogies and saints' lives, mostly set down long after the decease of their subjects, and annals, of which the **Annales Cambriae** are the most important. Useful too for the light they occasionally shed on society are the Welsh law codes and charters. Sometimes placenames are also helpful.

One concept which permeates modern scholarship in this area, is that of the 'high-status' site. This is distinguished by yielding material of a high quality, at variance with the general finds. The phenomenon is equated with a change in society whereby new leaders or an 'elite' is identifiable as the owners or controllers of such sites. There is however little at present to prove this theory is watertight. The 'high-status' objects could for example merely reflect a new-found wealth amongst an already existing 'elite'.

The archaeological evidence mostly comprises the information to be gained from hillforts and various types of hut group that represent the homesteads of Celtic farmers, and is appraised below under the convenience of regional headings.

South-west England

The native Celtic economy and settlement pattern prevailed in the south-west peninsula (Dumnonia), with a more romanized settlement and economy further east in what is now Dorset and part of Somerset. The precise location of the territorial division has been a subject of argument: for the purposes of this discussion, it will be assumed to lie somewhere on the Parret/Axe line, with the Somerset Levels (Thomas, 1966, 83-4; Thomas, 1976, 199). This region was a **civitas** of Roman Britain, and was neither strongly fortified after the initial conquest period, nor in possession of the trimmings of a Romanized lifestyle. Villas are non-existent east of

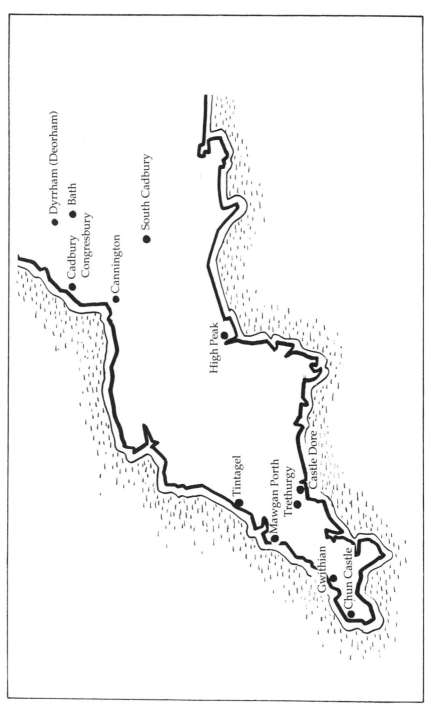

Map 2 South-west England

the boundary of Dumnonia, if the Romanized farmstead at Magor, Cornwall is discounted and Thomas is followed in seeing the Holcombe, Devon, villa as lying in Durotrigan territory (1976, 200).

DEVON AND CORNWALL

The later prehistory of Devon and Cornwall is still relatively little understood, a factor which is of relevance to its Roman-period and post-Roman fate. From the fourth century BC onwards however there seems to have been an expansion of settlement, with the spread of multiple-enclosure forts and hill-slope forts, as well as single farmsteads and village settlements (Silvester, 1980). Despite the apparent growth in population, there is no evidence that the Dumnonii, the tribe occupying the South-West at the time of the Roman conquest, was other than a very loose confederacy without strong leadership: no tribal centres have been identified, and the peninsula was not coin using.

The major settlement type in post-Roman Devon and Cornwall was the **round**: an enclosed farmstead (despite the name this can be oval or rectilinear), which is closely comparable with the rath of Ireland.

In Cornwall rounds were definitely pre-Roman, with origins in the last centuries BC. They are distributed at roughly the density of one per square mile (about 700 have been recorded), and similar sites are now known from Devon.

In Cornwall it is possible to identify continuity of settlement and traditions from the pre-Roman iron age into the Roman period on such sites as Chysauster and Carn Euny, which comprise villages of stone-built huts with associated plots. Breton influence has been seen as lying behind the planning of such villages, which seem to have a life-span from the first century BC to c. AD 300.

There is evidence however that differentiation among the occupiers of different rounds was beginning to be apparent as early as the late first or early second century AD. This has been identified through the increase in luxury goods denoting 'high status'. Such finds have been claimed as evidence for the rise of new local leaders (sometimes called 'potentates' in modern scholarly parlance). Whether these 'high status sites' can in fact be interpreted in this way is slightly open to doubt, though the presence of expensive goods would suggest an economic boom and new life-style. It is possible that the ostentatious display was of new-found wealth among long-established families, rather than a change in leading dynasties.

This economic change is identifiable through the evidence of coins, and the more varied evidence for specific sites.

Coin hoards The first increase in coin hoard numbers in the south-west is in the late Antonine period (later second century) (Isaac, 1976, 53). Another rise, that is clearly related to the inflation of the third century, was followed by a peak in the later third century, associated with the usurpers Carausius and Allectus. Finally, silver hoards were deposited in the early years of the fifth century (Isaac, 1976, 59-60).

In Cornwall there is a dense concentration of hoards in the period 250-340, particularly round the harbours on the West coast (Isaac, 1976, 62). This phase of hoarding has been associated with the contemporaneous boom in the Cornish tin mines (Isaac, *loc. cit.*; Thomas, 1966, 91-2 and map, fig. 10). However, there is good evidence that the Dumnonian peninsula was not a coin-using economy in the Roman period, and coins therefore must have been exchanged on another basis — as bullion, for example. Their subsequent hoarding would thus be comparable with the hoards found in other 'high status' contexts elsewhere in Britain beyond the frontiers.

It seems reasonable therefore to view the coin hoards as the possessions of chieftains in Dumnonia, whose accelerated wealth was no doubt partly connected with the tin industry. Clearly the process continued until after the collapse of Roman rule in Britain since silver hoards have been found in fifth-century contexts from Samson, in the Scillies (Archer, 1979, 54) and Zennor, Cornwall, the latter comprising no less than 80 siliquae (Archer, 1979, 64).

Settlements The material used to define 'high status sites' is varied. The round at **Carvossa** for instance, has produced a range of finds including pottery, coins, glass and brooches (Douch & Beard, 1970). This is perhaps one of the earliest of a series with features of rectilinear planning. **Grambla** is a rectilinear 'round' which produced pottery, a coin of the second century and post-Roman occupation (Saunders, 1972). Continuity of occupation of this site is indicated by fragments of a B iv jar possibly of the late fifth-early sixth century AD (Thomas, 1981, 15). **Stoke Gabriel** in Devon yielded pottery and coins of the mid-fourth century associated with a rectilinear banked enclosure (Masson-Phillips, 1965).

It may be that the planners of such rectilinear 'rounds' were influenced by Roman models, but they are probably best seen as reflecting the aspirations of their occupants for a more 'civilized' life-style, of which the Roman was the known apogee and therefore to be emulated. In these it has been implied that we can see the first signs of an emerging elite.

Thomas has suggested that the wealth of Carvossa might imply that it was an early **lis** or 'court'(1976, 203). In the same study he has drawn attention to the fact that the **lis** placename element is associated with several rounds in Cornwall, Leswidden, Lestowder (which contains the personal name Teudar) and Arallas ('the silver **lis**'), as well as surviving in town names, such as Liskeard (Thomas, 1976, 201).

Continuing prosperity of some rounds can be traced into the fifth and sixth centuries. The classic site is **Castle Dore**, Cornwall, with its timber halls and kitchens (Radford, 1951; Rahtz, 1971). The re-occupation in post-Roman times of what was originally an iron-age round has been associated with Cunomorus, whose memorial stone stands in the vicinity and is dated to around 500 (Thomas, 1976, 205).

The occupation at Castle Dore was apparently not continuous; the iron age phase was followed, after a period of abandonment, by one in the 'Dark Ages'. The implications that this re-occupation genuinely reflects a new political or social situation are strong.

The round at **Trethurgy**, Cornwall, was occupied between the third and sixth century and contained a series of round buildings, rebuilt many times, and a putative shrine. Imported Mediterranean pottery (classes A and B) attested its continued use into the sixth century, and occupation may have continued into the early seventh since finds included a putative fragment of E ware (Miles & Miles, 1973).

The stone-walled fort at **Chun Castle**, Cornwall, has been seen as reoccupied on the strength of B1 amphora sherds from a single vessel and a grass-marked pot, associated with insubstantial secondary structures (Thomas, 1956).

The long-standing identification of **Tintagel** as a fifth-century monastery has been questioned by Burrow (1974) and Thomas (1982). Thomas has suggested three phases for Tintagel, an 'unknown, perhaps small scale, occupation of the headland (as it was) during the fourth and possibly third centuries AD: then a much more interesting period, centred on the sixth century, lying between 450 and 650 . . . and thirdly, the construction and occupation of the medieval castle' (1982, 19).

Thomas has suggested that all the buildings of the 'monastery', belong to the castle-building phase. This view can perhaps be modified. Of the third and fourth centuries there is quite a reasonable quantity of Roman pottery, including Oxford colour-coated ware. In view of the general absence of Roman material from this part of Cornwall, it is probably reasonable to assume that the occupant of late Roman period Tintagel enjoyed high status, and could have been the predecessor of the local chief postulated by Padel (1981).

It cannot be assumed there was no occupation after the usage of the imported pottery until the coming of the castle-builders. The motif pieces from the site were dismissed by Thomas as 'undatable'. However they have a lot in common with a series of pieces from the Irish Sea province, for example from Dunadd, Argyll or Kingarth, Bute datable to around the ninth century. The interlace knot on one (Radford, 1935, pl. LX, 1) is not a type current in the medieval period.

The structures of the 'monastery' too are closely comparable with those from the tenth-century Cornish site at Mawgan Porth (Bruce-Mitford, 1956). It might be suggested therefore that the 'monastic' buildings are the ninth-tenth century successors of a fifth-sixth century site associated with a local chief.

Thomas has discussed the evidence for the establishment of a line of kings in Dumnonia, concluding that 'It is from this specifically, and typically, British background — a province divided and subdivided, ruled by kings and under-kings — that we can begin to construct a political model; a dominant class, prospering marginally under the **pax Romana**, dwelling in greater or smaller enclosures, and managing a stratified, tenurial, complex social system where wealth resided in cattle and land. From this we could expect a native line of **tyranni** to emerge in post Roman times' (1976, 207-8; see also Pearce, 1978 on this).

DORSET AND SOMERSET

In the pre-Roman iron age Dorset and Somerset were dominated by the coin-using tribe of the Durotriges, who had strong links with the Continent. To their north lay the Dobunni, whose territory extended into Gloucestershire, and to their east lay the Atrebates. In this area the pre-Roman landscape contained hillforts and scattered farmsteads. The area was part of the province of Britannia: with its Roman towns, villas and native farms. Any Celtic social change would inevitably be influenced by the Roman regime.

As elsewhere in Roman Britain, there is evidence, albeit slender, of a settlement drift in the fourth century out of the towns and into the countryside (see pp. 72).

Villas There is evidence for the growing importance of villas in the West Country in the third and fourth centuries — the increase being greater than in Roman Britain as a whole: about half the sumptuous villas in Britain lie in the south-west (Rivet, 1969, 209). The expansion began perhaps in the earlier third century, when some villas round Ilchester seem to have been established. It boomed in the last thirty years of the third century, when about forty villas commenced occupation, and when forty more, on less reliable excavation evidence, may have been founded (Branigan, 1976, 124-5). The arrival of immigrants from Gaul has been equated with this, and Gallic ownership has also been used to explain the exceptional prosperity of south-western villas in the fourth century.

Evidence for a Gallic immigration is not strong, so the increase in villas is more likely to show a growing prosperity in the late Roman south-west. Logic but little concrete evidence would suggest that post-Roman leaders would have emerged from such a background.

Hilltop fortifications The overall pattern of hilltop settlement in Somerset in the first millennium AD can be viewed as a result of the work of Burrow (1979, 81) who has argued that 'a substantial proportion of hillforts have produced Roman material' in Somerset (1979, 212). He has also pointed to late Roman rampart construction or refurbishment within small forts (1979, 217).

In reviewing this evidence, certain factors must be taken into account. Roman material could arrive at a hillfort for many reasons, ranging from military occupation by the Romans through casual/ agricultural use to religious use or illegal use (discussed in Burrow, 1981, 117). Roman material could also reach hillforts in the post-Roman period, as has been argued by Alcock for Dinas Powys, Glamorgan (1963, 22-5). Much of the material has come from badly-recorded excavations. However, where there is late Roman material with no evidence of post-Roman occupation, or where

103

there is post-Roman occupation without associated 'dark age' finds, it is probably reasonable to infer some use of the site in the late Roman period.

Only two hilltop sites in the south-west however have produced evidence for Roman fortification or for refurbishment of the existing ramparts — Kingdown, Somerset and Stokeleigh, Bristol (Burrow, 1979, 217).

The phenomenon of re-occupation in hillforts is not peculiar to Somerset. This is illustrated by the fact that forts further east have also produced some evidence for Roman usage, such as Cissbury, Sussex, where late Roman or post-Roman refortification was first recognized by Curwen (1929), Madmarston, Oxfordshire (Fowler, 1960), Wandlebury, Cambs. (Fowler, 1960, 30) or Oldbury, Wilts. (Fowler, 1971, 207).

The finds from **Ham Hill**, Somerset, include a coin series which, though spanning the Roman occupation, mostly belong to the late third and fourth centuries. The pottery series also displays a later-Roman emphasis, and the site sequence ends with B ware of the late fifth — early sixth century (Burrow, 1981, 268-77).

Tedbury produced a fourth century coin hoard (Burrow, 1981, 277), and Dolbury had Roman and Saxon coins of which the only identified was late Roman (Burrow, 1981, 277). **Norton Fitzwarren** has fourth-century sherds, notably Oxford ware (Burrow, 1981, 281). **Worlebury** yielded a fourth century hoard, 'coins of the late Empire' and fourth-century pottery. A late third century radiate, a coin of Gallienus (253-68) and late pottery (Burrow, 1981, 290), were found at **Ruborough**, and **Cadbury Tickenham** has given us a coin of Claudius Gothicus (268-69) and one of Valentinian II (375-92) as well as pottery (Burrow, 1981, 291). Fourth century coins came from **Clifton** (Burrow, 1981, 295), and **Brent Knoll** produced a coin of Victorinus (268-70) and third — fourth century pottery (Burrow, 1981, 297). At **Blaise Castle** coins of all periods in the Roman occupation were concentrated in the fourth century (Burrow, 1981, 300). There are also a series of sites with late Roman material which could be either late third or fourth century. As third century radiates do not appear to have remained in use in the fourth century (Casey, 1980, 40) it is reasonable to suppose that they reached the sites in the late third.

If the net is extended further afield, the evidence of forts in Gloucestershire producing late Roman material is much higher than in Somerset. About forty per cent of the forts have produced Roman finds or structural evidence, and three-quarters of all ex-

excavated sites have yielded late Roman material (Burrow, 1979, 217). Among these is the evidence from **Crickley Hill**, Glos. Here two settlements were constructed within the ruinous iron age hillfort. One was open, with rows of partly sunken huts, datable to the fourth-fifth century by late Roman metalwork and grass-tempered pottery. The other lay within a palisade with a gatehouse, enclosing a granary and at least one substantial timber-framed house. This was occupied at a comparable date (Dixon, 1988, 78). There was no evidence for 'late fifth century' occupation here, but presumably this is the residence of a late Roman-period 'chief' and the settlement of his followers.

Late Roman silver hoards The distribution pattern of late Roman silver hoards assumes particular interest in the context of newly forming leadership patterns. There is a concentration of hoards, both pre- and post-400, round the Bristol Channel in Somerset and Gloucestershire. These hoards were clearly 'bullion' hoards: silver ingots and a silver ring accompanied the East Harptree hoard (Archer, 1979, 40), and other hoards contained clipped siliquae. They should be taken, along with the villas and the reoccupied hilltops, as evidence for the accumulation of wealth by a number of individuals.

Memorial stones Memorial stones have some information to provide about the Roman legacy. The personal names that appear on stones of the fifth and sixth century in south-west England are Celtic, though Latinized. This is particularly relevant in the case of the five stones from Wareham, Dorset, which run from the late sixth century to the eighth or ninth and all of which, except the latest, carry British names. Radford has argued that Wareham represents a Romano-British settlement that became first a British (**clas**) and then a Saxon monastery (1975, 13).

Many of the stones stand beside old roads or trackways: the Tristan stone on the road from Padstow to Fowey and the Tavistock stone, which came from a trackway near Buckland Monachorum, are cases in point (Radford, 1975, 13). In Wales a similar phenomenon is noted (p. 111), but there the roads are of Roman origin.

The refortification of hillforts At the end of the fourth century, after the withdrawal of the Roman army from Britain, there is evidence that refortification of some hillforts commenced.

The clearest evidence for the post-Roman occupation of hillforts comes from **Cadbury Congresbury**, Somerset (Fowler *et al.*, 1970; Burrow,1979; Burrow, 1981). This iron age hillfort is divided by a post-Roman bank, dated to 400-700. Romano-British pottery mixed with post-Roman Mediterranean imports led Burrow to conclude that Roman pottery survived into the fifth century and beyond. Burrow sees the occupation at Cadbury Congresbury as a post-Roman phenomenon, a nucleated settlement controlling a territory probably containing smaller settlements (1981, 175).

While these arguments about the post-Roman date of Cadbury Congresbury may be acceptable, they cannot be applied indiscriminately to all the forts with late Roman occupation in Somerset. In the absence of any identifiable post-Roman material, post-Roman occupation cannot be postulated from late Roman finds alone. It seems fairly clear that forts were being increasingly occupied from the late third century onwards, not as fortifications but as regional centres. They were, in effect, the native counterparts of the villas.

Another classic site for demonstrating re-occupation is **South Cadbury**. It was defended by a new rampart with substantial Roman-style gateway around AD 500 and repaired towards the end of the sixth century. Inside was what has been called a feasting hall and bower (Alcock, 1982, 379). Apart from the presumed construction of a pagan temple, there is no evidence for late Roman usage of the site.

Wales

In Roman Wales, the pattern revolves around towns (Caerwent and Carmarthen) and a network of Roman forts, with a major legionary base at Caerleon and a major northern fort at Segontium (Caernarvon). Within this military network remained iron-age built hillforts, some of which were still occupied during the Roman period, and farmsteads, of which the most characteristic of the period was stone-built and set with other buildings within a stone-walled enclosure.

The general pattern suggests that the Roman administration had considerable influence on the post-Roman period. The evidence comprises the fate of towns and forts, the Church, hillforts, homesteads and various pieces of historical evidence including personal and placenames and memorial stones.

106

Map 3 Wales

107

Towns and forts Where towns existed in Romanized areas, they may very well have become the centres of fifth-century **civitates** and the focus of the nucleated kingdoms. The civitas capital for the Silures, **Caerwent**, survived into the middle ages. Radiocarbon dates for an extra-mural cemetery show it to have been in use in the fifth-sixth centuries, and into the seventh and eighth (Davies, 1979, 154). Finds from the town include a class G penannular brooch (Dickinson, 1982, fig. 4) and two double spiral topped pins, one bronze, one iron (Fox, 1946, 108 and fig. 12; Edwards & Lane, 1988, 37) which are probably seventh-century (Cunliffe, 1975, 211-4 for this type of pin).

Graffiti scratched on the walls of the Caerwent curia have been assigned to the fifth century (Wacher, 1974, 389), and there is some evidence that the forum and a bath house also survived (Wacher, *loc. cit.*).

Jeremy Knight has argued that four rectangular stone buildings in Insula 12 are of early medieval date, and that there may have been an Irish monastery established here in the sixth century (in Edwards & Lane, 1988, 37-8).

Carmarthen has not produced any evidence for occupation beyond the late fourth century; but the coin sequence includes some of the last issues circulated in Britain and the town is indirectly associated with Magnus Maximus (Wacher, 1974, 393).

Elsewhere in Wales, Roman forts may well have continued to function as the foci of local administrations. The evidence for continuing occupation in Roman forts has been discussed by L. Laing (1977). Segontium (Caernarvon), Pen Llystyn (Brynkir, Gwynedd), Castell Collen (Radnor), and Caersws (Mont) have all provided some indications of use into the fifth century. The putative 'Roman fort' at Aberffraw, Anglesey, is now seen as a post-Roman fortification connected with the kings of Gwynedd. The presence of Roman pottery from the excavations suggests a date for this in the fifth century rather than later (Edwards & Lane, 1988, 19-21). There is some evidence too that the Roman fort of Brecon (Y Gaer) has post-Roman usage (Davies, 1984, 24), and the same may be said for the legionary fortress of Caerleon, where there is possibly post-Roman occupation from the northern extra-mural area (Evans, 1986). Jones has suggested that some Roman forts were used in the later Middle Ages as the centres of estates (1960, 66-81).

It is now clear that **Chester** survived into the fifth century, probably as an administrative centre (Laing & Laing, 1984, 41-3).

Chester was certainly occupied into the later fifth or early sixth century, as is shown by imported Mediterranean pottery associated with a building with drystone sleeper walls and flagged floor. This underwent several modifications (McPeake, 1978, 43). The placename **Tarvin** (from Latin **terminum**, via Welsh **terfyn**) might suggest a political boundary for a territory centred on Chester (Laing & Laing, 1984, 43; Bu'lock, 1972, 24).

Ecclesiastical links It is notable that a feature of the later *maenor*, or estate, was the dual focus of **llys** ('court') and **llan** ('church'). There is some evidence that these fifth-century occupied Roman forts were also the foci of ecclesiastical continuity. In the case of Chester, the ecclesiastical focus was almost certainly Eccleston, where recent fieldwork has shown evidence for a late- or post-Roman church predating the Anglo-Saxon arrival (Laing & Laing, 1984, 20-24). This does not exclude the existence of a church in Chester as well (Laing & Laing, 1984, 26).

There are churches in the forts of Caerhun, Llandovery, Leintwardine (in Herefords, on the Marches) and Loughor and in the fortress of Caerleon (Lloyd-Jones, 1984, 82). At Caernarvon the church of Llanbeblig, with its cemetery occupying the site of the Roman garrison's cemetery, may equally well date from a late- or sub-Roman period (Lloyd-Jones, *loc. cit.*). The **llan** for Caernarvon may however have been further afield, at Penmachno, where there is a very important series of early memorial stones (Nash-Williams, 1950, 93). Early Christian memorial stones are also associated with the forts at Tomen y Mur, while Loughor has an altar with added ogham memorial inscription and Caer Gybi, Holyhead, was traditionally given to St Cybi in the sixth century as the focus for his monastery. The memorial stone from Brynkir, is near enough to the Roman fort to suggest some Christian focus in the vicinity.

Of course the association of a church, however early, with a Roman fort, however late, need imply no direct connection. It was fairly commonplace, for example, for a local ruler to give a Roman fort or other such site to a cleric for a Christian foundation: in England, Burgh Castle and Bradwell-on-Sea in East Anglia are good examples. However, the very fact that they were given as suitable sites might suggest that they were already associated with the local ecclesiastical administration especially if there were few or no conveniently placed Roman towns.

A similar situation perhaps can be seen in the Welsh borders, at Wroxeter, which certainly seems to have survived as the focus of a local administration into the fifth century and probably the sixth. Here Christian activity is suggested by a memorial stone and by the fact that the Anglo-Saxon church there is remarkably early, and may represent the Anglo-Saxon takeover of an existing British church.

Historical evidence It is difficult to estimate the extent of Roman involvement in the setting up of local administrations in Wales. It is likely that the Roman contribution was to 'regularize' emerging leaders and channel them into activities of benefit to the province by bestowing titles and specific powers. In this context, a number of quasi-historical or historical figures can be cited — in particular Maxen Wledig and Germanus. The former has been identified with Magnus Maximus, and the latter was a fifth-century soldier and bishop of Auxerre who led a mission to Britain.

Magnus Maximus is honoured in medieval Welsh tradition for having done something important for Wales, and is in fact the hero of the myth of Maxen Wledig in the *Mabinogion*. One of the things he may have done for Wales was just this 'regularizing'. This would explain why his name appears in so many of the genealogies of the later Welsh kingdoms.

John Morris suggested that Germanus was a Roman army officer sent out to set up an administration in Upper Deeside, where Catellius (i.e. Catel) was put in charge of administering the *pagenses* of the Cornovian hinterland who subsequently became the people of Powys. To do so, Germanus had to quash Benlli, a local ruler operating from possibly Foel Fenlli, a hillfort bearing his name, and lead a campaign against a Pictish-Saxon consortium trying to establish a base in Wales which terminated in the Alleluia Victory of 429 (Morris, 1973, 62-4; Bu'lock, 1972, 13; Laing & Laing, 1984, 27-8).

There are hints that this type of pattern prevailed in some measure into the fifth and sixth centuries. Wendy Davies has argued that in south-east Wales in the sixth and seventh centuries there were many minor kings who were progressively absorbed from the seventh century until the early eighth by new kings based near the mouth of the Wye (1978; 1982, 93-4 and map). This process can be documented in the south-east because it happened relatively late. Elsewhere in sixth century Wales any smaller 'kingdoms' apparently had already been absorbed into larger political units — Gwynedd, Dyfed, Powys and Gwent (Davies, 1982, 91). In the time of Gildas, writing around 540, these kingdoms were well established, and it is reasonable to suppose that they had been formed by the mid-fifth, since Gildas saw them as well established and was silent about their formation. It is probable therefore that the nucleation of kingdoms in Wales came about while Roman traditions were still strong.

There is evidence of survival from the pre-Roman iron age into the post-Roman period in the name of **Dyfed**, which seems to preserve that of the iron age tribe of the Demetae, with whose former area the later kingdom seems to have coincided. Gwent took its name from the Roman town of Venta Silurum, Caerwent.

Powys seems to take its name from **pagenses**, the occupants of a pagus or district of local government in Roman Britain. Ergyng, one of the small kingdoms of the south-east, took its name from Roman Ariconium (Weston-under-Penyard) (Davies, 1982, 95). The last two were formed in areas where Romanization included the foundation of towns, the first in an area that was not urbanised. Although boundaries are hard to define and were constantly fluctuating, both in Roman and in early medieval times, Gwynedd seems to coincide more or less with the tribal territory of the Ordovices, while Powys coincided with that of the Cornovii.

In Dyfed, the memorial stone of another subject of Gildas' disapproval, Voteporix (Vortipor in Gildas), commemorates him with the formula MEMORIA VOTEPORIGIS PROTICTORIS. Alcock has suggested the title **protector** is that of an officer-cadet in the late Roman army, and that in the genealogies it is used as a personal name — Protec map Protector. It is also held by Cyngar, brother of Tryffin. The relative obscurity of the title suggests it originates in a period prior to 410 (Alcock, 1987, 93-4). An alternative explanation, however, is that it is not a title, but merely the outcome of expressing the name trilingually.

Memorial stones Some further clues to surviving Roman traditions in Wales are provided by fifth and sixth century memorial stones. Interestingly, they were frequently set up not in graveyards but on road-sides. At Maen Madoc, Ystradfellte, in Brecknock, the sixth-century memorial stone of Dervacus had been erected where the Roman road from Coelbren to Brecon Gaer rises to a crest of a hill as seen from the valley of the river Hepste. The socket for the stone was cut into the edge of the Roman road metalling, suggesting that the margins of the road were overgrown (Fox, 1946, 109). In Glamorgan several memorial stones have been demonstrated to be sited on the course of roads linking auxiliary forts in the hills, and

Lady Fox has suggested that this may represent a survival of the Roman custom of setting up tombstones along roads (1946, 109).

The formulae on memorial stones hint at surviving Roman institutions. Thus a magistrate (magistratus) is commemorated on a stone from Penmachno, Gwynedd (Nash-Williams, 1950, 103) and a doctor (medicus) at Llangian in the same county (Nash-Williams, 1950, no. 92). Reference to the kingdoms from which the deceased came also appear on the stones — one from Elmet, on a stone from Llanaelhaiarn (Nash-Williams, 87), and one from 'Venedos' (i.e. Gwynedd) on a stone from Penmachno (Nash-Williams, 103). Particularly interesting for the Roman survival it implies, is the reference to an Ordous, i.e. Ordovician, on a stone from Penbryn, Cardigan (Nash-Williams, 126).

The Penmachno stone not only refers to a magistrate and to Gwynedd, but also notes that the deceased was a **civis**, citizen. Similarly, other stones imply a diocesan organization of the church with bishop (sacerdos) and priest (presbyter) recorded on four stones (Nash-Williams, 1950, 14). Personal names on the stones are sometimes Roman — Nobilis, Paulinus, Severus etc. — or sometimes have a family name which is Roman with a Celtic cognomen, e.g. Pumpeius Carantorius, Similinus Tovisacus, Eternalis Vedomavus, Lunarchus Coccus (Nash-Williams, 1950, 14). This implies a world in which Roman traditions still linger, albeit much debased. Whether this was simply due to a respect for the Roman world in an environment that was thoroughly Celtic, or represents a true lingering of Roman values, is a matter for conjecture.

Estate boundaries Wendy Davies has drawn upon the evidence provided by the Llandaff Charters of south-east Wales to study transactions involving estate boundaries. She has argued that the conceptual approach to property rights and the mechanisms of their donation in the sixth, seventh and eighth centuries was a Romano-British legacy, and that the estates themselves were in some cases the direct successors of their Roman predecessors (1979, 161). Alcock has argued that none of the charters is earlier than 555, and that therefore they cannot be used as an argument for the situation in the fifth century (1987, 95). But this reasoning could be applied to almost all the documentary sources that we have for the fifth century, and the survival of late Roman practices in the seventh century have still to be explained.

Hillforts Some hillfort settlements in Wales show no evidence for a break in occupation despite the Roman presence, others appear to have been abandoned with the arrival of the Roman army but re-used in the third or fourth centuries, other still demonstrate no occupation at all during the Roman period. This pattern is of course at variance with the civil zone of Roman Britain, where hillfort occupation was not permitted. The use of hillforts is therefore indicative of a different attitude to defended sites and thus a different relationship between Celt and Roman. In those hillforts where occupation was continuous through the Roman period one can postulate a tolerance and even a political pact with the chiefs. Presumably such a social/political situation would form a strong basis for post-Roman developments in leadership. However, many of these hillforts are notable for producing no evidence for post-Roman occcupation — indicative of a change in leadership fortunes.

The various types of occupation discussed below indicate that in a few instances hillforts seem to have been occupied in some measure throughout the period: both Braich-y-dinas and Tre'r Ceiri in North-west Wales have produced finds of Roman pottery of the second to fourth centuries (RCHAM 1956, 252; RCHAM 1960, 1056), and Tre'r Ceiri, Gwynedd, also produced a magnificent gold-plated brooch, Roman iron tools, a late bronze torc and part of the stem of a pewter jug (Baring-Gould and Barnard, 1904; Hughes, 1906; Richmond, 1965, 174).

Tre'r Ceiri, Gwynedd, is a strange anomaly. Richmond suggested that its stone rampart was modelled on Roman ramparts 'strong enough to keep out marauders, yet not so strong as to defy a Roman force' (1965, 174) and suggested its status was similar to that of Traprain Law, East Lothian, an 'oppidum' on good terms with the Romans. Certainly Segontium would have been more or less in sight of Tre'r Ceiri, and its continuing occupation would not have been tolerated had it been a threat. Possibly it helped to maintain Roman control in an otherwise difficult area, and that the 'high status' goods were exchanged for support. Braich-y-Dinas, (at Penmaenmawr), now destroyed, and Dinorben, Clwyd, may have served some similar function: most of the Roman finds at Braich-y-Dinas seem to have come from the space between the ramparts, suggesting that the fortifications were not used for defence. All three sites are located along the North Wales coast, and could have been elements in a wider scheme of control, since they were defensive.

In north-east Wales and the Marches the counterparts of Tre'r

Ceiri can be recognized at **Dinorben**, Clwyd, occupied in the late first-early second century AD and again in the late third-fourth century (Gardner & Savory, 1963; Savory, 1971; Guilbert, 1979, 182 and 186) and **Sutton Walls**, Hereford occupied down to the third century (Kenyon, 1954). The assemblage at Sutton Walls includes considerable quantities of pottery up to the third century, the quantity of which has eclipsed the fact that there is a significant amount of fourth-century pottery as well, including at least one sherd datable to late in the century (Kenyon, 1954, 55-6). In view of the difficulty of recognizing third-century Romano-British pottery, it is probably reasonable to assume that occupation continued until the end of the Roman period, albeit on a reduced scale. Both sites should perhaps be seen as being of 'high status'.

In **south Wales** the pottery from Caer Dynnaf, Llanblethian, may suggest continuing occupation there from the iron age to the fourth century (Davies, 1967, 77-8).

In the **Marches**, late Roman pottery is known from Dinedor and Aconbury (Kenyon, 1954, 25-6),Oldbury and Wall Hills (Brown, 1965, 85), Poston and Timberline Camp (Anthony, 1958, 6-10, 14-18), the Berth and the Breiddin (Gelling & Stanford, 1967, 83; O'Neil, 1937, 97; Musson, 1976, 302) and from the promontory fort at Oliver's Point, occupied apparently from the late second to the fourth centuries (Hume & Jones, 1961, 130-2).

In **south-east Wales** a concentration of sherds of the second to fourth centuries have been recovered from Castle Ditches, Llancarfan (Alcock, 1960b, 299; Hogg, 1977, 34-7).

Particularly convincing of late Roman use of a hillfort is the material from **Coygan Camp**, Glamorgan. Here in the later third century some forgers set up their workshop (Wainwright, 1967, 70-1, 157-8).

At **Dinas Emrys**, Gwynedd, the presumed dark age occupation seems to have been preceded by a late Roman phase, (Savory, 1960; Laing & Laing, 1988, 213; see also above, p. 57). At **Degannwy**, Gwynedd, there is clear evidence of the use of the hilltop from the mid-third century onwards, with a coin sequence extending from Gallienus (260-8) to Valens (364-78), matched by a comparable pottery sequence. This occupation was within a pre-existing stone-faced wall, the date of which was uncertain, though at least as early as the second century AD (Alcock, 1967, 199-200). **Moel Fenlli**, Clwyd, associated in the *Historia Britonnum* with a King Benlli in the fifth century, has produced late Roman coin hoards and a sherd of Argonne ware, an import of the fourth century seen by some as evidence for fifth-century occupation (Alcock, 1987, 59). **Carreg-y-llam**, Gwynedd, often discussed in the context of post-Roman occupation, is a small hillfort with some abraded Romano-British sherds from a hut paving (Hogg, 1957; Edwards & Lane, 1988, 39; Alcock, 1987, 59-60 and 158 for 'fifth century' date).

In Pembroke, Roman pottery of the third and fourth centuries has been recovered from the fort at Crocks-y-dam (Grimes, 1931, 394-5), and second-century pottery from the promontory fort at Buckspool (*loc. cit.*).

Other sites show no evidence for continuing Roman-period occupation: for example Conway Mountain, Pen-y-Gaer or Craigdinas (Lloyd Jones, 1984, 49). In the Marches the larger hill-forts seem to have been abandoned at the time of the Conquest: for example, the Breiddin, Mont (Stanford, 1974a, 50-1), Croft Ambrey, Titterstone Clee, the Berth and the Roveries, the Wrekin, Credenhill and Midsummer Hill were all abandoned at the beginning of the Roman period (Lloyd-Jones, 1984, 53).

This material is uneven in both quantity and quality. When set alongside the comparable but better evidence from Somerset (see above, p. 103-4), it does nothing to contradict the view that hillforts in Wales from the later second century onwards were, in some cases at least, seeing renewed occupation.

Farmsteads and homesteads　Other types of settlement in Wales illustrate a clearer pattern. In north-west Wales the dominant rural settlement type was the homestead or hut-group, often associated with terraced fields. It has frequently been suggested that these represent a deliberate introduction of 'colonists' into a under-populated area from outside, through Roman agency (Hogg, 1966, 33; Hogg 1979, 295-6). The origin of the incomers has been suggested as Iberia (Griffiths, 1951, 181) or north Britain (Hemp & Gresham, 1944, 191). For Gresham, the enclosed hut group was 'an exotic tradition introduced into Gwynedd by the Romans' (1972, 60). Most scholars now would not accept this.

A detailed statistical study of the morphology of enclosed home-steads in north-west Wales has been able to show a continuous development from prehistory through to the fifth century. However, development in the later second century AD has been shown of 'round and sub-rectangular buildings with surrounding enclosures, complex and regular plans, and associated with systems of 'terraced fields'' (Smith, 1978, 50) which Smith has seen as 'the regional equivalent of the smaller Romano-British **villa** of Lowland Britain'.

In some cases new enclosed hut groups were built on top of earlier ones in this period: the polygonal settlement at **Caerau,** Clynnog, overlay an earlier, probably oval, homestead of the late first/early second century (White, 1973, 10-13). At **Cefn Graeanog II** another (probably not enclosed) timber settlement, dated by second century pottery, was overlain by a polygonal hut group in the late second or third century. The original report suggested this was occupied from the third to fifth centuries AD (White, 1977, 406), and subsequently occupation was suggested to have con- tinued through the fifth into the sixth or seventh century (Davies, 1982, 27-8). Although the late Roman occupation is not disputed, there has been some disagreement over the continuing use of the site in the fifth century onwards (Edwards & Lane, 1988, 42). At **Cae'r Mynydd**, Gwynedd, a thick-walled homestead built in the third or fourth centuries overlay an earlier settlement of uncertain plan. A third phase of occupation was aceramic, and could have continued into the fifth century (Griffiths, 1959b, 57-60; Edwards & Lane, 1988, 31).

At **Graeanog,** Gwynedd, a multi-period hut-group has produced Roman pottery of the second to fourth centuries in residual contexts. A remanant magnetic date from a hearth shows occupation in the period 500-900, and radiocarbon dates from a corn-drying kiln span the period from the ninth to twelfth centuries. Excavation is still in progress, but it seems likely that a late Roman-period occupation was followed by at least one phase in the medieval period (Edwards & Lane, 1988, 79). Other polygonal hut groups occupied in the late Roman period include Pant-y-Saer, Anglesey (Phillips, 1934), Din Llugwy, Anglesey and Hafoty-wern-las, Gwynedd, built probably in the third century (Hogg, 1966, 36).

In Pembroke, **Walesland Rath** can be shown to have occupation in the second-third centuries AD, when huts and a rectangular building were erected (Wainwright, 1971, 77-82).

The evidence for Wales, then, might suggest that in the late Roman period enclosed hut-groups may have been built as the homes and farmsteads of an increasingly rich elite.

North Britain

In Northern Britain the areas to the south of Hadrian's Wall, which lay within the military zone of Roman Britain, are distinguished from the territories that lay beyond it. In Lowland Scotland, between Hadrian's Wall and the Antonine Wall, a military zone existed in the first two centuries AD. The lands beyond the Forth-Clyde line were outside the Empire. Agricola penetrated it in the first century, and Septimius Severus campaigned there at the turn of the second/third century, but it remained hostile to Rome. This area is discussed separately in the following chapter.

Roman activity north of Hadrian's Wall The landscape south of the Forth-Clyde line was one dominated by farmsteads of various types, including crannogs or lake dwellings, and a scatter of hill-forts, most of which were abandoned at the time of the Roman occupation in favour of a more dispersed settlement pattern of farms.

Sites occupied in the Roman period often produce some datable Roman artefacts. After the Roman period this type of dating evidence is lacking, and other types are sparse. Environmental studies suggest that the fifth and sixth centuries were a period of relative prosperity for the people of the North, but south of Hadrian's Wall there is no site with provable Dark Age occupation. Between the Walls the evidence is almost as sparse: apart from a few hillforts with occupation in this period most of the evidence comes from a few crannogs in Ayrshire.

The military occupation in the zone between the two Roman Walls did not continue later than AD 210 and there were no towns to form the centres of local administrations. Furthermore, unless the forts were taken over immediately after the withdrawal of Roman forces, they were unlikely to have been adapted for native administrative use. It is likely however that farmsteads might have been established within some of the Scottish forts, though excavation has produced little evidence for it. At Birrens, Dumfriesshire, some sherds found in 1936-7 were believed to be assignable to the third and fourth centuries (Robertson, 1975, 8). Given the standard of many of the early excavations, in the absence of diagnostically-late Roman artefacts it is unlikely that late occupation would have been recognized.

On Hadrian's Wall and to its south, the Roman military occupation continued until the end of the Roman period, and there is

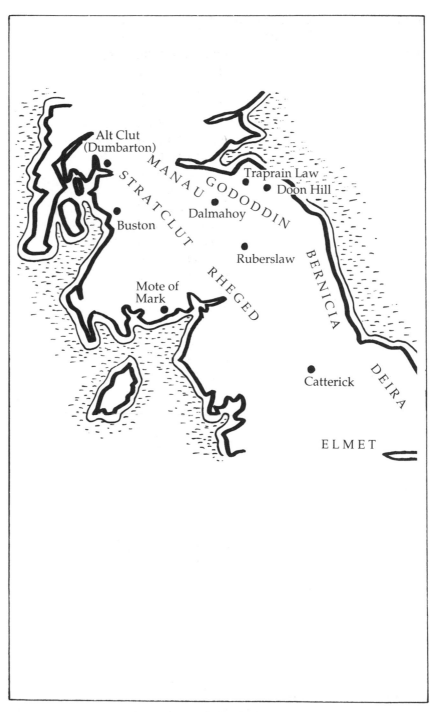

Map 4 North Britain

evidence for Roman forts continuing to be used in some way into the fifth century: in some cases churches were established within them. It is notable that the forts with churches on Hadrian's Wall are at the western end rather than the eastern — Bowness, Burgh by Sands, Carlisle, Brampton, Bewcastle — possibly indicating that the focus of late Roman Christianity was Carlisle. Elsewhere Roman forts with churches include Ribchester, Piercebridge, Ilkley, Castleford, Ebchester, Chester-le-Street, Moresby, Brough, Bowes, Piercebridge, Lancaster, Ilkley, Aldborough and York.

Forts with some evidence of fifth-century usage in North Britain include Carlisle (McCarthy, 1982), Ravenglass (Anon., 1977, 378), Corbridge (Laing, 1987, 271), Chesterholm (Macalister, 1945, no. 498 — fifth century memorial stone), York (Biddle, 1976, 117), Halton Chesters (Laing, 1987, 272), Brough (Thomas, 1968, 100), Brougham (Thomas, 1968, 97), Maryport (Thomas, 1968, 97) and Carrawburgh (Breeze & Dobson, 1976, 230-1). Recent excavations at **Birdoswald** have revealed three Dark Age halls on top of two granaries, with apparently continuing use of Crambeck Ware (the latest Romano-British pottery in North Britain) into the fifth century, if not the sixth (Selkirk, 1988b, 158). Some of these could easily have been the foci of both small local administrations and churches in the fifth century, which failed to survive the arrival of the Anglo-Saxons.

The difficulties of the evidence are made clear by Catterick, Yorks., which was certainly occupied in the late Roman period. It has been identified with the **Cattraeth**, which was the British kingdom commemorated in the **Gododdin** poem. However, as Alcock has pointed out, Catterick has produced an amount of early Anglo-Saxon material of the later fifth century, and nothing diagnostically 'British' to equate it with an important seat of Urien, as Taliesin suggests it was (Alcock, 1983, 15-17). A dearth of convincing archaeological material however does not automatically exclude the possibility that Roman forts became the centres of Dark Age administrations and/or kingdoms.

The lack of evidence for the continuing usage of Roman forts in southern Scotland might suggest that here the foci must have been purely native. Thomas (1981b, 278) and others (e.g. Smyth, 1984, 16) have seen the occurrence of 'Roman' names in the southern Scottish genealogies as due to the prestige of Rome and not necessarily to any direct Roman involvement. Prestige may indeed explain the widespread usage of Roman personal names in fifth- and sixth-century Lowland Scotland, as indeed may the influence of the Church. It does not however rule out the possibility of Roman influence on the 'regularizing' of local administrations in the interests of law enforcement in frontier lands. The case in favour of such a process was advanced by Chadwick (1949, 150), Morris (1973, 16-18) and Johnson (1980, chapter 1).

The strongest argument archaeologically for Roman involvement in affairs south of the Forth-Clyde line is the continuing fortunes of Traprain Law, East Lothian, the stronghold of the Votadini. Finds from the site show it to have had prolonged occupation to the end of the fourth century, and possibly the fifth. Roman involvement in this area must account for the spread of Christianity at an early date as far as the Forth (attested by the Catstane cemetery, radiocarbon dated to around the fifth century — Cowie, 1981).

Native settlements south of Hadrian's Wall Immediately south of Hadrian's Wall the dominant settlement type of the early centuries AD was the enclosed farmstead or hut group, which display a great diversity of forms.

Few sites have been excavated so sound pronouncements about social or economic changes in the early centuries AD in the region as a whole are not possible. Certainly the origins of most of the types of palisaded settlement in the area go back to pre-Roman antecedents.

One element can be identified as new in the Roman period — enclosed stone walled or stone foundation houses. There is no evidence to suggest that these developed in the region until the second century AD (Higham, 1986, 194). This has frequently been claimed as evidence for Roman influence upon the native economy, but this is not an unimpeachable inference. Higham for instance has seen the incidence of stone walling as coinciding with areas where timber had become in short supply due to deforestation, and where a ready supply of suitable stone for building was available (1986, 196).

While in the north-east the evidence indicates longevity of settlement, in Cumbria the enclosed farmstead seems to have arrived relatively late: of the five per cent of Cumbrian settlements sampled by excavation, all have been shown to have commenced within the Roman period, and most of them were not occupied until after 200 (Higham,1986,196).

Roman imports on native sites in North Britain are fairly common in the second century, and thus facilitate dating. But after

200 AD there is reason to suppose that artefacts did not travel as extensively, and their use for dating is thus limited.

Native settlements between the Walls Between the Walls, the evidence is equally sparse. Farmsteads, hillforts and crannogs were used, but a lack of datable material makes it impossible to pinpoint with any certainty the date of the re-occupation of hilltop sites. The metalworking site at the Mote of Mark was certainly not defended until the late fifth or sixth century, and there is no convincing dating evidence for the commencement of the 'Dark Age' occupation at Trusty's Hill, Kirkcudbright or Tynron Doon, Dumfries (for all these, Laing, 1975). **Castlehill, Dalry,** Ayrs, however, appears to have been occupied in the second century AD (finds including a dragonesque brooch and Roman pottery, notably samian, and a sword mount of late first-early second century date). It was also occupied at a date centred on the sixth century: a class G penannular, and Germanic glass are the finds from this phase (Smith, 1919). It is not impossible that occupation began in the second century, and continued until the sixth.

Another stone walled fort, **Castlehaven,** Kirkandrews, Kirkcudbright, has produced a late Roman D7 brooch and a spiral finger ring and trailed glass bead; both the latter would fit with a late Roman reoccupation (or occupation) of the fort (Barbour, 1907).

There is evidence for an active phase of building in lowland Scottish forts in the late first century AD. At **Hownam Rings,** Roxburgh, rubble ramparts were built at this period. A storage pit and two huts were excavated, dating from within the Roman period — one hut produced pottery of the period AD 250-300 (Piggott, 1948, 208), while the other produced a fragmentary glass armlet of probably second-century date. Built into the wall was a Roman nail cleaner (Piggott, 1948, 215 and 219). Piggott suggested that this hut could have been post-Roman, and drew attention to a post-Roman knife blade from the robbing of the gateway of an earlier (phase II) defensive work on the site. She saw the rubble-rampart building as a defence against the Romans, but the re-fortification and continuing occupation at Hownam could just as easily be equated with a phase of building connected with the rise of new chiefs in the Roman period.

Three other Roxburgh forts show similar signs of rampart construction in the Roman period — Shaw Craigs, Woden Law and

121

The Castles, Swindon (Piggott, 1948, 222). Late, but at present undatable, constructional phases are apparent in some other southern Scottish forts, namely Harelaw and Stobshiel, East Lothian, and Chatto Craig and Peniel Heugh in Roxburgh (references and discussion in Laing, 1975b, 10).

Crannogs More evidence is forthcoming from crannogs which have many similarities with those in Ireland.

Prehistoric occupation of crannogs is likely, though evidence for it is rare. That at Oakbank, Perths, has radiocarbon dates centred on the sixth century BC (Dixon, 1984, 218), while radiocarbon dates for three other crannogs all lie within the second half of the first millennium BC (Morrison, 1985, 24). Milton Loch, Kirkcudbright, was originally dated to the second century AD on account of its associated find of an enamelled bronze dress fastener (Piggott, 1954). Radiocarbon dating of a timber pile from the crannog and of a wooden ard found at its base suggest that the crannog appears to have been constructed in the fifth century BC (Guido, 1974).

Apart from these instances there is no reason to suppose that most crannogs were constructed before the late first or second centuries AD. The earliest of the 'Roman iron age' crannogs is perhaps that at Langbank, Renfrews, which was the target of an elaborate hoax in the late nineteenth century. The crannog however was genuine, even if many of the finds were not, and seemingly genuinely associated were a decorated comb and an early penannular brooch. The comb may belong to the later first century, but could have been lost, like the brooch, in the second (Callander, 1929). The crannog at Hyndford, Lanarkshire, also produced material of the late first century (Flavian samian) in its rich array of finds (Munro,1899).

It is probably reasonable to see the southern Scottish crannogs as representing the homes of a rich elite — the range of finds from several is impressive, and apart from Roman brooches and the like include such 'high status' objects as the horse-bit and mirror handle from Lochlee (Macgregor, 1976, nos. 4 and 272) or the ornamental collar from Hyndford (Macgregor, 1976, no. 202). These crannogs have a south-westerly distribution in Scotland, in the part closest to north-eastern Ireland, and Irish influence on their construction should not be ruled out.

Another group of crannogs, in north-east Scotland, have produced medieval and later material (with the exception of **Loch**

Glashan crannog, Argyll, which is Dark Age), and these may perhaps represent a separate tradition introduced from Ireland to Dalriada in the post-Roman centuries.

6

THE ORIGINS OF THE PICTS

The Romans called the Celtic barbarians living to the north of the Antonine Wall 'Picti'. As such, the Picts owe their existence to history rather than archaeology. Without documentation, it is extremely unlikely that they would be recognizable as a distinct entity in the archaeological record. Only the distribution of 'Pictish' symbol stones might suggest some kind of political, social or other alliance in northern Scotland that is otherwise unreflected in material culture. Their cultural remains are generally sparse, but similar to those of the other Celts.

The Picts first appear in history in AD 297, as northern tribesmen hostile to Roman Britain (Eumenius, *Pan Lat Vet* viii (v), 11, 4). Although the Picts figure in Roman records from the end of the third century, they are more particularly documented in the fourth century. They are named in connection with hostilities against the Romans in 305-6, in 360 (when they are associated with the Scotti (Irish) and are accused of breaking a peace treaty — Ammianus, xx, 1, 1), in 364-5, when Dicalydones and Veturiones along with Scots, Attacotti and Saxons are seen to be exerting pressure on Britannia's frontiers, and in 367-9 when along with Scots and Attacotti the Picts are again in a 'barbaric conspiracy' against the northern frontiers. After the 'conspiratio barbarica' chronicled by Ammianus, they again appear to be involved in an invasion of Britannia, with the Scots, to be repulsed by Magnus Maximus. In 396-8 there was a further onslaught when the Picts alone were driven back from their raid by Stilicho (for summary of all these, Maxwell, 1987, 43, and see also Miller, 1981).

Clearly, the Picts were not newcomers to the arena of Roman frontier raiding (Maxwell, 1987, 31): but how much earlier they had evolved as a distinct group is debatable. The evidence available to us is entirely archaeological and inevitably the colourful warriors

Map 5 Pictland

of the literature are not to be found. The most distinctive of Pictish material remains are their symbols stones, discussed in chapter 10.

There is no evidence for any major intrusive cultural group in Scotland from the arrival of the Beaker people in the third millennium BC. The ancestors of the Picts must therefore be sought in the native late bronze and early iron age cultures of northern Scotland. This corroborates the historical evidence that the Picts evolved rather than 'arrived'.

Significantly, throughout northern Scotland the archaeological evidence points to changes in a long-established pattern of settlement types somewhere between the second and fourth centuries AD: the point at which the Picts came to Roman attention.

The material available for the period consists of settlements, of which the chief types in use in what became historical Pictland were brochs, wheelhouses and souterrains, and an associated assemblage of artefacts which, with the exception of the pottery, is not particularly diagnostic of either culture or date, comprising mainly basic subsistence equipment common to Celts.

Brochs and wheelhouses In the Northern and Western Isles and north Scottish mainland the dominant iron age monument was the broch, a stone fort with cavity walling, a single entrance passageway and guard chambers, and internal timber ranges. Recent work on two Orkney brochs has produced radiocarbon dates in the eighth-fifth centuries BC (Hedges, 1987, 31; Carter *et al.*, 1984) suggesting they have much earlier origins than was formerly supposed (for earlier views, Hamilton, 1966; Hamilton, 1968; MacKie, 1965; MacKie, 1970, canvassing origins in either the Northern Isles or the Hebrides). Recent work on brochs has also shown that the settlements round brochs once believed to post-date the usage of the brochs themselves, were present, in the Orkneys at least, from the earliest stage in broch history. Rather than being abandoned in the second century, broch sites continued in use into the third and probably even the fourth century AD (Hedges, 1987, 32).

In Shetland, the evidence is slightly divergent. There are signs that brochs were being replaced by 'wheelhouses' — round stone huts with radial piers — by the early second century AD. The association of new artefact types with the wheelhouse at Jarlshof suggests some kind of break (Hamilton, 1956, 59-60). Wheelhouses also make their appearance in the Hebrides around this time, for example at Dun Mor Vaul on Tiree (MacKie, 1965, 139).

In Shetland wheelhouses may have continued in use until the

coming of the Vikings, but in the Hebrides the sequence from **the Udal**, North Uist, (where there is a long series of radiocarbon dates), shows evidence for an important break. 'Between 200 and 400 AD ... the structure and artifacts of all types change character abruptly and completely from the classic wheel house types to a range of material comprehensively alien thereto' (Crawford & Switsur, 1977, 129). Crawford has termed this phase 'Scotto-Pictish' and has pointed to pottery similar to Irish souterrain ware, suggesting a migration to the Hebrides from Ulster though he admits the assemblage as a whole is difficult to parallel in Ireland (Crawford & Switsur, 1977, 130).

Souterrains South of the area of brochs and wheelhouses were souterrains — subterranean passages with walls of upright slabs and with capstones, terminating in a chamber. The excavations of F.T. Wainwright showed that far from being isolated features, they were the below-ground elements of large round farmsteads, occupied in the first two centuries AD (Wainwright, 1963).

Current work shows that souterrains were a comparatively short-lived type of structure on settlements of round timber houses that seem to have been occupied from the mid-first millennium BC (if not earlier) until the sixth century AD (possibly even the ninth).

Recent excavation has shown that the settlements which later contained souterrains began much earlier than formerly supposed, in the first half of the first millennium BC, as attested by radiocarbon at Douglasmuir, Angus. Here there was an under-floor passageway probably ancestral to souterrains (Kendrick, 1980; 1982; Watkin, 1984, 66). Dalladies, Site 2, Kincardine, was dated to in the first century BC (Watkin, 1984, 66).

The settlements of which souterrains formed a part were long-lived. Radiocarbon dates from Dalladies 2 showed occupation continued from the first century BC to at least the sixth century AD (Watkin, 1981, 164), and at Bankfoot, Perthshire, occupation seems to have continued until the eighth century (Watkin, 1981b, 179-80; 1984, 68).

The souterrains themselves however appear to have been deliberately dismantled, around the end of the second century AD. At Newmill the souterrain roof was removed and the chamber obliterated in the late second or early third century; at Dalladies 2 there was similar evidence for destruction of the souterrain around this time (Watkin,1984, 71-2). Wainwright found similar evidence for destruction and infilling at Ardestie and Carlungie (1963, 25, 74, 77).

Recent aerial photography has shown that souterrains are much more densely distributed in Fife and Angus than was supposed by Wainwright, and that in some cases they form part of larger complexes (Maxwell, 1987).

From this rapid survey of Northern Scottish prehistory is illustrated a long tradition stretching back to the early first millennium BC, with some social changes taking place between the second and fourth centuries AD.

Language and history

Linguistic study of the names given to the Picts by ancient writers provides some clues to Pictish origins. If the name 'Pict' means in a literal sense 'the painted people' then it should probably be seen not as a political or tribal label but a generic description for a group of barbarians, (in much the same way that the term 'Black Foreigners' was applied to Viking raiders in Ireland at a slightly later period, regardless of ethnic origins). Indeed, since it would seem that the Picts were known in their own lands as *Cruithni*, 'the native people' (perhaps implying a bronze age origin), it seems likely that the term *Picti* was originally without any kind of political significance, and was applied indiscriminately to barbarians north of the Forth-Clyde line.

The term *Cruithni* has the same meaning as **Prydein** or *Priteni*, which was used by their contemporary Celtic-speaking neighbours to describe the Picts. Both terms are represented in Latinized form by *Pretani*, the name given to the people of Britain or the 'Pretanic Isles' by the earliest classical travel-writers such as Diodorus Siculus, who reported the accounts of travellers of the second century BC (Chadwick, 1949).

Writing in the eighth century Bede reflects a bipartite division by distinguishing between Southern and Northern Picts. This bipartite confederacy is also implied by references from the late second century onwards — Maeatae and Caledonii (*c*.200 AD), 'Caledonii and other Picts' (*c*.310), then Dicalydones and Verturiones (*c*.367) and finally Southern Picts and Northern Picts (*c*.600).

Herodian and Cassius Dio in recording the campaigns of Severus at the turn of the second century refer to Caledonians and Maeatae, the two most important nations in the 'hostile part of Britain'.

Significantly, too, they mention the other tribes 'having been merged within them'.

Marjorie Anderson in discussing the reference to Dicalydonas and Verturiones in Ammianus Marcellinus' description of the major raid of 367, has argued that this merely indicates that these two groups of Picts were involved in the attack, not that all Picts were divided into these two groups. She has pointed out the name Verturiones survives in the later Pictish province of Fortriu, and that the Verturiones may have been sea-borne raiders from Perthshire and Fife (1987, 7).

Rivet and Smith have suggested that the name of the Maeatae means 'the people of the larger part' (1979, 438-40). Placename evidence indicates the Maeatae were to be found immediately to the north of the Antonine Wall, in Stirlingshire. A sixth-century battle fought at Circind in the north-east of Strathmore involving *Miathi* might suggest that the name survived into the Dark Ages and that their territory extended to the Mounth. As Maxwell (1987, 32) has pointed out, Bede's reference to Oswiu's campaigns against the Southern Picts describes them as 'the greatest part of the Picts' which may reflect a survival of the identity of the Maeatae.

Before the second century our source of information for the people north of the Forth-Clyde is Tacitus. He simply groups them together as the people occupying the geographical region of Caledonia, i.e. as Caledonians. There is no suggestion of tribal division in Tacitus' writings. However, this need not imply that the Caledonians represented a unified political group: it could suggest that they were composed of large numbers of separate tribes which it seemed irrelevant to list. If that is so, we can possibly see in northern Scotland in the first four centuries AD the gradual formation of centres of power or chiefdoms out of a much looser tribal structure.

From the foregoing, it seems reasonable to believe that from the later second century onwards there were in northern Scotland two large tribal confederacies. Within these there may well have been several tribes which changed, amalgamated and re-allied with the passage of time. The archaeological evidence from the sites has been seen above not to contradict this view.

Roman imports and Pictish chiefs

In the light of the historical evidence, it is instructive to consider whether there are any clues to new political configurations among the Picts in the second to fourth centuries AD. Both Watkin (1984) and Alcock (1987a; b) have been concerned with the process of state formation and the rise of 'potentates'. For both however the crucial period in Pictland was later, in the fourth-fifth centuries (Alcock, 1987, 85).

There is archaeological evidence, however, that the process began perhaps in the second century when significantly we can first detect Pictish political alliances in the literary sources.

The evidence for this takes the form of Roman imports from native contexts in Scotland. Coarse pottery, the commonest type of merchandise traded by the Romans to the barbarians, is extremely rare on native sites in Scotland, as are coins of base metals (Robertson, 1970). Instead, the Roman objects found are high-quality pottery (samian) and high-denomination coins in gold and silver. To quote Robertson: 'The most striking features are the fine quality of the material, and the scarcity of the mundane and the pedestrian such as coarse-ware pots whose fragments form the bulk of the material recovered from the excavation of Roman sites. . . . The lists of Roman coin finds . . . underline the "preference of the native North Briton for Roman gold when he could get it, and for high-quality early Roman silver " ' (Robertson, 1970, 200).

Robertson saw the Roman material as being acquired mostly through direct trade, initially with the forts then subsequently through 'drift'. This would not seem to be supported by the evidence which suggests that ordinary trade played a small part. Essentially the Roman objects were status symbols, and the presence of Roman material on native sites should probably be taken as an indication of the wealth and importance of their occupants. The presence of Roman objects in iron age burials of the second century at Tarland, Aberdeens (playing men), Airlie and Kingoldrum, Angus (glass cups) and Westray, Orkney (glass cup) (Robertson, 1970, 212) perhaps indicate chiefs' burials in second-century Pictland. The relatively frequent occurence of Roman material on excavated broch sites in the Northern Isles bears out the idea that these may have been the strongholds of northern chiefs.

Recently, it has been suggested that the Falkirk hoard of Roman silver denarii constitutes payments made to a barbarian dynasty or leader to 'buy off' aggression north of the Antonine Wall in the period AD 160-230 (Todd, 1987).

In this context souterrains assume a special prominence. Firstly, a high proportion of excavated souterrains have produced Roman finds: for example Dalladies 2 (Watkin, 1981, 155), Carlungie, Ardestie, Conon, Fithie, Pitcur I and II and Tealing III (Wainwright, 1963, 23).

Secondly Watkin has suggested that the souterrains were stores for excess farm produce by wealthy individuals, and were thus of themselves 'status sites'. For this suggestion he has drawn upon comparative material from early Mesopotamia (1984, *passim*). It therefore seems clear that the sites with souterrains reflect a rise in the wealth and status of certain individuals: presumably Pictish leaders. Apparently contradictory to the historical evidence these sites were abandoned at precisely the point we are told the Picts were becoming stronger as a political force. This may be explained in several ways.

Watkin has suggested that the abandonment of souterrains came about when they became too small to store the produce from the area subject to the local leader, who abandoned them in favour of a more prestigious site.

For Watkin, the abandonment of souterrains in the last years of the second and the early years of the third centuries AD suggests the rise of more powerful elites around this time. He asserts that we need not expect to find larger souterrains in the new centres of power because souterrains were no longer suitable due to their limited size for storage in very large quantities (1984, 78).

The abandonment of souterrains c. AD 200, thus might be seen as providing a date for the growth of chiefdoms in Pictland. It is the very time at which our documentary sources suggest there were new tribal configurations taking shape in north-east Scotland. This coincides with the campaigns of Septimius Severus in the North in 208-11 against the Maeatae and Caledonians, and the building of the legionary fortress at Carpow in the heart of souterrain country. It is possible that the disturbances that prompted the Severan campaigns were associated with new political alliances and new 'potentates' in southern Pictland.

Breeze has argued that the few examples of souterrains in southern Scotland are all late. They could therefore well represent some kind of movement south in the 180s or 190s when the Roman army lost control. The finds from the southern souterrains that are closely datable all belong to the late second century (1982, 144).

Halls and hillforts

Two types of site may reflect the centres occupied by the chiefs of Pictland after AD 200: halls and hillforts.

Least informative are the **timber halls** mostly revealed by aerial photography. Since crop-marks do not provide evidence of date, there can be no certainty that all the halls thus discovered are of 'Dark Age' date. Since one of these halls, excavated at Balbridie, Perths, proved to be neolithic, there has been a natural reluctance among archaeologists to assign dates to those that are only known from crop marks (for original identification Reynolds, 1980; Ralson, 1982 for neolithic date). The Balbridie hall was reminiscent of the earlier of two Dark Age halls at Doon Hill, near Dunbar (Reynolds, 1980, fig. 11), but is rather different from the more elongated structures with bowed-out end(s) that appear on most of the aerial photographs (e.g. Maxwell, 1987, fig. 2, illustrating Lathrisk, Fife, where there is a complex of halls with annexes, reminiscent of similar features at Doon Hill, Yeavering, Millfield and Sprouston in Northumbria).

The sites most closely conforming to the assumed 'Dark Age' form seem to be concentrated in central Pictland with a fairly even east-coasterly distribution (Maxwell, 1987, 34 and fig. 1).

That timber rectangular halls were a feature of historic Pictland is shown by the putative example excavated at Clatchard Craig, Fife, though the character of this building was not properly determined (Close-Brooks, 1988, 144-5).

Hillforts are not much more informative. Characteristic of north-eastern Scotland are forts with timber-laced ramparts, some of which have been fired and vitrified through the burning timbers creating draught channels which heated the stones of the rampart-core to melting point — only possible with silica-based stones.

A series of radiocarbon dates from Scottish forts (only eight from Pictland) presents an interesting picture. The table shows two phases of building activity, one in the earlier part of the iron age (from the seventh century bc onwards), another extending from the third to the tenth centuries ad (Alcock, 1987, 86, fig. 4). From this Alcock properly recognized that the later phase of fort-building is to be associated with the rise of 'potentates', and that, recalibrated, they show that this new phase of fort-building belongs to the fourth and fifth centuries. There are only four forts in Pictland that have produced a set of radiocarbon dates, and on such slight evidence it is unwise to draw too far reaching conclusions, but taken along with the evidence from other regions in Scotland is not incompatible with a fort-building stage which may be stretched back to the third century AD.

In this context it is worth considering more closely the finds from radiocarbon-dated sites in Pictland. The excavated example at **Clatchard Craig** has been discussed previously in this book (p. 59), where it was suggested the finds indicated occupation as early as the second or third century AD.

A similar argument can be advanced for **Burghead**, Moray, where the series of radiocarbon dates point to rampart construction around AD 290 (Edwards & Ralson, 1978, 207) though the problems involved with the radiocarbon dating of Burghead are all far from resolved (Ralston, 1987, 16; Edwards & Ralston, 1978, 206-9). Here reported finds include a Roman coin (Small, 1969, 61), which certainly did not arrive in Scotland later than the fourth century.

One fort in Pictland, **Cullykhan** in Banff, has produced a radio-carbon date of AD 317-40 (BM-445), for a wooden object associated with a wooden structure, which implies use of the pre-existing iron age fort at a recalibrated date centring on the early fourth century (Edwards & Ralston,1978, 209; Grieg, 1972). Other finds from Cullykhan are compatible with a 'Pictish' occupation phase.

The Picts and Rome

The emergent Pictish leaders of the later third and fourth centuries clearly had objectives in mind behind their alliances and large scale raids. On the analogy of other barbarians outside the frontiers of the Roman Empire at this time the promise of loot must have been an important factor.

A fact which does not seem to have been commented on is the large quantity of silverwork which has survived from Pictland. There are four major hoards of Pictish silverwork on record — Norrie's Law (Fife), St Ninian's Isle (Shetland), Burgar (Orkney) and Gaulcross (Banff), as well as a series of massive silver chains and an array of silver penannular brooches. Some of these, such as the 'Cadboll' brooches of the late eighth century, seem to have come from otherwise inadequately recorded hoards. There is no native source of silver in Pictland, and we can only assume that these objects were made from silver originating in the late Roman world, some of which may have come as loot, more of which may have come as diplomatic gifts from the Romans in an attempt to 'buy off' Pictish aggression.

We have an insight into the process from the Traprain Treasure, deposited at **Traprain Law**, East Lothian, in the early years of the fifth century, which included over a hundred pieces of late Roman silver plate, mostly crushed and flattened (Curle, 1923). Whether the hoard was lost by a returning sea-borne Pictish raiding party, or was a treasure of the native British occupants of Traprain Law, the Votadini, is not easy to determine, since the crushed state of the silver simply shows it was hoarded for its bullion value. Inside the province similarly-crushed silver is found in fourth-century hoards, such as that from Water Newton, Hunts (Painter, 1977). British or Pictish, the Traprain treasure is as likely to have been part of a 'pay-off' as a hoard of plunder (Alcock, 1979, 135).

Of the purely Pictish treasure hoards, the earliest is probably that from **Norrie's Law**, Fife. Recent research has shown that when the hoard came to light in around 1819 it was found 'crushed in pieces to permit convenient transport and concealment' and comprised 'not much under 400 ounces of pure bullion' (Buist, 1838). The hoard contained what was identified as scale armour along with a helmet, shield and sword hilt, armlets, finger rings, plate silver (in one case decorated with repoussé bosses), hand-pins, a pair of silver plaques and Roman silver coins.

In the past the Norrie's Law hoard has been dated to the sixth or seventh century through its supposed association with a Byzantine bronze coin. It is now clear that this, and an early Roman coin, have no association with the hoard, the only coins from the find being three silver siliquae of Constantius II, Valens and Valentinian I, pointing to a date of deposition sometime after 380 (Laing, forthcoming). The hoard also contains part of a Roman spoon bowl, inscribed with its owner's name (Stevenson, 1956, 229) and various pieces of scrap including what seem to be fragments of vessels similar to cups from Traprain and fragments of ingots of a type common in late Roman silver hoards. Of the other surviving pieces the disc with repoussé spirals is similar to various Caledonian and Irish pieces of metalwork usually assigned to the second century AD: the closest parallels are the 'Monasterevin' discs from Ireland (see p. 185). Armlets and finger rings are compatible with a Roman iron age date, and a large thin silver disc may well be the mount for a votive shield of native manufacture. The armour appears to have been a version of Roman **lorica squamata**. All the other pieces are compatible with the suggested dating of the deposition of the

134

hoard around 400 or 450 AD, and it can be seen as a mixture of Roman silver and Pictish products, some or all of which were fashioned from melted-down Roman coin and plate.

Four objects in the Norrie's Law hoard are of exceptional importance, since these bear symbols which are characteristically 'Pictish'. Two are proto-hand pins (the one a copy of the other), which can be dated to the late fourth or early fifth century on comparative evidence (see p. 204). The other two are leaf-shaped plates (again one copying the other) which appear to be Pictish versions of Roman votive plaques. Such plaques were often made as offerings at shrines: there are a series of similar (Christian) plaques from the Water Newton hoard of silver (Painter, 1977, nos. 10-27) and there are pagan versions from Barkway, Herts, from a shrine to Mars (Walters, 1921, 59-60) and from Stony Stratford, Bucks (Walters, 1921, 62-4). Similar leaf-shaped plates are illustrated in the **Notitia Dignitatum**, a list of dignitaries in the late Roman Empire, where they are associated with donatives distributed by the 'Comes Sacrorum Largitiorum'.

If a fifth-century date for Norrie's Law is accepted, then it shows that Pictish symbols were in use by this time (see p. 232-3), and that accumulations of Roman treasure must have been attendant on status-building among the early Pictish leaders.

The silver armlets in the Norrie's Law hoard are exactly matched by another from the mostly-destroyed Gaulcross (Grampian) hoard, which also had a proto-hand pin of similar type to the symbol-decorated pins from Norrie's Law. The Gaulcross hoard, which originally contained pins and brooches, was of comparable size to that from Norrie's Law (Stevenson & Emery, 1966).

Two of the objects in the Norrie's Law hoard may have been 'symbols of power'. These are a pair of torcs (sometimes erroneously identified as large penannular brooches), which were clearly not worn round the neck in the manner of traditional torcs but more probably on the chest, as Romans wore the torques awarded them as military decorations (for these, Maxfield, 1981, 87-8). In this context the somewhat different torc from Ballinderry 2 crannog (Hencken, 1942, fig. 18, 609 and 44-5) might stand as a Dark Age parallel. Their models are however traditional and iron age. In this context it is worth noting that the *Gododdin* poem alludes to the wearing of gold torcs in the sixth century, which has usually been taken to be an anachronism.

Probably to this period belong the series of massive silver chains found mostly in southern Scotland but presumed to be of Pictish origin. There are ten of these, with heavy links terminating in penannular rings, sometimes with Pictish symbols. These have been catalogued by Edwards (1939) and briefly discussed by Henderson (1979) and Stevenson (1956, 229), who has argued that they are made from melted-down Roman parcel-gilt silver, on the basis of the analysis of a chain from Hordwheel which had a high (4.24%) gold content.

One of the chains has been found at Traprain Law, and another, from Walston, Lanarkshire, has on its terminal ring hammer marks of a distinctive character that are matched on some of the Norrie's Law silver and the Gaulcross armlet. All the evidence points to the chains being contemporary with the silver hoards and belonging in the fourth-fifth centuries. The Lowland Scottish distribution may perhaps be connected with either Pictish raids to the south or more probably with Pictish alliances with their southern neighbours. However, Alcock has suggested that they were not Pictish but originally made in southern Scotland and subsequently acquired and marked with symbols by the Picts (1987, 248).

Literary sources may provide some clues to the usage of chains. Enright (1983) has suggested that Welsh sources indicate that they were worn as marks of kingship in the Dark Ages until crowns were introduced in the time of Rhodri Mawr (877). There are abundant references to chains as signs of rank, divinity or magical power in Irish literature (Enright, 1983, discusses various occurrences). They too are mentioned in the *Gododdin* poem.

There are other possible 'symbols of power' from early Pictland. In discussing the Sutton Hoo whetstone/sceptre, Enright has suggested that it is a Celtic object, as are the related whetstones from Hough-on-the-Hill and Collin, Dumfries. The Sutton Hoo and Hough whetstones are carved from silty greywacke from the Scottish southern uplands (Evison, 1975, 79). The Collin whetstone is of Dumfries sandstone (for its affinities, Laing, 1975d), as appears to be the whetstone from Portsoy, Banff, in Pictish territory (Ralston & Inglis, 1985, 56-7). The decoration on the Portsoy whetstone is 'Pictish' in character, and although it is possible that ceremonial whetstones originated among the North Britons and that the stone itself was an import from further south, they seem to have been taken up by the Picts.

Also possibly Pictish and symbols of power are the bronze double discs joined by septa from a Viking burial at Ballinaby, Islay (Anderson, 1980; Grieg, 1940, 36-7). The plates are of repoussé bronze, with tinning, and have concentric ornament of bosses in zones separated by a raised moulding. They are very badly preserved, but each disc originally had a diameter of about 7 cm. They recall the 'double disc' symbols of Pictish art, which may be intended.as representations of them, and they could have been worn on the chest.

Returning to Roman silver, certain items in the St Ninian's Isle treasure, deposited *c*.800, appear to be modelled on Roman objects, suggesting they were copied from objects that had survived in late Roman hoards. These include the spoon (Wilson *et. al.*, 1973, 113) and more certainly the claw-like object (Wilson *et. al.*, 1973, 115-18) and two of the bowls with friezes of punched animal ornament (Wilson *et. al.*, 1973, 125-6).

Also possibly a borrowing from the Roman world may have been the kind of *carpentum* or processional vehicle that appeared on a now-lost stone from Meigle, Perthshire (no. 10). The Meigle vehicle is not descended from the known iron age chariots, nor from those shown on the Irish High Crosses. A possible explanation for it is that it was borrowed by the Picts from Roman ceremonial usage (Laing & Laing, 1987b).

Ritual sites

It was suggested above that some, if not all, of the objects in the Norrie's Law hoard were votive, destined for a shrine. The hoard was found in an artificial mound on the side of a hill. There is no evidence for associated burial, though a stone cist is reported as being found adjacent, possibly an unconnected prehistoric burial. It is therefore not impossible that the Norrie's Law hoard was buried on a 'traditional' ritual site. There is reason to believe that a class II Pictish symbol stone (that now re-erected at Largo Church) was set up on the same mound. The **Old Name Book** of the Ordnance Survey (1854, 18c, 27) said that one portion of the stone was found when the north side of Norrie's Law was removed. If this is the case, the hoard could have been a votive offering at a cult centre, possibly subsequently buried (with the conversion of the Picts?) and marked with a class II stone, which on present evidence cannot predate the eighth century.

The comparable hoard from Gaulcross, Grampian, was found on a prehistoric burial site in a stone circle (Stevenson & Emery, 1966).

Although usually regarded as a stronghold of pro-Roman Votadini, it is not impossible that Traprain Law, East Lothian was held for a period at least by the Picts, and was one of their ritual sites. This would explain the presence of the Traprain Treasure as a votive offering, the silver chain and a number of artefacts of distinctively 'northern' type, such as the projecting ring headed pin series culminating in the proto-hand and hand-pins — no hand-pins or projecting ring-headed pins are known otherwise from southern Scotland with the exception of one ring-headed pin from Moredun, Midlothian, associated with a couple of brooches of the late first/second century AD in a cist burial (Curle, 1932, 396 and Ritchie & Ritchie, 1972, 60). The later association of Traprain with St Monenna (around AD 600) might imply a continuation of the tradition of a religious importance of the site (Hogg, 1951, 207).

There are other clues about the existence of cult centres among the Picts at this period. Jackson has suggested that the series of bull carvings found in the sea at Burghead are not Pictish symbols as such but votive offerings deliberately thrown into the water (Jackson, 1984, 20), Taken in conjunction with the subsequently Christianized well at Burghead, this might point to a water cult there in Pictish times. In this context there is the reference in Adamnan's **Life of Columba** to sacred wells and a connection between Pictish druids and a bull cult in pagan Pictland (Smyth, 1984, 57).

The Sculptor's Cave, Covesea, Moray, has produced a considerable series of late Roman coins and native pins, hardly compatible with an orthodox settlement. Following the argument about Roman coins as status symbols, Covesea must surely be seen as a ritual site.

Other caves may also have served as cult centres, such as the East Wemyss caves in Fife, with their engravings of Pictish symbols, and the 'weem' names in Scotland which might point to Pictish usage of caves.

The survival of paganism into later times in Pictland is not unlikely, and pagan iconography may have been borrowed for some Class II stones. Cernunnos the pagan Celtic god appears on a stone from Meigle (Henderson, 1967, fig. 32), and there are such scenes as the two bird-headed men with a severed human head between their beaks from Papil, Shetland, an axe-carrying centaur from the Aberlemno Roadside cross (Henderson, 1967, fig. 32), a hammer-carrying giant who could well be Sucellos from Barflat, Rhynie (Shepherd & Shepherd, 1977-8), a bird-headed man carrying a (?) cross from Rossie (convenient figure in Shepherd &

Shepherd, 1977-8, fig. 3b) and a tree that may represent a cult grove that appears on the back of the Eassie stone, which has what may be severed heads on it (Henderson, 1967, pl. 43).

7

IRELAND

Since the Romans never occupied Ireland, the traditional
argument goes, we can use the archaeological material to trace
the development of at least a portion of Celtic 'Dark Age'
culture from the iron age straight through to the medieval period.
This is however less easy than might at first be imagined, because
not only are there problems about dating sites to particular
centuries (p. 39f.), but we are also hard-put to find a diagnostic iron
age culture out of which to see evolving that of the Dark Ages.
Furthermore, there is a certain amount of Roman influence, which
is discussed separately in the following chapter.

It is universally understood that the term 'iron age' is one which
indicates the widespread use of iron for edge tools, and an accom-
panying material assemblage that is distinguishable from that of
the preceding bronze age. In Britain and Ireland what is generally
sought is an artefact assemblage with objects comparable with
those associated with Hallstatt C and D and La Tène I-III on the
Continent, i.e. a 'Celtic' iron age culture.

When we come to review the evidence for Ireland however, there
is remarkably little material of Hallstatt or La Tène type. Yet it is
indisputable that Ireland was Celtic. We must bear in mind during
the review of Irish material that whilst it can be argued that all those
who adhered to La Tène and Hallstatt cultures were Celts, not all
Celts were of the La Tène or Hallstatt cultures.

This underlines the very important fact that term 'Celtic' is
linguistic, and as such cannot be equated directly with any one
archaeological assemblage. Many features of Celtic society were to
be found among speakers of other Indo-European languages. An
elected ruler; a council of elders; graded series of social obligations;
a three-caste system and possibly also shared farming systems have
all been seen as common characteristics of Indo-European societies
(Palmer, 1955).

Map 6 Ireland

It is possible that this simple proviso is sometimes overlooked by scholars, causing unnecessary difficulties. In Ireland far more than in any other area, the period from the fifth to the seventh centuries AD displays very little to mark it out from previous or subsequent ages in the archaeological record. The changes obvious from the sparse historical records, and from the Church traditions are at variance with the material remains, a salutory and important lesson for archaeologists and historians alike to remember. In view of this discrepancy it is useful to review briefly the linguistic and written evidence first, followed by a discussion of the long traditions to be found underlying the settlements and artefacts used in the 'Dark Ages'. Put very simplistically, the period of upheavals in society both in sociological and religious terms in particular appears to have had remarkably little effect on everyday life in Ireland.

The language

Irish is a form of Q-Celtic (or Goidelic Celtic) and is closely related to its offshoots Manx and Scots Gaelic. Linguistically-speaking, it is held to be more archaic than the P-Celtic languages (Welsh, Cumbric, Cornish). A form of P-Celtic seems to have been spoken in La Tène iron age Europe as well as Britain — the few Q-Celtic placenames that survive in Gaul, such as *Sequana*, the name for the Seine, have been seen as older survivals (Piggott, 1965, 222).

There are strong arguments in favour of a form of Celtic being spoken in Continental Europe in the late bronze age Urnfield cultures: they are the direct predecessors of those of the Hallstatt Celts; and place-name evidence suggests that Celtic names are found in areas settled by Urnfield peoples but not by later Hallstatt and La Tène Celts (Piggott, 1965, 173-4 for summary of evidence). Although Celtic can only be attested in the late Urnfield period (*c.* 8th century BC), the Urnfield cultures go back to the late second millennium BC. A certain measure of continuity could be argued back to the arrival of the first Indo-European speakers in Europe towards the end of the third millennium BC or earlier, if Renfrew is correct in attributing the spread of Indo-European speech to the spread of farming from *c.*7000 BC (1987).

From the foregoing, it would appear that as the La Tène Celts seem to have spoken a form of P-Celtic, the Q-Celtic language is likely to have arrived in Ireland before that time. If it were introduced by Hallstatt incomers, it must have happened with the arrival of at most a handful of Hallstatt chiefs, since there is no evidence whatever for a large-scale Hallstatt migration to Ireland. If we require invaders to introduce the language, we must probably look back to the Beaker people, who recent research has shown reached Ireland in the later third millennium BC. The Beaker people probably possessed an Indo-European speech which could have been the ancestor of Irish.

It is of course also possible that Celtic was introduced to Ireland as the language of trade, as French was in Norman England. If that is the case, we need not seek any migrations at all to explain its adoption.

THE HISTORICAL SOURCES

Although there is no 'history' for Ireland before the time of Patrick in the fifth century, there is nevertheless a body of information about early Celtic Ireland that relates to the period before AD 400.

Epic tales were set down by monks in the ninth century and later, but until that time handed down faithfully by oral tradition. There is little doubt that they were composed at least as early as the fourth century AD, and the most celebrated of them, the Táin Bó Cuailnge, certainly reflects a real period of conflict between Ulster and Connacht (Jackson, 1964 on this literature).

Also informative are the complex law tracts, some of which were set down in the seventh century AD, which reveal a great deal about early Celtic society. From such sources as these a clear picture emerges of society in Ireland in the first millennium AD, a society which was 'tribal, rural, hierarchical and familiar' (Binchy, 1954, 54).

On the basis of legends and pseudo-history, O'Rahilly put forward a model of 'invasions' of Ireland in late prehistory (1946). This was taken up by later writers, who distinguished **Cruithin**, the same people as the Picts, the **Fir Bolg**, or Belgae, the collective invasion of **Lagin, Galioin** and **Fir Domnann**, seen as coming from Gaul and settling in Leinster and Connacht, and the **Goidels**, who were seen as coming from Gaul and being the introducers of Q-Celtic in the first century BC (Dillon, 1954, 18). While there is an argument for intrusive scatters of incomers from Britain and Gaul in the latter centuries BC, there is no evidence for invasions, and we must think at most in terms of immigrant chiefs who siezed power among certain tribes, or gained power through trade and influence.

The beginnings of the Irish iron age

Only a few sites can confidently be assigned to a chronological horizon between the fifth century BC and the fifth century AD. In any study of social or economic change in Ireland in the last centuries BC and early centuries AD, the absence of distinctive sites and assemblages makes it difficult to date changes closely, and say whether outside influence had any part to play in them.

A scatter of finds in Ireland have affinities to **Hallstatt** iron age objects, and constitute evidence for the adoption of ironworking towards the end of the Dowris phase of the late bronze age, perhaps around 700-600 BC. At the crannog of Rathtinaun, Co. Sligo, for example, after a purely 'Dowris' assemblage, a second occupation phase comprised Dowris objects along with iron items. One of these at least may be a native product (Raftery, 1984, 11). At Aughinish, Co. Limerick, two stone-walled enclosures appear to be associated with Dowris material a Hallstatt C bronze pin, and part of what is probably a very corroded Hallstatt C iron horse bit (Kelly, 1974, 21). Of course, such an import is not evidence for native iron working.

Scant evidence points to a period after ironworking was introduced c.600 BC in which some objects with **La Tène** affinities were used in Ireland: but the assemblage is effectively without an archaeological context. Although certain items of metalwork are associated with particular raths, crannogs and other settlements, their real relationship to the settlements is unknown, and may be merely fortuitous.

The only two sites to produce La Tène style metalwork in an archaeological context are the ritual hilltop sites of Emain Macha (Navan, Co. Armagh) and Dun Ailinne (Knockaulin, Co. Kildare), which have royal associations and are thus not normal domestic sites. To quote Raftery (1984, 335): 'The La Tène art style, technology and artifact types clearly represent a foreign, introduced tradition in the country. They appear fully developed but, from the very beginning, in a wholly Irish manifestation. The number of imported items is insignificant, and, with the exception of a few late burials, we lack any intrusive assemblage of artifacts. There are no foreign burials in the country contemporary with the earliest metalwork, and no proven exotic settlement types. . . . The total absence of recognizable La Tène pottery from the country is striking'.

Although hillforts exist, they cannot be linked to intrusive La Tène traditions, but appear rooted in a native past (Raftery, 1976, 352-3). At Emain Macha there is a long sequence of occupation from the Later Bronze Age until the last centuries BC (Selkirk & Waterman, 1970; Wailes, 1983).

One possible explanation for this apparent anomaly lies in the fact that all the La Tène derived objects (horse gear, brooches, swords etc.) are 'high status' objects or ritual objects, not to be associated with the general populace. Presumably the ordinary population continued to live in a 'late bronze age' style until the early centuries AD. The apparent absence of a native iron age thus becomes less inexplicable. This theory would incorporate the apparently anomalous evidence for the second phase at Rathtinaun. Here the radiocarbon dates have been rejected as they appear to be too late (grouping around 2150 bp = 200 bc, McCauley and Watts, 1961). They need not be so if we consider a prolonged late bronze age phase (for the dating and sequence, see also Raftery J, 1972, 2-3f, where a prolonged late bronze age is suggested).

Although arguments have been advanced in favour of a La Tène colonization of Ireland (notably by Rynne,1958), recent commentators have rejected the idea for a variety of reasons including those set out by Raftery in the passage quoted above (see for example Laing, 1975, 145-6 and Champion, 1982). A consensus of modern opinion favours the view that the La Tène objects were the property of a ruling elite, though whether this was native, and had acquired La Tène status objects through trade and treaty, or whether it was intrusive is far from clear.

Hawkes has suggested on the evidence of brooches that there may have been an influx of 'Belgae' from Britain around 250 BC. These, he postulated succeeded in establishing a La Tène culture in northern and north-eastern Ireland, 'but disappear once the deeper-rooted Irish had gained enough power to expand from those quarters, for a wider re-assertion of insular cultural identity' (1982, 71). Hawkes saw these 'Belgic immigrants' as giving their name to the legendary tribe called the Fir Bolg, an equation canvassed by O'Rahilly as long ago and 1946, though at that time without the archaeological supporting evidence.

A continuing late bronze age culture in Ireland?

If we cannot find a definite iron age, perhaps we should attack the problem from another angle and look for examples of bronze age traditions that survived in Ireland into the early centuries AD.

There are two avenues of approach, through the study of pottery and that of settlement types. The evidence provided by pottery, although presenting problems, is useful, and settlement types and ritual sites are available for scrutiny.

As the only native pottery of Dark Age Ireland appears to be rooted in in an iron age or even bronze age past, it cannot be used reliably for dating.

One of the distinguishing features of the Dowris phase of the Irish bronze age (*c.* eighth century BC — Eogan, 1964) is the occurrence of pottery (absent in the previous phase).

The ceramic assemblage is often collectively grouped as 'flat-rimmed ware' despite the fact that it also includes pots with rims with an internal bevel, cordons (sometimes with impressed dots), slightly everted rims and even lugs. The main forms are bucket urns and globular pots.

The Irish pottery has been identified as related to a 'conventional' bronze age tradition in Britain, namely 'Covesea Ware', named after the site at which it was first recognized in Grampian, Scotland (Benton, 1931). Covesea Ware has been identified at Loanhead of Daviot, Old Keig and Balmashanner in eastern Scotland, where Coles is of the view it is an intrusive tradition from north-west Germany around 700 BC (1960, 44). The Scottish east coast pottery is hard and thin-walled, with a slurried surface producing a sandy but smooth finish (Coles, *loc. cit.*). Similar pottery is known from Jarlshof, Shetland, where again the fabric is hard and fine (Hamilton, 1956, 29). This relatively high quality ware is peculiar to Northern Scotland, and suggests that the tradition is distinctive, and that Coles' origin for it is possible.

However, where similar forms occur in the Irish Sea province they are in quite a different fabric, coarse, badly fired and frequently gritty. The coarse variant of Covesea Ware is widespread. It occurs at Ballinderry 2 (Hencken, 1942, 19), at Knocknahollet, Co. Antrim (Henry, 1934, 264) and in Yorkshire (map in Hecken, 1942), as well as in Wales (Griffiths, 1959). Flat rims, inturned bevels, cordons and a lug occur at Ballevullin, Tiree (MacKie, 1964), and a lug appears in the assemblage from the late bronze age occupation of the hillfort at Mam Tor, Derbyshire (Coombs, 1970, 100), where it may represent a skeuomorph of a bronze cauldron handle. Similar types of pottery occur at Plumpton Plain, Sussex (Hawkes, 1935, 39), at Eldon's Seat, Dorset (Cunliffe & Philipson, 1968, fig. 10) and at

Ronaldsway, Isle of Man (Laing & Laing, 1988b, 409-12). Its widespread occurence in the late bronze age is undoubtedly because it developed out of native bronze age ceramic traditions in different areas. The use of cordons may go back to Grooved Ware neolithic antecedents, as indeed may several features of the tradition: similar pottery was found in the neolithic court cairn at Dunly, Co. Antrim (Proudfoot, 1956, 25).

The tradition certainly persisted into the iron age in Britain. To cite one example, some of the features in the pottery of Brigantia and south-east Scotland in the early centuries AD start much earlier. This 'Votadinian' and 'Brigantian' ware is represented at Stanwick, Yorkshire, where Wheeler compared the assemblage to pottery from Traprain and discussed its affinity to late bronze assemblages such as Ballinderry 2 (1954, 40): the pottery of 'Votadinian' type from Traprain showed more 'bronze age' features than the Stanwick (Hogg, 1951, Laing, 1975, 276-8).

In the Isle of Man the tradition seems to linger even down to the Middle Ages, where twelfth-century pottery from St Patrick's Isle, Peel, shows some of the characteristics (Wright, 1985).

In Ireland, the same 'bronze age' features occur on the 'iron age' pottery from Freestone Hill, Co. Kilkenny (Raftery, 1969, 91-6), and recur in souterrain ware (Ryan, 1973, 621).

Thus it seems that we have a choice of two arguments. Firstly, if we see 'bronze age' traditions surviving in Ireland into the early centuries AD, then souterrain ware can be seen simply as the continuation of a long tradition of native pottery of late bronze age origin that recurs down to the middle ages. If this longevity is seen as improbable, then the second argument maintains that separate occurences of these features in coarse pottery must be seen as random and fortuitous developments on many separate occasions in prehistory and early history: such pottery cannot be seen as diagnostic of any period or area.

Settlement types in Ireland

In recent years extensive debate has surrounded the dating of the main classes of field monument of the early Christian period.

Ireland has relatively few types of settlement, and apart from a few hillforts and promontory forts, the bulk of these comprise ringforts (raths and cashels), crannogs (lake dwellings) and souterrains.

Raths are circular enclosures, with single, or more rarely multiple, banks, and a single entrance. The interiors usually contain various structures. Raths vary in size, the average being about 30m in diameter or slightly larger, and it has been estimated that there are 40,000 in Ireland.

Cashels are similar forts, with stone walls rather than earthen ramparts.

Crannogs comprise a single dwelling on an artifical island constructed of layers of brushwood in lochs.

Souterrains generally consist of a stone-lined passage way leading to a terminal chamber, though they may also be segmented by narrow tunnels into several chambers. They can have lintelled chambers or beehive corbelled cells offset from the passage, which can be straight, curved, or sharply angled. Some are found in forts, some in open countryside.

Raths and crannogs are frequently but misleadingly grouped together. Crannogs are relatively rare, estimates suggesting that there are about 250 known (though on Lough Gara and elsewhere the number of sites that might be crannogs would multiply this), in contrast to the raths.

Only a tiny proportion (perhaps 150-200 sites) of the raths and crannogs of Ireland have been sampled by excavation. Therefore the picture is necessarily distorted, particularly since major sites with known historical associations have attracted the most attention from excavators.

Less than ten per cent of the excavated sites have produced a range of finds; the great majority of ringforts investigated are devoid of diagnostic finds, producing (if any finds at all) the debris of relatively impoverished farming communities.

Penannular brooches and other ornamental metalwork, imported pottery, bracelets, glass etc are all indications of 'high status' sites. The presence of even one or two ornamental bronzes on a site may show some of its occupants to have been of a relatively high social order.

Although frequently cited as a 'classic' ringfort, Garranes, Co. Cork, is distinguished from the majority by its multiple ramparts, as for that matter was Ballycatteen, Co. Cork, the Rath of the Synods and some of the other ringforts at Tara. At the opposite end of the scale, some ringforts seem to have been only used as cattle compounds — this was the case of the second rath at Garryduff, Co. Cork (O'Kelly, 1962).

Crannogs seem in the main to have been 'high status' sites. Again

148

relatively few have been sampled by scientific excavation, but most of those that have have produced 'high status' artefacts. A similar pattern is apparent from stray finds reported from older excavations (see Wood-Martin, 1886).

DATING

The majority of excavated raths have produced evidence of 'Early Christian period' occupation. The discussion of key sites (above, p. 50), shows that there is no reason on many of the major excavated sites to date commencement of occupation as late as the fifth century, but in most cases there is no reason either to date occupation before the fourth or possibly third century. Despite the detailed arguments about individual sites by Lynn (1975; 1977; 1983), the fact remains that *some* ringforts are definitely older than AD 400, and many could be. The array of finds from the Rath of the Synods at Tara (Ó Riordáin, 1947; Bateson, 1973) shows it to have been in occupation in the second or third century.

EARLY RATHS

The arguments for dating many raths before the third or fourth century AD are however not strong. The Rath of Feerwore (Raftery, 1944) is usually cited as a 'classic' example of an iron age structure, on account of the proximity of the Turoe Stone. It is now suggested that the Turoe stone (decorated with La Tène art and dated to around the end of the first century BC — Duignan, 1976) is unconnected with the rath, and a La Tène iron fibula from the rath was under the bank and thus pre-dated the rath construction. The iron axe from the site could now be seen as medieval not iron age (Caulfield, 1981, 208). Before an 'early iron age' date is assigned to the rath, certain objects require our attention, namely an iron bell and clapper (Raftery, 1944, fig. 3) which is of 'Early Christian period' date, a Viking period pin (Raftery, 1944, fig. 4, no. 25) and a triangular crucible fragment (Raftery, fig. 4, no. 22). The first of these finds were not from a diagnostic context, but the crucible came from the yellow clay that Raftery assigned to period 2, before the building of the ringfort proper (1944, 39). Such crucibles are characteristic of the Early Christian period. Thus there is strong evidence to suggest that the rath was built, probably in the Early Christian period, on top of earlier occupation.

Of some significance in the dating of the Rath of Feerwore is a cist cremation burial reported as dug into the bank (Raftery, 1944, 41). It came to light prior to Raftery's excavation, and the top of it was 2.5 ft below the surface of the rampart. . . . A local herd informed me that the bank was considerably higher twenty years ago than at the time of the excavation, so that the top of Knox's cist would have been about in the middle of the bank' (Raftery, 1944, *loc. cit.*).

If the 'local herd' was wrong about the height of the bank at the time of the discovery of the cist, then the cist could have been beneath the bank, which at the time of excavation averaged about 1 m above the interior of the fort (Raftery, 1944, 26). Indeed the published sections suggest that the rampart was for the most part exactly 2.5 ft high. The arguments in favour of the bank not having been reduced in height and the burial underlying the bank have been advanced in detail by Lynn (1983, 50).

In his survey of the chronology of raths, Proudfoot could cite only Feerwore as dating to before the Early Christian period (1970, 41-4), though pointing to pre-rampart occupation on rath sites.

In summary, there is good reason to suppose that raths developed around the second or third centuries AD out of earlier types of enclosure.

Similar chronological remarks can be made about hillforts. Only a few have been extensively excavated. Freestone Hill, Co. Kilkenny, was shown by Barry Raftery to have been occupied in the fourth century AD from an imported Roman coin (1969). Cathedral Hill, Downpatrick, has a long sequence of occupation on the summit starting in the bronze age and continuing in the iron age and medieval periods (Proudfoot, 1957). Rathgall, Co. Wicklow, seems to have had a late bronze age occupation, followed by an iron age phase, in the early centuries AD, and re-occupation in the thirteenth century (Raftery, B. 1970; Raftery, J. 1972, 9).

In his survey of hillforts Barry Raftery (1972) suggested that excavated examples indicated that hillforts were being constructed in the fourth and fifth centuries AD, but as Rathgall showed, in some cases at least have occupation which goes back to the late bronze age.

RITUAL SITES IN IRELAND

The **Martyrology of Oengus** associates with paganism the 'royal' sites of Tara, Cruachain, Dun Ailinne and Emain Macha, and implies that they were abandoned by *c.* AD 800. Other sources lead to the supposition that they were already abandoned by the fifth century, and were subsequently replaced by monasteries (Wailes, 1983, 5). Literary sources also regarded these sites as fortresses and settlements: in the **Táin Bó Cuailgne** Cruachain and Emain Macha were the capitals of Connacht and Ulaid respectively (Wailes, 1983, 6).

Two other sites, Cashel and Uisneach, are not mentioned by Oengus, though they were regarded as important centres later. Cashel has been rejected by Wailes as having produced no pre-ecclesiastical material (1983, 6), but it probably should not be discounted totally in view of the find of a Roman brooch from there. **Uisneach** has produced some finds of iron age or probable iron-age date, such as the catch-plate of a La Tène III fibula. Despite the assertion to the contrary of Wailes (1983, 18-19) and before him the excavators, Macalister and Praeger (1928), there is evidence for Early Christian period occupation. Several of the finds from Uisneach are in fact of Early Christian period date, such as the penannular brooch (Macalister & Praeger, 1928, pl. XVIII, 11), the possibly similar brooch (*loc. cit.*, pl. XIX, 20), the slotted iron object (*loc. cit.*, no. 12),and the ringed pin (*loc. cit.*, pl. XVIII, 10). The jet bracelets suggested by Wailes as iron age could equally well belong to the early Christian period, and the assemblage as a whole is characteristic of the early Christian and medieval periods rather than earlier.

Whether or not these last two sites are included, taken collectively there is evidence as Wailes has shown that these sites were important ritual centres in the early iron age if not before, but 'There is no evidence so far for high-status residential use contemporaneous with pagan religious (ritual, ceremonial) use. During their most impressive phases, Emain Macha and Dun Ailinne appear on present evidence to have been entirely ceremonial' (Wailes, 1983, 21). The evidence from Uisneach might suggest that here is a pagan ritual site taken over as an administrative centre in the Christian period, and if this is the case would point to growing political centres of power from the later iron age onwards.

CRANNOGS

Crannogs, like raths but in contrast to the ritual sites, appear mostly to date from the Early Christian period. Lynn has tried to demonstrate that while lacustrine settlements may date back to the bronze age in Ireland, true crannogs, i.e. artificial islands made of brush-wood and stones and consolidated by wattle fences and substantial timbers driven into the bottom of the lake, did not appear until the 'Early Christian period' (Lynn, 1983). In the main, Lynn's arguments appear to be fairly sound, and his detailed arguments need not be repeated here. There *are* undefended platforms in shallow water or on lake margins in prehistoric Ireland, and they *do* differ from the substantial crannogs of the Early Christian period.

One site however remains an anomaly — Island MacHugh, Co. Tyrone. Originally identified as a bronze age crannog, recent re-excavation has shown that there was a late bronze age or early iron age crannog, followed by an Early Christian one (Ivens, Simpson & Brown, 1986, 102), the sequence confirmed by dendro-chronology.

From this, it can be concluded that while crannogs existed in Ireland in the late bronze age, for the most part they were lakeside settlements, and the true piled crannog does not become common until after *c.* AD 300. The supposed iron age crannog at Lisna-crogher, from which a series of decorated La Tène sword scabbards reportedly came, could have been an iron age crannog, despite arguments by Lynn to the contrary (1983).

SOUTERRAINS

The remaining class of monument in Ireland is the souterrain. These are mostly confined to Ulster. Finds from souterrains are mostly of the Early Christian period, though sometimes later medieval material is recovered from them. Ogham inscribed stones are sometimes found roofing or re-roofing souterrain passages (Thomas, 1972, 76), and souterrain ware which is widely asso-ciated with them cannot confidently be dated before the fourth century AD (see p. 40). The finds from souterrains are generally meagre, but do not include anything diagnostically datable earlier than this.

SETTLEMENT AND SOCIAL CHANGE

The foregoing survey would seem to suggest that there was a considerable degree of cultural continuity in Ireland from at least the late bronze age, with little evidence for intrusive elements in the population. Although all the main types of settlement appear to have been constructed as early as the late bronze age, there is good evidence that in the early centuries AD there was a notable expansion of the population. This may well have led to the kind of conflict that is mirrored in the **Tain**, or in the Irish raids on Roman Britain. We cannot put a date on the events that lie behind the **Tain**, if indeed the great struggle recounted in that epic had any basis in historical fact. But as Byrne has noted, 'Such turbulent days were over when the sagas were being written in the monasteries of Christian Ireland. Not of course that Irish kings of the period were particularly peaceful. But they had ceased to be great military potentates' (1973, 49).

As Byrne has shown us, Early Christian Ireland was a country ruled over by a multitude of kings: he has suggested there were no less than 150 kings in the country at any given date between the fifth and twelfth centuries. Given that, the proliferation of raths and crannogs in the third and fourth centuries onwards might suggest that here is the archaeological evidence for the beginnings of the kingdoms of Early Christian Ireland, and as in Britain it is to the period before AD 400 that we should turn to seek the roots of Dark Age Celtic society.

8

THE CELTS ABROAD

A lthough displaying regional characteristics, the people we identify as the Dark Age Celts shared a very homogeneous culture, which in turn had much in common with that of their Anglo-Saxon or Continental neighbours. Alcock has canvassed for an 'Irish Sea province' in the Dark Ages (1970), and has also stressed the common cultural elements between Celt and Saxon (1973). As a result the interactions between Celts and Saxons are not dealt with in any detail in this book.

To a considerable extent the development of a common Celtic culture was due to a process of movement in all directions across the Irish Sea in a complex series of political negotiations, migrations, raids, settlements and trade. The cultural interplay between the various groups of Celts was of paramount importance in the Dark Ages.

The Irish in particular ranged far afield in their activities and all groups interacted strongly with their neighbours, both in Britain and on the Continent. The Irish probably raided Roman Britain, and had direct contact with the Roman world, which resulted in certain Roman influences becoming discernible in Irish culture. The Irish settled in Scotland, the Isle of Man, Wales and Cornwall. The Picts and Irish were in constant contact, and even areas as far distant as Egypt may have had an impact on Ireland.

Raids on Roman Britain

The evidence for the Irish Raids on Roman Britain is less firm than that confirming their activities after the Roman period, both within Ireland and outside.

Roman Britain was subject to raiding from the Continent and

Northern Britain. It is generally assumed that it also suffered raids from across the Irish Sea. This is implied by the heavy defences put up along the operative coastline.

The lack of direct material evidence for the Irish raids in late Roman Britain would be expected: by definition raiders, as opposed to settlers, leave none of their belongings behind them.

As there is no direct evidence either historical or archaeological for Irish raids in the West, we can only assume the defensive measures introduced at the end of the third and beginning of the fourth century remained effective during the fourth century. The evidence centres on coin hoards and the fate of various forts in Western Britain.

For a period at the end of the third century and beginning of the fourth **coin hoards** were deposited in Wales and not recovered. Economic factors may in part account for the large numbers of coins of Carausius and Allectus, the British usurpers, since after the collapse of this 'British Empire' in 296 Diocletian and Maximian demonetized their issues (Casey, 1984, 58). However, almost half the coin hoards of Carausius and Allectus found in Britain have come to light in Wales, and the distribution of hoards of the period AD 253-96 (the period of Carausius, Allectus and their immediate predecessors) is also coastal, suggestive of general unrest and insecurity experienced in areas where the threats would be unlikely to be from, say, the continent or the interior (Simpson,1964, for discussion).

Coins of Carausius occur as site finds on Roman forts, but coins of Allectus are absent at, for example, Caernarvon, Forden Gaer and Brecon Gaer.

The fortifications of Roman Britain imply a threat, possibly from Ireland. Rebuilding was put in hand at Chester around the turn of the third century, for example, and a new fort was built at Lancaster. Constantius Chlorus probably founded forts at Caer Gybi on Holyhead and at Cardiff. Although firm dating evidence for the latter is lacking, its design puts it in the closing years of the third century (Johnson, 1979, 89) and Caer Gybi probably fits into a similar context. Though again dating is uncertain it seems probable that Constantius was responsible for the lower fort at Caernarvon, built like the others to accord with the new styles of fortification that were being seen in the forts of the Saxon Shore. Stephen Johnson has suggested that Cardiff, Chester and Caernarvon were linked to the fortified towns of Caerwent and Carmarthen in south Wales as part of a defensive scheme. This may also have involved Gloucester and possible signal stations at Loughor and Pembroke, linking Carmarthen with the sea (1979, 89). Caerleon, a legionary base for Wales since the late first century, seems to have been abandoned at the end of the third century (Boon, 1972, 65-6). The dating of Lancaster poses some problems, since the fort there does not seem to pre-date the 330s (Jones, 1976, 240).

There may have been a fleet based on the Bristol Channel, as is suggested by the inscription from the temple site at Lydney, Glos., mentioning a 'prefect in charge of the fleet's supply depot' which is assumed to have been nearby (Johnson, 1980, 90).

ROMAN MATERIAL IN IRELAND

Since Ó Riordáin compiled the first catalogue of Roman finds from Ireland (1947) there has been an awareness that Ireland was not totally isolated from the Roman Empire. Although many of the finds have now been shown to be spurious or modern losses (Bateson, 1973; 1976), an appreciable body of material remains. Bateson has shown that this falls into two chronological groups, an early one, during the first and second centuries, and a later one in the fourth (Bateson, 1973, 28). The Roman finds of the earlier period seem to have arrived in a fairly random manner (though some may have come through a trading base at Stoneyford on the Nore), and cannot indicate any regular avenues of trade with either Britain or the Continent (Warner, 1976, 267). The discovery in 1852 of a Roman glass cremation urn with glass tear bottle and bronze mirror in a rath at **Stoneyford** has recently been shown to be a genuine find, and as these cannot be construed as luxury items in a native grave, the find can only be interpreted as that of the burial of an emigré Roman of the late first century AD (*Irish Times*, 23 June 1989).

Third-century finds are effectively absent from Ireland (Warner, 1976, 267), and the bulk of the material belongs to the fourth and can be explained in a number of ways.

Firstly, there is a body of material which is only explicable in terms of loot hoards. An example of this is the late Roman hacksilver from **Balline**, Co. Waterford (Ó Riordáin, 1947) and **Coleraine**, Co. Londonderry (Mattingly & Pearce, 1937). The Coleraine hoard is of particular interest since it contains 1,506 Roman coins and seven silver hide-shaped ingots with, in one case, official stamps. These ingots have recently been studied by Painter (1970) who has shown that they were used as donatives to troops

156

and others at the end of the fourth century. The Balline hoard was smaller, with four ingots and three chopped-up pieces of plate, (again bearing stamps). The ingots may have been part of a pay-off to Irish raiders, or just possibly, payment to Irish federates.

Material could have been brought to Ireland as gifts or offerings by Roman emissaries. This must surely be the reason for the Roman finds from **Newgrange**, Co. Meath, which included 25 coins, ranging from a worn *as* of Domitian (*c.* AD 81) to six late Roman gold coins and a clipped *siliqua* of the House of Valentinian or Theodosius (*c.* AD 380). As well as these there was a cache of five Roman gold ornaments (associated with some of the gold coins) (Carson & O'Kelly, 1977).

Claire O'Kelly was of the view that the gold cache at least was a votive offering (1977, 44-5). She emphasised that this, and the majority of the other Roman coins, came from the then perimeter of the mound and adjacent to three tall standing stones which are the surviving segment of the Great Circle.

The presence of a clipped silver *siliqua* at Newgrange is of particular interest, since clipped *siliquae* belong to the final phase of monetary history in Roman Britain and appear to have been hoarded at the end of the fourth and beginning of the fifth century (Archer, 1979; Casey, 1984, 58-60). Hoards of such *siliquae* are notably found concentrated in the West Country, whence some Roman metalworking traditions may have reached Ireland.

The remaining Roman finds from Newgrange would fit in with a fourth century dating: the disc brooches are of types which are now known to have been current at this period, and which occur as residual finds in Anglo-Saxon graves. Also present at Newgrange were 26 glass studs or 'pin heads' with iron shanks 'one of them eyed, reminiscent of those on Victorian boot buttons' (Carson & O'Kelly, 1977, 46). Dark blue, with insets of swirled glass, they have their counterparts at the Rath of the Synods at Tara and from Cairn H at Loughcrew, which produced the Loughcrew bone slips (*loc. cit.*) (see p. 183). Claire O'Kelly suggested that they are pendants, perhaps ear-rings, and could not offer parallels for them. The closest parallel possible takes the form of a similar dark blue (effectively black) bead without swirled inlay from the Mote of Mark, Kirkcudbright, occupied in the sixth-early seventh century.

Newgrange was regarded as a place of religious significance, and it is referred to in Early Christian period sources as a residence of the gods (Carson & O'Kelly, 1977, 48). The 'pin heads' may belong to an Early Christian period phase of veneration, rather than earlier, but it does not detract from the probability of pilgrims from Roman Britain leaving offerings there in the late fourth or early fifth centuries.

The Roman coin-list from Ireland shows a distinct clustering around the period represented by the Newgrange finds. Dolley concluded from this numismatic evidence that the coins pointed to a period of activity centred on the 420s and 430s (1976, 188). This calculation was based on the fact that coins later than the opening years of the fifth century are not found in Britain, and are likely to have still been current in the 420s and 30s.

The Roman imports in Ireland point to a period of considerable contact in the last years of the fourth century and the early years of the fifth. Worn fourth-century coins occasionally appear as site finds, for example from Freestone Hill, Co. Kilkenny, an iron age hillfort (Raftery, 1969, 62).

This period of contact coincides with a period of active Irish raiding on Roman Britain. Irish legendary history sets the tale of Niall Noigiallach (Niall of the Nine Hostages) in this context, and recent scholarship would suggest that Niall was a historical personage who lived around the 420s or 430s (Byrne, 1973, 70-74). More significant historically is the raiding in which St Patrick was abducted from North Britain along with 'thousands of others'.

ROMAN INFLUENCE IN IRELAND

It is against this background of Irish raiding and settlement that cultural traits of Roman origin in Early Christian Ireland can be viewed. It is apparent that sometime between the fourth and sixth century the material culture of Ireland was heavily influenced by types of Roman-derived object. These material manifestations of Roman influence in the archaeological record are distinct from other signs of influence from the Roman world, which belong rather to an intellectual climate fostered, probably, by the Church and by contact through ecclesiastical channels with the Continent, particularly the Mediterranean.

The influence of the Church would account for Latin loan words of ecclesiastical origin, and might account for other Latin loan-words which could have reached Ireland through clerical interest in Latin literature. These include such words as **legion** (legio), **trebun** (tribunus), **long** (navis longa), **Mercuir** (dies Mercurii) and **Saturn** (dies Saturni). The first three might be seen as borrowings necessary to define the late Roman organization of neighbouring

Britain, but the last two, being the names of pagan gods used for days of the week, seem difficult to explain in a Christian context and might suggest an earlier, pre-Christian date (Carney, 1971, 70).

Again, a pagan background is probably necessary to explain the close similarities between the **Iliad** and the **Táin Bó Cuailnge**, unless both are seen as a traditional type of Indo-European epic.

One technological innovation might be ascribed to ecclesiastical influence — the extraction of purple dye from the **purpureus** shell at Inishkea North, Co. Kerry (Henry, 1952).

The remaining evidence for Roman influence in Ireland is exclusively secular.

This Roman-influenced material assemblage has been discussed in detail elsewhere (Laing, 1988), and the salient points need only be summarized here. By far the largest category of material comprises items of personal adornment — penannular brooches, pins, rings, bracelets, dress-fasteners, combs and toilet articles. Collectively they may be seen to represent a revolution in dress, or at least in the adjuncts of it. There are however few areas of life that do not seem to have been influenced by Roman design. Tools derivative of the Roman world include barrel padlocks and tumble locks (the latter represented by their keys), certain types of axe, saucepans, beaten bronze bowls, and weapon types. A few types of object, such as billhooks, leaf-shaped spears, iron shears with notches at the base of the blade, stave-built wooden vessels and certain types of iron knife might be either of Roman or Celtic (La Tène) derivation — if the latter, there is no evidence as yet for their presence in pre-Christian Ireland (Hencken, 1950, 15 original discussion; Laing, 1988, 262 reappraisal).

Two questions must be asked of this material. When did these Roman-influenced traits in the material assemblage reach Ireland, and from what source?

THE DATE OF THE APPEARANCE
OF ROMAN TRAITS IN IRELAND

Much of the assemblage comprises object types that are incapable of precise dating: they were fashionable through much of the duration of the Roman Empire and could have reached Ireland at any point from the second to the fifth century. Some objects, however, are more closely datable. These comprise certain types of penannular brooch and pins.

Of the penannular brooches current in Britain during the Roman period, most of the 'early' types (notably Elizabeth Fowler's A, B, C and D brooches — Fowler, 1960) are totally absent. The E brooches are similarly largely absent, though they are relatively abundant in Britain. E brooches do not outlive the fourth century in Britain, and the couple of examples from Ireland are fourth-century imports from Britain rather than native Irish products. It is notable that one of these brooches is from Newgrange, which we have already discussed in terms of other Roman votive objects. Two brooches of a type which Fowler saw as belonging to a development of her E group (E1) are represented in Ireland and likely to be Irish brooches, but these are unrelated to the main E series and need not pre-date the sixth or seventh century.

In contrast, Fowler's class F brooches are not only present in Ireland as imports from Britain, but also develop into a series of distinctively Irish forms (see pp. 207-8). On the evidence of the E and F brooches, it would seem that 'Romanization' took place after the fourth century, at a time when E brooches were no longer fashionable. As the evidence from Clogher shows, F brooches were probably current in the fifth century in Ireland, and indeed by the sixth century if not earlier Irish types were being evolved (see pp. 207-8).

The evidence provided by penannular brooches seems to be endorsed by that provided by hand-pins. Again the ancestral types (projecting ring headed pins, ibex pins, beaded-and-corrugated pins) are absent in Ireland: of these the ibex pins generally seem to belong to a fourth century milieu. Certainly proto-hand pins had evolved by the mid fourth century as is shown by the Oldcroft example, coin dated to this period (p. 204). Elsewhere in this book we argue that penannulars and pins along with certain techniques of metalworking and ornament reached Ireland from the Bristol Channel region in the early fifth century (p. 208), and this date, if not necessarily the source, would be quite compatible with the appearance of other 'Romanizing' traits in Early Christian Ireland.

Of course it need not be assumed that the arrival of Roman-derived object types in Ireland was the result of a single, short period of cultural influence. The process may have begun in the later fourth century, and continued for half a century or more.

THE SOURCE OF ROMANIZING TRAITS
IN IRISH MATERIAL CULTURE

The Bristol Channel region was an area which retained a

flourishing Roman culture, until it was extinguished by the Anglo-Saxon advance and victory at Dyrrham in 577 (or 8), with the attendant capture of Cirencester, Gloucester and Bath. It is unlikely however to have been the only source for Roman traits. The other possibility is North Britain. Only the writings of St Patrick need be considered here.

Patrick makes it clear that he came from a Romanized background in Northern England, a background which included '(undefended?) country properties with servants, *curiales*, the use of an education in formal Latin and an urban-controlled hierarchical church' (Thomas, 1979, 93). It was a strong tradition, and one which contributed to the formation of Northumbria. This was the world from which Patrick was abducted, and he and his fellow slaves must have taken with them items of personal adornment as well as technological skills that were firmly rooted in Romano-British tradition. Who more likely than slaves would have been employed in the manufacture of tools and weapons in the courts of Irish chiefs? With the growing influence of the Church, more and more in Ireland would wish to aspire to Roman values and taste. Penannular brooches (and possibly also composite bone combs?) became with the passage of time part of the vestments of Irish clerics. Provincial though they might have been in origin, by the seventh and eighth centuries they were equated with 'Romanitas' and became symbols of the Christian church.

Irish settlements in Scotland

Irish settlements in Scotland are implied by the documentary sources and have been extensively discussed over the last century. Attempts have consequently been made to recognize the settlements archaeologically with no success before the end of the fifth or the beginning of the sixth centuries, to which period belong the earliest of the ogham-inscribed memorial stones found in Britain. Their absence in Scotland (where the earliest ogham-inscribed stones are eighth-century Pictish) suggests that the Irish settlers responsible for the Welsh and Cornish ogham inscriptions did not also migrate to southern Scotland.

The settlement of **Dalriada** in western Scotland around AD 500 is well attested from documentary sources. The main source of information is a seventh-century text preserved in a later medieval copy, the **Senchus Fer n-Alban**. Bannerman has argued there is no material in this later than the seventh century (1966; 1968; 1974). This text relates how Fergus Mor, son of Erc, established a dynasty in Scotland derived from Dal Riata, in present-day Antrim. Fergus mac Erc's descendants ruled over both the holdings in Ireland and Scotland down to the early years of the seventh century (Bannerman, 1974).

Bede, in discussing the Dalriadic colonization, refers to the leader as Reuda, and an Irish origin-legend tells of Cairpre Riata, who supposedly lived some ten generations before c.501, the traditional date of Fergus mac Erc's death (Duncan, 1975, 41). This would produce a date in the third century AD, if not earlier, and might point to Irish traditions of long associations with Scotland. It is however possible that Lorn and Islay were colonized before the arrival of Fergus. **The Senchus fer n-Alban** states that these areas were colonized by the Cenel Loairn and Cenel nOengusa, named after Loarn and Oengus, two sons of Erc. Duncan has pointed out, however, that this seems to be an explanation for the sake of convenience, and that these two tribes were kindred from an earlier migration: the Cenel nOengusa are known in Ireland before the time of Fergus (Duncan, 1975, 42). Bannerman has also taken the view that the first Dalriadic settlement may pre-date 500 (1974, 122-6).

Dunadd is a citadel of the Dalriadic Scots in Argyll. No finds however from this site need pre-date 500. Dunadd is usually assumed to be the Dalriadic capital, but as Lane has pointed out, there is no firm evidence to assume this is the case (1980, 1-3; 1984, 43). He has suggested that the existing defences of this 'nuclear' fort, like those at Dundurn, Perths, (in Pictish territory), do not necessarily pre-date the seventh century. In recent excavations E ware was found under an extension to the original rampart (1984, 45). Lane has suggested that the metalworking from the site belongs to the eighth century or even ninth (1984, 55). While this is possible for some of the moulds, other moulds appear to be for objects more at home in the seventh century, and this might seem to be supported by the fact that D ware was present on the site (for fuller discussion, see p. 59).

In **south-west Scotland** apart from placenames (see below) there is no indisputable archaeological evidence for early Irish settlement.

The ecclesiastical site at **Ardwall Isle**, Kirkcudbright, for example, is frequently cited as a classic 'Irish' early Christian chapel; but the interpretation of the sequence set out by Thomas (1967) is open to doubt. Thomas' ingenious sequence of 'special burial — corner post shrine — relic cavity in altar' is not convincing. The evidence for a corner-post shrine consists of a series of post holes set in a random arrangement (Thomas, 1967, plan, fig. 26). All known shrines are rectilinear, not polygonal, and it is notable that none of the presumed posts or slabs have been found. The hollow from which the relics were supposedly translated similarly cannot be shown to have ever contained a burial.

More convincing is the timber oratory of Thomas' Phase II, despite the fact that only three post-holes can be lined up. There is no dating for either Phase I or II, though an inscribed stone from the site, presumably associated with burials, seems to belong to the mid-eighth century (Thomas, 1967, 154). This inscription, naming Cudgar, is Germanic rather than Celtic, and has affinities that might point to the period of Anglian occupation as are a series of later cross-slabs. There is nothing from the site to suggest its usage before the eighth century, and the sole object which might suggest an Irish connection is a stone which has been interpreted as part of a butterfly gable finial (Thomas, 1967, 157 and fig. 31, 12), though other interpretations for it are possible. The stone chapel of Phase III to which this finial has been assumed to have been attached need not be any earlier than the tenth century and could be as late as the twelfth.

An alternative sequence to that published by Thomas, is that a cemetery of the seventh century was furnished with a timber chapel or oratory in the eighth century which was followed by a stone replacement of the tenth century or later.

It has been suggested that a penannular brooch from **Luce Sands**, Wigtown, is of Irish manufacture (Rynne, 1965), but the case against this has been argued by L. Laing elsewhere (1975c).

Recent excavations at **Brydekirk**, Annan, Dumfriesshire, have produced what may be the ring from an Irish ringed pin in a primary context: the dedication is to St Bride (Bridget), an Irish saint, and the name is a **Kirk** one probably of the Norse period (Crowe, 1987).

PLACENAMES

The place-name evidence is in keeping with a relatively late date for the Irish colonization of Galloway. Nicholaisen has drawn attention to the place-name element **Slew** in south-west Scotland, pointing to its origin in the Gaelic **sliabh**, which in Ireland means a 'mountain', in Scotland a 'hill' (1965). In addition, MacQueen has discussed the place-name elements **Kirk** and **Kil** in the same area, and has concluded that **Kirk** placenames are inversion compounds of the Norse period (ie. around the eleventh century) but that the **Kil** names predate this (1956). It has been suggested that logically this phase belongs to the period before the Anglian colonization, but this remains open to debate. It is sometimes suggested that the monastic foundation at Whithorn had an Irish phase (Thomas, 1987), but current excavations have not yet demonstrated any clear Irish connection.

Irish settlements in the Isle of Man

The evidence from the Isle of Man is firmer, and attests Irish settlement around 500. The earliest names recorded in Man are P-Celtic (i.e. British or Welsh), such as Tudwal (Tutuvallus), who appears in an early Manx dynasty. A late fifth or early sixth century ogham stone, with bilingual inscription commemorating AMMECATUS (Macalister, 1945, 479; Jackson, 1953, 173), suggests that both British and Irish were spoken in Man at the time of its erection. Subsequently Manx, which is a form of Q-Celtic (Gaelic) was developed, though not before the thirteenth century.

Archaeological material indicative of Irish contacts with Man comprises the head of what is probably a latchet brooch of the seventh century from **Kiondroghad** (Gelling, 1969) and a series of finds from a complex multi-period site at **Ronaldsway** (Neely, 1940; Laing and Laing, 1988b). Ronaldsway appears to have begun as a secular settlement but subsequently became ecclesiastical, with at least two phases before the arrival of the Norse. The ecclesiastical site may have been a minor monastery, with two **leachta**, outdoor altars of the Irish type that is well represented by St Patrick's Chair, Marown (Kermode, 1907). **Leachta** are well-known in Ireland, for example at Inishmurray, but are not well authenticated in Britain. Structures at Tintagel, Cornwall and Birsay, Orkney, have been put forward as leachta, but neither is persuasive, especially in view of the current interpretation of Tintagel as a secular trading base. The Ronaldsway finds also include Irish brooches, notably a zoomorphic penannular of class F3 and a pseudo-penannular ring brooch, of the seventh and ninth centuries respectively.

Irish settlements in Wales

The evidence for Irish settlement in Wales has fequently been discussed (Richards, 1960; Richards, 1962; Alcock, 1971; Laing, 1975; Thomas, 1972a; Thomas, 1975 are some of the main studies). Once more, the bulk of the evidence is documentary and toponymic rather than archaeological, though the archaeological evidence is more convincing than from other areas.

Some Irish settlement is indicated before the end of the Roman occupation. The name of the extreme west of Gwynedd, 'Lleyn', and some placenames, such as Mallaen and Dinllaen, incorporate the Irish name **Laigin**, 'Men of Leinster' (Williams, 1966). Ptolemy in the second century referred to Lleyn as the 'promontory of the Gargani', who were a north-west Irish tribe (Alcock, 1970, 65). Archaeologically this is perhaps supported by the distribution of decorated rotary querns, which are concentrated in Anglesey, the adjacent part of Gwynedd, and Ulster (map and discussion, Griffiths, 1950). Though difficult to date, they appear to belong to a Roman iron age horizon rather than later.

Welsh folk tradition describes the enclosed hut groups of the Roman iron age in North Wales as **cytiau'r Gwyddelod**, 'Irishmen's huts'. The term was current at least as long ago as the sixteenth century, as Camden refers to them as **Hibernicorum casulae** (1590, 723). With certain exceptions, these huts appear to be developed in the third and fourth centuries, possibly through official Roman encouragement. Roman influence would explain the rectilinear planning of some, and there is no reason to associate them with Irish settlers (Hogg, 1966 for general discussion) since similar hut groups are not found in Ireland. Nevertheless, the tradition shows that in late medieval Wales there was a belief in Irish settlement at a remote period in the past. A possible explanation for this might be found in the hut groups being the homes of deliberately-settled natives encouraged to act as a buffer against the Irish raids by the Roman authorities. In the order of things, some may have come into Irish immigrant possession.

A number of stray finds show sporadic contact with Ireland from the sixth century to the Viking age, but are generally conspicuous by their absence. They suggest that Irish settlement in Wales was not a continuous process and that links were not maintained by the colonists with their homeland.

They include a hinged pin and 'slotted object' from Lesser Garth Cave, Glamorgan (Alcock, 1958), which need not pre-date the

165

eighth or even ninth century, and a similarly datable ringed pin from presumed secondary occupation on a Roman iron age site at Gateholm, Pembroke (Lethbridge & David, 1930). There are also two pins with double-spiral heads from Castlemartin Burrows, Pembroke, and Caerwent, Mont (Fox, 1946, 105-22). Spiral-headed pins are relatively rare, though they are known from pagan Anglo-Saxon England (Pretty in Cunliffe, 1975). There are only two in Scotland, from Pictish areas. The Welsh pins are closer to the Irish than the Anglo-Saxon, which are smaller. A lead pattern for an Irish penannular brooch and a millefiori rod from Dinas Powys, Glamorgan, of the late sixth century (Alcock, 1963, 121 and 187), implies no more than an itinerant smith. Three late brooches, from Llanmadog, West Glamorgan, Llys Awel, Clwyd and Trearddur Bay, Anglesey, are of the eighth or ninth centuries (Lewis, 1982).

The remaining evidence comprises ogham-inscribed memorial stones of the late fifth/early sixth century, and a body of placename and literary evidence.

The documentary evidence for Irish settlement in Wales takes three forms. The first is a tradition preserved in Nennius' **Historia Brittonum**, compiled in the ninth century, that the 'sons of Liethan' ruled in south-west Wales, Gower and round Kidwelly until driven out by a certain Cunedda and his sons from 'all British districts'. This, as Charles Thomas has pointed out, is a garbled tradition, since there is nothing to connect Cunedda with south Wales, as his activities were in the north (1972a, 256).

It should be emphasised that the only tradition associating Cunedda with the Irish in Wales is that to be found in the ninth-century compilation of the **Historia Brittonum**. According to this, Cunedda left Manau in Gododdin territory (round the Firth of Forth) with all his sons except the eldest and migrated to Wales, where he held out against the Irish. On his death his kingdom was divided amongst his sons, who founded separate kingdoms. Nennius' date for the migration was 146 years before the date of Maelgwn, a contemporary of Gildas, which takes the date of the migration to around AD 400. Welsh genealogies include the name of Cunedda and his sons, but attempts to correlate particular reigns with historical dates have foundered (Nicholson, 1908, 63-105; Blair, 1947, 28-37; Hogg, 1948, 201-5; Alcock, 1971, 125-9).

Therefore a date cannot be assigned to Cunedda, though the migration is most easily explicable in terms of the Roman practice of **foederatio**. It is frequently pointed out that Cunedda's ancestors are given Celtic versions of Roman names — in particular Padarn

(Paternus) Pesrut (Red Tunic). From this it has been argued he had perhaps been invested with a red or purple tunic or cloak as a mark of his status in the last days of Roman Britain. It is equally possible that the Roman names in Cunedda's family tree belong to 'systematic pseudo-ancestries' devised much later to tidy up the earliest parts of genealogies (Jackson, 1955, 80; Miller, 1978). Mann has also suggested that the Latin names were devised in the light of later Christian practice (1974). If all this is so, Cunedda's Roman lineage dissolves and he becomes a pseudo-historical figure whose migration could have taken place much later in the fifth century.

It is more rewarding to compare the tradition of the sons of Liethan (the Uí Liathain, a south-east Irish tribe) with a second tradition concerning another tribe from the same area, the Deisi (Dessi), who were said in an Irish story (the earliest text of which goes back to the eighth century) to have been driven out of Ireland with their king to settle in south-west Wales (Pender,1947, 209- 27; Hull, 1957, 14-63; Alcock, 1963, 58-9; Thomas, 1972a, 257). A list of the rulers of the Deisi are preserved separately in Irish and Welsh sources, and attempts have been made to arrive at a date for the migration from these. Current opinion puts it around AD 400, though it could possibly have taken place later.

The only firm evidence for Irish settlement in Wales that exists takes the form of ogham inscribed stones, which are concentrated in the north, in Gwynedd and Anglesey, and in the south, particularly in Pembroke.

The study of ogham inscriptions raises a number of interesting issues. Kenneth Jackson argued (and it has not been disputed) that the ogham alpahbet developed from a fourth-century classification of the Roman alphabet, as used by grammarians in the late Empire (1953, 151f). More recently, Harvey has suggested that there was some degree of naturalized latinity in Ireland at an early date, before the sound change of lenition had occurred, in his view sometime before the middle of the fifth century (Harvey, 1987, 9). In Ireland ogham is mainly found in the south; in Britain it is absent from early Scotland and is found in a few inscriptions from North Wales but mostly in the south, with a concentration in Pembroke. It has been suggested that the alphabet might have been developed among Irish colonists in south-west Wales — Thomas has suggested that the earliest ogham stones are pagan, and date from around 400 (1972a, 259-60; 1981, 299). Certainly the earliest Irish stones employ a formula 'Of A, of the son of B' which seems to echo late Roman tombstones. While it is possible that ogham in Ireland pre-dates the fifth century, there is good reason for thinking it was a development of the early fifth, in the same millieu as the other Roman-derived innovations in Ireland discussed above (p. 159f.). The stones need not be pagan, and the alphabet could have been introduced to Wales from southern Ireland around the middle of the fifth century, perhaps with the earliest colonists. The Welsh stones are bilingual also carrying inscriptions in Roman letters which represent a translation of the ogham (or vice versa).

In considering the distribution of ogham inscribed stones, Thomas has pointed out that Irish-style memorial formulae are found in Latin inscriptions in Wales, with, instead of the more usual HIC IACIT A, we find 'OF A FILIUS OF B' or 'OF A' or even mixed Latin-Irish formulae 'HIC IACIT OF A FILI OF B'. These two traditions have been plotted by Bu'lock (1956), and Thomas has argued that they represent the period of Irish expansion in the sixth-seventh centuries and commemorate people of mixed origin, perhaps of bilingual speech. They show Irish penetration most strongly in south-west Wales and Brecon, with weaker penetration in the north. From this he has deduced that Irish settlement in north-west Wales was earlier, more localized, and more rapidly assimilated (Thomas, 1972a, 260).

The remaining evidence for Irish settlement in Wales takes the form of place-names. Melville Richards has studied the element **cnwc**, 'Hillock', which he sees as derived from Irish **cnoc**. Its distribution is concentrated in Pembroke, the former kingdom of Dyfed, and is remarkably localized (Richards, 1960). Possibly related is the element **meid(i)r** or **moydir**, a 'lane' or 'road', which may ultimately be derived from Irish **bothar**, a 'road'. Again the distribution is localized in Pembroke (Richards, 1962).

In summary, there is a body of documentary, archaeological and toponymic evidence for Irish settlement in Wales. There is no conclusive evidence for date, although there are some suggestions that settlement in the North was early, perhaps within the fifth century, and was relatively minor and rapidly assimilated. In the south the settlement was denser and had much greater impact, and need not have taken place before the sixth century.

Irish settlers in Cornwall

Amongst the limited archaeological evidence, the most important is ogham-inscribed memorial stones, or stones bearing Irish names in Latin letters. These are concentrated on the plateau of north-east Cornwall, at a date around the beginning of the sixth century. It indicates a secondary colonisation from the Irish communities of south Wales (Fox, 1964, 158 and map; Thomas, 1973, 6), rather than direct colonization from Ireland.

Charles Thomas claims a separate colonization of West Cornwall and Scilly based on the evidence of the occurence of **grass-marked pottery** on a variety of sites. The grass-marked pots are distinguished by their inelegant jam-jar shapes and the impressions on their bases of chopped straw on which they had stood to dry out. The pottery sequence for Cornwall is fairly clear, so it is fairly certain that they make their appearance in the area in the later sixth century AD. Thomas has studied the tradition (1968; 1973) and has reached the conclusion that the pottery is most closely comparable to the **souterrain** ware of Ulster, which has been the subject of study by Ryan (1973). While pointing out that grass-marked pottery is absent in Wales, Thomas has drawn attention to the presence of it in Scotland, at Iona, Sollas (N. Uist) and Killegray, off Harris (1972, 265), 'in a region where the first Irish settlement was derived exclusively from north-east Ireland' (1973, 7).

A number of arguments militate against Thomas' claim. Firstly, none of the Cornish vessels match very closely their Ulster counterparts, and grass-marking can now be shown to be a widespread phenomenon in southern Britain, occuring in Anglo-Saxon contexts, such as Portcheter, Hants (Cunliffe, 1975, 177-82). Secondly, Richard Reece's excavations at Iona have suggested that there the grass-tempered pottery belongs to a later, perhaps tenth-twelfth century, horizon (1973, 40), which would fit in with the dating of grass-tempered pottery in N. Uist (Crawford, 1972). In Reece's scheme, there were two periods of grass-tempering, one beginning in late Roman Britain and surviving in the south into the sixth century, and another in the north in the tenth to twelfth century (1973, *loc. cit.*). The Cornish pottery would thus best fit in with the end of the Romano-British tradition, and be indigenous rather than intrusive. It is worth remembering that poor pottery (which the Cornish grass-marked and Irish souterrain wares both are) does not lend itself to complex shapes or decoration, and similar baggy vessels are found in many different contexts at different periods. In support of this theory it is to be noted that the local Cornish type of sub-Roman platter was produced in grass-marked fabric (e.g. Thomas, 1968, fig. 72, nos. 8-15).

The remaining evidence for an Irish colonization of Cornwall can be summarized briefly. A few finds of objects from **Gwithian**, a native site with stone-walled huts, may be Irish (Thomas, 1958; 1972, 265) but which by themselves say little. Historical sources are twofold — dedications to saints of Irish origin and an enigmatic statement in the late ninth-century **Cormaic's Glossary** which states that the Irish were established in some part of Britain, fairly clearly the south-west, where they had two fortresses, **dind map Lethain** and **dun maic Liathan** which were in the lands of the Cornish Britons. The names incorporate the tribal name already encountered in south Wales, and would support a secondary Irish colonization of Cornwall from this area rather than a direct settlement from northern Ireland.

The Picts and the Irish

It is extremely unlikely that any Pictish alliances in the fourth century were the outcome of suddenly-formed friendships. In the chapters on art some attention will be given to the links between Scotland and Ireland in the Roman iron age. There the case will be set out for links between Scotland and Ireland as attested by ornamental metalwork in the first to third centuries AD.

That these links continued through the third and fourth centuries is perhaps attested by a variety of objects. Examples of these objects commonly found in Scotland and occasionally found in Ireland include the 'Donside' or 'Massive' terrets. These were produced in north-east Scotland from the second century onwards, and which we have argued were still being produced in the fourth (Laing and Laing, 1988, 212). Other objects include the 'knobbed spear butts' current in Scotland from the second or third century but surviving later (Laing & Laing, 1988, 214), and objects decorated with the 'crested bird's head' that also survives into 'Dark Age' metalwork (Laing & Laing, 1988, 215-8, with other examples).

There is literary evidence for Pictish connections with Ireland, and indeed some for 'Irish' Picts. The Irish before the eighth century were of the view that the **Cruithin** (the word is the same as the Cruithni of Pictland) were of the same origin as the Picts. Bede narrated how Picts came from Scythia and sought refuge in Ireland, but were refused a landing and went instead to Scotland. Macneill pointed out (1933, 20) that references to the Irish **Cruithin** ceased to be made after 773, at a time when the Scots and Dalriada were at war with the Picts, who were thus now regarded as inferior peoples. The homeland of the historical **Cruithin** was eastern Ulster, and seven, possibly nine, small kingdoms are recorded for them as late as 563 (NacNeill, 1933, 10). The **Annals of Ulster** refer to them intermittently from this date until the late eighth century, when they disappear from the records. It is clear therefore that there were non-native peoples in eastern Ulster in the early Christian period who were regarded by the Irish as Picts.

A further group of Picts are recorded in medieval Irish tradition which maintained that the **Loigis** of Leix in Leinster were Cruithin or Picts. They were believed to be divided into seven tribes or segments, like the Picts of Scotland. This view is endorsed by modern scholarship (Smyth, 1982, 76).

Later links, from the end of the fifth century AD, between Picts and Irish were clearly fostered through Dalriada. The assemblage of moulds from Dunadd include specifically Pictish types (Lane, 1984, 51-7), and Ritchie has argued that the Picts and Scots also shared board games (1987, 60-2), though the Ballinderry 1 board may in fact be Manx, and an import in Ireland not a native product.

Some of the interplay of ideas between Scotland and Ireland in the design of penannular brooches has been discussed by L. Laing, (1977).

It is likely that the ogham alphabet reached Pictland from Dalriada, along with Gaelic loan words, presumably transmitted via Iona (Smyth, 1984, 79; Ritchie, 1987, 64-6), though Ritchie has seen the transmission as less the outcome of direct contact with the Scots and more the result of the influence of the Church in spreading the idea of memorial stones. She has suggested that in Pictland their usage is comparable to their usage in Ireland, with a late, secular application in cryptography (1987, 66).

Ireland and the Continent

Much attention has been focussed on Irish missionary activity on the Continent, and the evidence has been stretched to argue for a strong intellectual interplay between Ireland and Atlantic Europe, and, at a further remove, Coptic Egypt, Armenia and Spain. That Irish monks founded monasteries in Gaul is not in doubt; that cultural interplay between Ireland and the Continent was the result is a thesis based more on inference than sound fact.

In the fifth century, the Atlantic ports of Aquitaine that had operated in Roman times continued to trade with Spain, the British

Isles and northern Gaul, and the Garonne and Loire ports were the hub of a trade route which stretched from Iberia through the Irish Sea to Dalriada. Pirates may have been a problem in the fifth century, but by the sixth and seventh this axis of trade was well established (James, 1977, 221). Throughout this province, the cult of the fourth-century monk St Martin may well have been a unifying factor. This would explain how the cult of St Martin reached Ireland at a relatively early date (Mayr-Harting, 1972, 84-6).

It is fairly clear that early Irish monastic foundations owe much to Martin's model. The rectilinear planning that characterizes Iona and Clonmacnois, for example, owes a direct debt to the fort-like plans of the monasteries of the East, which had been Martin's inspiration (Thomas, 1972, 32). Columba was a monk in the Eastern mould: Adamnan relates that Columba's bed was the bare rock, and a boulder provided him with a pillow. Like the desert fathers who had inspired Martin, Columba was known to retreat to a hut on a remote island to fast for three days.

Links were clearly maintained between Iona, Ireland and the Loire. Gaulish sailors are reported by Admanan as regularly visiting Iona (though he does not say what part of Gaul they came from) (**Life of Columba**, I, 28), and when Columbanus was deported from Gaul in 610 he found an Irish boat to take him back at Nantes (Mayr-Harting, 1972, 85). A late **Life of St Cybard** relates that when Nicasius of Angoulême founded a church at Bordeaux 'ships from Britain equipped with sail and oar arrive at the port of the city to do trade there' (James, 1977, 223). It is in this context of Martinian monasticism that the popularity in Ireland of Sulpicius Severus' writings on Martin should be viewed.

The archaeological evidence for contact between Ireland and Aquitaine is less clear. If Thomas and Peacock are correct in ascribing E ware to the Bordeaux region (1967; Thomas, 1981), it suggests a flourishing trade throughout the Irish Sea province in the later sixth century onwards.

From the sixth century onwards too Irish monks were travelling abroad, in Gaul and Italy and slightly later, Germany, and some Continental clerics were travelling to Ireland to study. As Kathleen Hughes commented, monks like Columbanus sought to abandon earthly ties, for life was a 'roadway whereon none dwells, but walks' (1966, 91). Already by the sixth century some Irish monks had fled to the deserts. Deep-rooted in the Irish personality was a desire to travel, and pilgrimage appealed as a form of perpetual exile.

Columbanus set up a hermitage on the Vosges at Annegray, where he attracted disciples who lived like him on a near-starvation diet. From these austere beginnings grew the monastic foundations of Luxeuil, St Gall and Bobbio. Another Irish monk, Fursey, first established a monastery at Burgh Castle in Norfolk, then went to north-east Gaul. Bishop Ronan went to Gaul on a pilgrimage in the late seventh century, and stayed to become abbot of Mazerolles (Hughes, 1966, 92). The intellectual current was two-way. Agilbert, for example, who became bishop of Paris, was educated in Ireland. It is in this context that the cross-fertilization of intellectual life between Ireland and Gaul in the sixth to eighth centuries must be viewed.

One of the areas in which cross-fertilization can be seen most clearly lies in the travels of books. At Bobbio, in Italy, Irishmen worked in the scriptorium, where they learned Italian scripts but employed their own systems of abbreviation, their glosses and decorative devices. Manuscripts were taken to Bobbio from Ireland, including the late seventh-century **Antiphonary of Bangor**, while others executed at Bobbio, such as the **Codex Usserianus Primus,** of the seventh century, found their way back to Ireland (Hughes, 1966, 93; see also for these manuscripts Nordenfalk, 1947).

Irish monks in the **paruchia** of Fursey in north-east Gaul were probably responsible for the dissemination of the cult of St Patrick there: relics of Patrick were said to have been brought to Gaul by Fursey, and abbot Cellan (who died in 706) composed verses on the saint. Patrick's Confession was probably brought to Peronne, where it was copied by a continental scribe in the late eighth or early ninth century (Hughes, 1966, 94).

The Irish monks were wide-ranging in their intellectual interests. At Bobbio they held three North African manuscripts of the fourth and fifth centuries, one reputedly carried by Columbanus in his book-satchel (Lowe, 1934-63, iv, 465).

The works of Isidore of Seville had a profound effect on Irish thought. Of the nine seventh-century manuscripts of Isidore that survive, three were copied at Bobbio and one in either Bobbio or Ireland (Hillgarth, 1962, 180). Isidore, like the Irish monks, was interested in Hebrew, Greek and Latin, and in etymology; grammar was rated highly in seventh-century Irish monasteries. Pagan classical texts were not ignored: a seventh-century commentary on the Bucolics and Georgics of Virgil shows that he was studied in Ireland (Kenney, 1929, 285-7).

Considerable study has been made of possible links between Iberia and Ireland, most notably in the works of Hillgarth (1963). The evidence usually cited takes two forms, (1) the familiarity in Ireland with texts of Spanish origin and (2) the influence of Iberian manuscripts on Insular art.

The studies of Hillgarth show very clearly that the works of Isidore (c.570-636) reached Ireland very rapidly. Laidcenn of Lismore, who died in 661, quoted from Isidore, and an Irish contemporary of Aldhelm used several of Isidore's works (Hillgarth, 1963, 187). Other Spanish writers were also known in Ireland, such as Juvencus and some Priscillianist writers (Hillgarth, 1963, 168). Hillgarth saw the export of Spanish manuscripts as via Southern France to Britain and Ireland, reaching Ireland directly from the Continent, not via England (1963, 180). The source was seen at Britonia, a Celtic see in Galicia, probably founded from Britanny in the late fifth or early sixth century (Hillgarth, 1963, 189; for Britonia, Thompson, 1968).

Artistic links have been noticed by Werkmeister between Visigothic illumination and Insular manuscript art. Werckmeister studied three manuscripts — the Paris Isidore (held to be an eighth century copy of a Visigothic manuscript executed in northern France), the Echternach Gospels, and the Durham A II 17 (Werckmeister, 1963). The last contains a miniature of the Crucifixion, which Werckmeister suggested was by the same hand as the *Imago Hominis* page in the Echternach Gospels. The lobed treatment of draperies, which is also found in the Book of Dimna, the Book of Deer and the St Gall Gospels, of the eighth and ninth centuries, led Werckmeister to put forward a Visigothic model for this distinctive treatment of figures. However, Werckmeister's examples, though of Insular tradition, can be regarded as of very different provenance. The Echternach Gospels were probably produced at Echternach, if not in Northumbria, the Durham A II 17 almost certainly in Northumbria, the Book of Deer in Pictland (Hughes, 1980, 22-37). Only the Book of Dimna is certainly a product of an Irish scriptorium. Added to which, most recently and convincingly, Nordenfalk has suggested that the lobed drapery owes its origin to the Far East, namely Persia (1968; 1987, 4-5). Even if Werkmeister is correct in believing the device was transmitted to Insular manuscripts via Spain, there is no evidence that it came directly from Spain to Ireland, rather than through some intermediary channel, and the same may be said for Hillgarth's arguments regarding texts.

What has been seen as an archaeological clue to a possible Irish contact with Spain is provided by the crosses countersunk above the doors of some Irish churches with architrave lintels (Leask, 1955, for series). Examples can be seen at St Fechin's Church, Fore, Westmeath and at Inishmurray (Leask, 1955, figs. 31-2). This device is found in Spain, but there is no reason to date any of these Irish churches to such an early period as the seventh or even the eighth century: they are likely to belong at the earliest to the ninth or tenth centuries.

Cumulatively, the case for direct links between Ireland and Spain in the sixth to eighth centuries cannot be proved, though indirect links are certainly apparent.

ARCHAEOLOGY AND CONTINENTAL LINKS

There are a few traces of Continental links in Irish archaeology. Again, these mostly date from the period later than that covered by this book. Of the period under review are a number of Chi-Rho inscribed stones which are distributed along the west coast of Ireland and west coast of Britain. Hamlin in studying these has pointed out that the 'monogram' form of Chi-Rho was current in Gaul from about 400 to the mid-sixth century, and in Spain until the seventh, appearing on Merovingian coins even in the eighth (1972, 24). All the Irish Chi-Rho stones are seen by Hamlin as belonging to the sixth or seventh, possibly eighth century, and to be part of the network of Continental contact implied by imported pottery and manuscripts (Hamlin, *loc. cit.*). There is a solitary Frankish tremissis found near Trim (Lindsay, 1860, 12), and two Byzantine coins from a garden in Ballymena (Hillgarth, 1963, 177). In a recent study James has pointed to Visigothic influence on the Moylough Belt Shrine, and has drawn attention to the similarity between the kind of multiple cross found for example at Inishmurray and similar crosses from the region round Nevers (James, 1982, 384-5). James has also pointed to other possible links in sculpture between Aquitaine and Ireland, while pointing out, however, that only four objects of probably Irish origin are recorded from Merovingian sites in Gaul (1982, 381). Thomas has discussed possible continental influence in early ecclesiastical art (1972, 114-7; 1987).

175

Ireland and Egypt

Much has been made of connections between Ireland and the Coptic church of Egypt. Certainly the influence of the Coptic church extended beyond the East Mediterranean, and was a factor in the development of Merovingian art in Gaul (Lasko, 1971, 76-89).

The evidence for Ireland receiving influence, either direct of indirect, from Egypt, is not however strong, and was cogently questioned by Joseph Raftery (1965). The strongest advocate of Coptic influence has been Paulsen (1952-3), who argued that Irish monasticism was Coptic, that Irish monks painted their eyelids in the manner of the ancient Egyptians, Egyptian monks were buried in Ireland, Irish monks met Egyptian ones abroad, Coptic manuscripts, paintings and sculptures were copied in Ireland, the use of red, yellow and green favoured by Irish illuminators was derived from Egypt, red dotting outlining letters and dotting on garments in manuscripts is Coptic, as are frontally arranged evangelists and the use of Carpet pages, and finally, the five-fold gathering of folios is a Coptic device (Paulsen, *loc. cit*).

Raftery has trenchantly dismissed much of this 'evidence' as improbable or fallacious. The colour choices were dictated by the pigments available, and, as Raftery has argued, were colours favoured for enamels in the iron age. There is no evidence that Irish monks ever painted themselves (Raftery, 1965, 199), while there is only one instance recorded of Irish monks meeting an Egyptian (in Rome, in the seventh century), and no evidence whatever that the only Egyptian recorded as buried in Ireland (in 799) was a Copt: as Raftery has argued, it could have been an Egyptian from Gaul, where some are known to have settled (1965, 199).

When these random instances are dispelled, we are faced with a body of assertions about Coptic influence in Irish art. Despite arguments by one of us to the contrary (1975), there is no reason to suppose Coptic Egypt provided the model for Celtic interlace, which more probably has other roots (see p. 215).

No Coptic manuscript earlier than the eighth century survives, and had they existed, it is likely that one or two might have survived, in view of the arid conditions of Egypt that have allowed other Coptic antiquities (and later manuscripts) to survive extremely well. The carpet pages of insular manuscripts seem closer stylistically to Coptic textiles, but these too are too late to be useful for dating.

Perhaps the most commonly cited 'Coptic' element in Irish art is the use of red dots for outlining letters, or for infilling. James, in studying the use of dotted backgrounds on Merovingian metalwork in Aquitaine, came to the conclusion that it originated not in Egypt but in late Roman metalwork (1977, 120-1). In view of the Late Antique background of much of Christian Irish art, this is probably the explanation for its occurence in Insular manuscripts — if a model is required, it can be found on the **largitio** *missorium* plate of Theodosius I in Madrid.

The case for Coptic influence in Irish art is not strong, and for the influence of Coptic Egypt in other spheres even weaker.

9

CELTIC ART BEFORE *c*. 400

There has long been a tendency to regard Celtic Art of the fifth to seventh centuries AD as an essentially Irish phenomenon. Modern scholarship now avers that there was influence from Britain on Irish art in the period. It is, furthermore, impossible to demonstrate a thriving artistic tradition in Ireland in the third and fourth centuries AD. During that period it can be seen that various Roman provincial motifs were developed in Britain in designs that were ancestral to those of the post-Roman centuries. Thus the development of Dark Age art is considered more complex than originally thought.

The tendency to insist that Celtic art was synonymous with 'Irish' presumably arose through the desire to take as the definitive model an area of 'pure' Celtic tradition 'uncontaminated' by any other influence. This view was proprounded by the late Mlle Françoise Henry in a series of works starting in 1933, which saw an unbroken line of development from La Tène art of the pre-Roman iron age through to the full flowering in Irish monasteries of a style best exemplified by the Book of Kells. This thesis generally viewed manifestations of Celtic art in Britain as essentially of Irish inspiration. Thus objects as diverse in style and provenance as the largest hanging bowl from Sutton Hoo, Suffolk, the Book of Durrow or the High Crosses of Iona were regarded as displaying Irish influence.

Recent thinking allows greater possibility of Roman influence on Celtic art and argues that as there is very little evidence for 'La Tène' culture in Ireland (see p. 144), by definition, there would be relatively little La Tène art. The truth of the matter is that, apart from one or two early imports, almost the sum total of Irish La Tène art consists of a few scabbards from Co. Antrim, a small cache from Broighter, Co. Londonderry, containing a torc, some decorated bone slips, and a number of pieces of the early centuries AD of which the most notable are a group of decorated horse bits. This is hardly demonstrative of a flourishing tradition. Furthermore, there is no indisputable reason to insist that the 'tradition' was unbroken to the Early Christian period. In consequence, there is very good reason to look for sources other than Ireland for the origins of Early Christian period Celtic art.

A strong case can be made out in the present state of scholarly thought for the origins of Dark Age Celtic art lying fairly substantially in the Romano-British repertoire.

During the first and second centuries AD, Ireland and Britain benefitted from an interplay in which objects and motifs were transmitted both ways across the Irish Sea. Among these must be counted objects and designs of Roman and provincial Roman origin, though in some cases these may have reached Ireland directly from the continent. In addition, there was a flourishing artistic repertoire in Britain, which can conveniently be considered separately (below, p. 185f).

Ireland before 400

A consensus of modern opinion indicates that there was no native La Tène art in Ireland before the late third or early second century BC (Raftery, 1987, 13). Before this date it is possible to distinguish a number of imports, such as the Clonmacnois (Co. Offaly) gold torc, which was a product of the Middle Rhine of the late fourth/ early third century BC (Raftery, 1984, 177). Imported too is an anthropoid sword hilt from Ballyshannon Bay (Co. Donegal) (Megaw & Megaw, 1986, 48), which originated in southern Gaul perhaps around 100 BC.

The first native manifestation of Celtic art can be seen in a series of sword scabbards from **Lisnacrogher**, Co. Antrim, and from adjacent areas centred on the River Bann in Antrim and Londonderry. Dating from around the early second century BC, the scabbards are by different hands but share features in common, notably their use of engraved ornament of S-curves and C-commas, combined with occasional birds' heads. They share stylistic elements with the horns associated with a pony cap from Torrs, Kirkcudbright, and a recently discovered bronze box from Wetwang Slack, North Humberside (Megaw and Megaw, 1986, 19-32; Raftery, 1987, 13-15). Nothing in these attenuated foliage

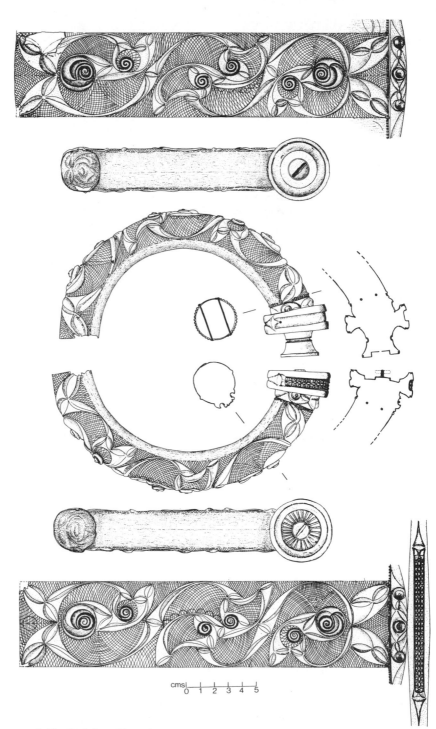

cms | | | | | |
0 1 2 3 4 5

6 The Boighter Torc, from a drawing by courtesy of Dr Barry Raftery.

patterns bears any close resemblance to Early Christian Irish art however.

Irish versions of La Tène art

The first manifestation of a motif that remained popular in Irish art down to the Early Christian period can be found in the hoard from **Broighter**, Co. Londonderry, dated to the first century BC. This hoard comprised a gold torc with rich decoration (fig. 6) and a series of other gold artefacts including a model boat, two plain torcs, a bowl and two chain necklaces (Evans, 1897; Raftery, 1984, 181-92; Megaw & Megaw, 1986, 48). The tenon and mortice fastening of the torc and beading on the terminals betray its prototypes as emanating from north-east France or Belgium. It is possible that the terminals were imported and added to a hoop made and decorated in Ireland.

There are no precise affinities for the Broighter ornament, which comprises slender, raised trumpet patterns with lentoid boss endings, snail-shell spirals and compass drawn arcs. It is notable for being a purely native Irish version of La Tène art, though it shows a remote relationship to some torcs found in eastern England. Its interest lies in the distinctive slender trumpet patterns which remained in the Celtic artistic repertoire into the Dark Ages.

After the Broighter torc, there is no evidence of an Irish La Tène style until the first century AD, when it is possible to point to two important groups of objects in a native Irish version of La Tène style. They are of particular note, since nothing can be dated with certainty between them and the fifth-century penannular brooches.

The first group comprises a series of decorated bone slips discovered in the nineteenth and early twentieth century during excavation of the cemetery of neolithic passage graves at **Lough Crew**, Co. Meath (fig. 7). The iron age material came mostly from cairn H, which was claimed to have produced 4884 fragmentary flakes, of which 4350 survive, including some portions of bone combs (Raftery, 1984, 251-63). Very few of the flakes are decorated, but those that are seem to have been ornamented using compasses (a compass arm, but of dubious antiquity, was among the other finds from the site). The Lough Crew flakes have been seen as metalworkers' trial pieces, but there was no evidence for metalworking there, and they are more likely to have been votive plaques, perhaps inspired by Classical models. The motifs em-

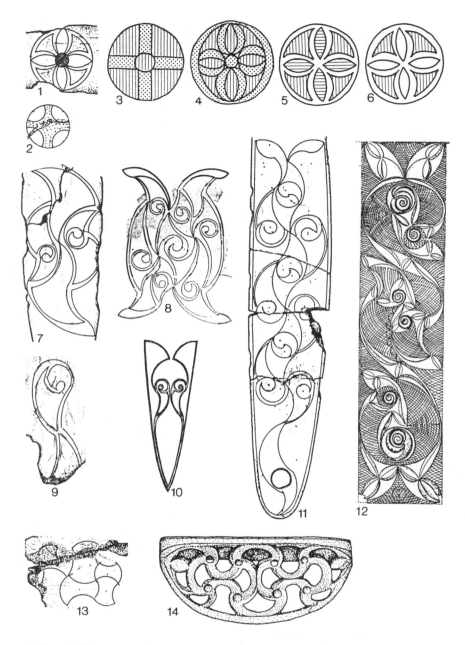

7 Lough Crew art and a selection of stylistic analogies. 1-2, 7, 9, 11, 13 bone
flakes, Lough Crew, Co. Meath. 3-4 enamelled studs, Pitkelloney, Perthshire,
Scotland. 5 enamelled inlay, Rise, Holderness, Yorkshire, England.
6 enamelled inlay, Seven Sisters, Glamorganshire, Wales.
8 stone, Derrykeighan, Co. Antrim. 10 ornament on Irish tubular spearbutt.
12 gold collar, Broighter, Co. Derry. 14 scabbard mount, Lambay, Co. Dublin.
Various scales. After B. Raftery, *La Tène in Ireland*, 1984, by courtesy.

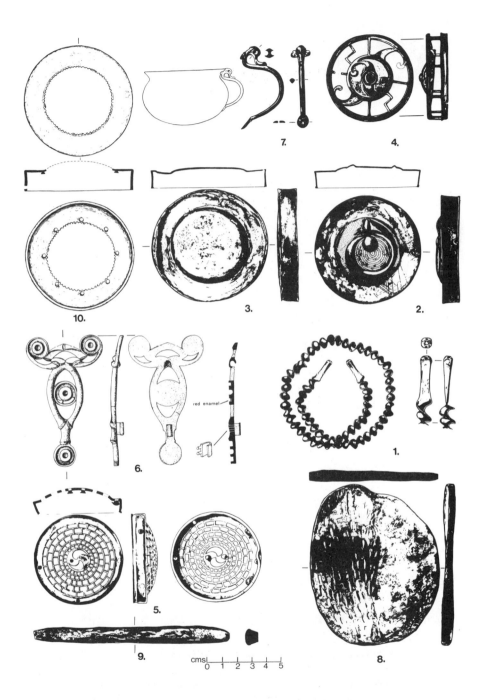

8 The Somerset, Co. Galway, hoard. After B. Raftery by courtesy.

183

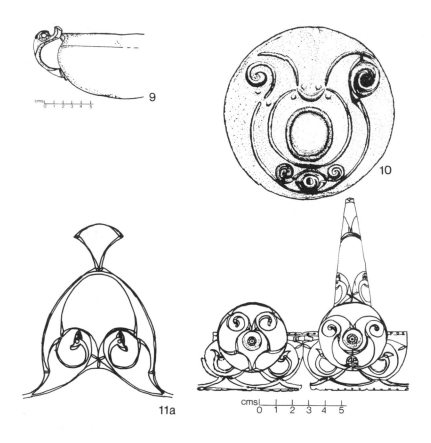

9 Keshcarrigan bowl, handle.
10 Bronze disc, Monasterevin type, unprovenanced (diam. *c*. 7 cm).
11a The 'Petrie Crown; with detail of ornament.
11b-c The Bann Disc (diam. *c*. 10 cm) and detail of ornament from the Cork Horns.

employed are broken-backed curves, yin-yangs and simple triskeles, as well as concentric circles, simple pelta and quartrefoil flower patterns. Elements of the Lough Crew style are shared by other Irish products, notably a series of bronze 'spoons'.

The second group of objects comprise the items from the hoard found at **Somerset**, Galway (Raftery, 1960; Raftery, 1984, 244 etc.). The Somerset hoard was a smith's assemblage, and included a bronze box, a brooch of the 'Navan' type (named after a find from a classic hillfort), a series of bronze mounts, a bird's head cup handle and a gold-ribbon torc, among other items (fig. 8).

In the Somerset hoard's ornament there are elements not encountered at Lough Crew. These include cast relief trumpet and lentoid bosses and the three-dimensional bird's head handle.

The Lough Crew-Somerset style as Raftery has termed it (1987, 15) has other manifestations in Ireland, notably on the bronze cup from Keshcarrigan, Co. Leitrim (Jope, 1954), which has a bird's head handle reminiscent of the Somerset example (fig. 9).

The Lough Crew-Somerset style overlaps with another, characterized by a series of high-relief decorated discs of unknown function, named after the best as 'Monasterevin' discs. Here the spirals are produced by repousse hammering, and the finest have a narrow crest. The spirals are combined with elongated confronted trumpet patterns, with lentoids where they meet (fig. 10).

Elements of the designs appear on a series of objects without the same high-relief modelling, the 'Cork Horns', the 'Petrie Crown' and the Bann disc (O'Kelly, 1961; Jope & Wilson, 1957; Raftery, 1984, 268-75) (fig. 11a and b-c). These pieces have attenuated 'fine line' trumpet patterns, and also employ crested birds' heads on the ends of spirals. The relief is much shallower than on the Monasterevin discs, and it has been shown by O'Kelly that it was produced by cutting away the ground (1961). The restraint, as Raftery has noted, is 'almost classical' (1987, 18).

Stylistically, the Monasterevin discs and the Bann Disc/Petrie Crown/Cork Horns group of objects represent an advance on the Somerset-Lough Crew tradition. In the Somerset box can be seen the beginnings of high relief trumpet patterns, which are developed on the Monasterevin discs. Similarly, the Somerset type of bird's head may be one of the precursors of the crested bird of the Petrie Crown and related pieces.

Artistic links with Scotland

As Raftery has noted, good parallels for the Lough Crew ornament can be found in Scotland, on pieces such as the Mortonhall scabbard (MacGregor, 1976, no. 150), the Lochar Moss collar (MacGregor, 1976, no. 204) or the Langbank bone comb (MacGregor, 1976, no. 275) all of the first-second centuries AD (fig. 12); the quatrefoil flower is to be found on some Caledonian armlets (see below) and

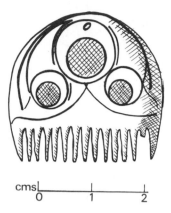

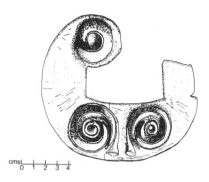

12 Bone comb, Langbank Crannog, Renfrews.

13 Silver plaque, Norrie's Law, Fife.

on a terret from the Seven Sisters hoard deposited in the first century AD (Glamorgan) (Raftery, 1984, 261).

Raftery has emphasised the limited repertoire of this compass ornament, and pointed to the lack of skill shown when the Lough Crew artists tackled a subject for which compasses were inappropriate, for example in drawing a deer. The hatched infilling recalls a similar animal on a sherd of wheelhouse pottery from Bragar, Lewis (MacGregor, 1976, no. 327), and all in all links with Scotland seem inherently probable. Dating is problematical, but probably lies in the first-second centuries AD.

None of the Monasterevin discs come from datable contexts. The closest parallel to the ornament found on them has been found outside Ireland, again in Scotland, in the hoard of silver from Norrie's Law, Fife. In this hoard was found a silver circular plaque decorated with high-relief spiral bosses composed of attentuated trumpets. Even the crest of the spiral found on the best of the Monasterevin discs is reproduced on the Norrie's Law plaque, which has had a sub-rectangular hole cut in its centre and an attachment projection on the back filed off (fig. 13). The Norrie's Law hoard was possibly deposited in the early fifth century (p. 135), but some of the pieces, such as this one, are probably much older.

The same type of high-relief modelling and slender trumpet patterns appears in the Brigantian and Caledonian Schools of metalworking (see below). They can be seen, for example, on the boar's head trumpet from Deskford, Grampian (Piggott, 1959, 24-32), and on the series of massive armlets discussed by Macgregor (1968 and 1976). Dating evidence is lacking for these Caledonian pieces, though they seem to fit in best with a horizon in the late first-early second centuries AD.

The links between Scotland and Ireland in metalworking, traditionally exemplified by these items, are part of a more general pattern (Raftery, 1984, 328-30; Warner, 1983; 1987) that was already operating before the birth of Christ. Raftery and Warner have suggested at this period the areas of Scotland particularly involved were the south-west and the Hebrides.

In the first and second centuries AD these links became even stronger. A Caledonian armlet has been found at Newry, Co. Down, and Scotland and Ireland share knobbed spearbutts (which were certainly made at Traprain Law, East Lothian, as well as in other places). Such spearbutts are found scattered as far afield as Bute, Tiree and Mainland Orkney, where the types are virtually indistinguishable from the Irish. Their contexts are purely local, and indicate a coming-and-going rather than settlement (Raftery, 1982). Irish-style ring-headed pins from Coll and Skye reinforce the connection between the two areas, as do organic-hilted swords (a distinctively Irish type) in the Isles.

The opposite end of the exchange is exemplified by an Orcadian type of weaving comb from Glassamucky Brakes, Co. Dublin and a Hebridean projecting ring headed pin from Keady Mountain, Co. Derry (Raftery, 1984, 329).

Apart from the material trade in objects, decorative elements seem to have reached Ireland from Scotland. The tooled ornament on the Monasterevin discs and Petrie Crown is similar to that on a collar from Stichill, Roxburgh. This object bears 'swash-N' ornament, as does an armlet from Plunton Castle, Kirkcudbright, and this unusual device can be seen on a 'spoon' from Ireland now in Liverpool Museum (fig. 14).

14 Swash-N from (a) Stichill Collar, Roxburgh and (b) Irish spoon in National Museums & Galleries on Merseyside. Not to scale.

Warner (1983) has defined two separate groups of objects in Scotland, of Irish inspiration if not origin, which he terms EIA1 and EIA2, the latter of the first and second centuries AD and possibly later. Warner's EIA2 objects have a different distribution from that enjoyed by his EIA1 material, and he has pointed out that this 'avoids crossing the Antonine line into 'proto-Pictish' territory, though compares with the distribution of Roman finds, other than coins, from non-Roman sites of the second century' (Warner,1983, 172). Warner's overall conclusions are that this interplay between Ireland and Scotland in the first-second centuries AD was the result of settlers and craftsmen arriving in the areas of the buffer tribes south of the Antonine Wall. The reflux of objects and artistic influences from Scotland to Ireland could be explained in terms of a flight by Irish emigrés to their native land during the disturbances attendant on the Roman advance.

Artistic links: Ireland and Roman Britain

There is evidence for contacts between Ireland and Roman Britain in the later first-early second centuries AD. In studying the Roman material in Ireland, both Bateson (1973) and Warner (1976) have stressed that Roman imports in Ireland are concentrated in the first to second centuries and again in the fourth-fifth. Warner saw the first-century phase of trading between Ireland and Britain as generally haphazard, though possibly via (among other places) a trading base at Stoneyford on the Nore (1976, 267).

The artistic links with Roman Britain are apparent, in particular, from the use of triskeles, the type of relief decoration on Irish horse bits and horse pendants, and the use of certain zoomorphs.

TRISKELES

In addition to the clear links with Scotland, the Monasterevin-Bann Disc style seems to owe something to Roman Britain. The triskele design of the Bann disc, though taking up a design found on the Lough Crew bone slips, probably owes its strict symmetry to Romano-British triskele-decorated objects. The triskele of spirals can be seen on a series of Romano-British applied disc brooches, from Silchester (Hants.), Victoria Cave, Settle (Yorks.), Brough (Cumbria), Greatchesters (Northumberland), Richborough (Kent)

15 Romano-British disc brooch, Silchester, Hants.
16 Romano-British triskele brooches from Chesters, Northumberland, Richborough, Kent and Brough, Cumbria
Actual sizes: a) 3.3 cms; b) 2.6 cms; c) 3.2 cms.
17 The Aesica (Greatchesters) Brooch.

cms |_____|_____|_____|
0   1   2

A   B   C

cms |__|__|__|
0   1   2   3

and St Albans (Herts.) (figs. 15-16). The best of these brooches, (for example that from Silchester), have slender-stemmed trumpet patterns. The contexts from which most of these brooches come indicate a second- or third-century AD horizon for them, though the St Albans brooches appear to have been lost in the third and fourth centuries respectively (Frere, 1972, fig. 51, no. 24 and Wheeler & Wheeler, 1936, 217). Other applied plate brooches of the Roman period in Britain appear to imitate Hadrianic coins (Collingwood & Richmond, 1969, 299), so a second century date is likely for them. Their wide distribution makes them difficult to provenance, though they may be from a northern factory or factories.

The '**Aesica Brooch**' from Greatchesters is related in style. This gilt bronze fan-tailed brooch of the second century is decorated with trumpet patterns and a pair of confronted creatures with swan's heads and sea-serpents' bodies on the footplate (fig. 17). The heads of these creatures are very close in style to those that appear on the Cork Horns.

189

The link between this group of Romano-British objects and Ireland is a bronze disc displaying a triskele with a rosetted centre found in a cemetery at Lambay, Co. Dublin (fig. 18). The beaded border at once betrays its relationship to Romano-British disc brooches. It has been discussed by Rynne (1976) and Lloyd-Morgan (1976, 217-221). Lloyd-Morgan suggested that the closest parallels for the piece lie in the Lower Rhine, and both she and Rynne have pointed to the similarity in the design to that on a now lost lozenge- shaped plaque from Moel Hirradug, Clwyd, usually dated to the first century AD.

cms 0 1 2 3 4 5

18 The Lambay (Dublin) Disc, restored.

Another Romano-British piece with broken-backed triskele is a disc brooch of uncertain provenance in Newcastle Museum (Macgregor, 1976, fig. 5:7). This has, as its central element, a berried rosette, with three further rosettes in the angles of the triskele. Round it is a running scroll of debased palmettes.

The broken-backed triskele appears on a mount from Navan Fort, Co. Armagh, where it is surrounded by a border of large concentric circles flanked by smaller (fig. 19). The whole flavour of the ornament is Romano-British, though the object itself is dis-

tinctively Irish, and closely related to a series of ten 'Somerset-type' mounts, well represented in the Somerset hoard (Raftery, 1984, 284). Of these mounts, which are characterized by openwork, one example from Ballycastle, Co. Antrim, has an ancestral version of the 'crested bird' that appears on the Bann disc (for this motif, see below).

cms 0 1 2 3 4 5

19 Bronze box, Navan, Co. Armagh, after B. Raftery, by courtesy.

Lambay has produced five Roman brooches, which have aided the dating of the cemetery to the late first century AD. As Raftery has noted (1984, 282) the finds from the site suggest contacts with Northern

190

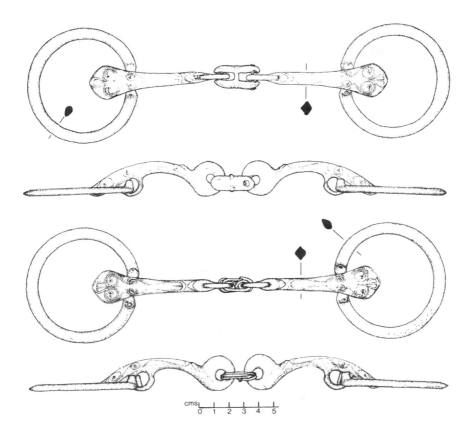

20 Bronze bit, Attymon, Co. Galway, after B. Raftery, by courtesy.

England and it is quite possible that elements of Romano-Celtic art were reaching Ireland around the late first century AD, to influence the Monasterevin Disc-Petrie Crown tradition of metalworking.

HORSE BITS

The most common decorated objects of the last century BC/first century AD in Ireland are a series of horse bits and 'pendants', amounting to 231 items in all. They have been studied by Haworth (1971) and B. Raftery (1984), and can be seen to have been first made in the second or first centuries BC. From the point of view of this study of later Celtic art, it is the bits of types D and E that are of the greatest interest, since they belong to the early centuries AD, and by common assent show Roman influence (fig. 20).

Some of the designs are reminiscent of those on Romano-British fantail brooches, while slender trumpet patterns as well as linking

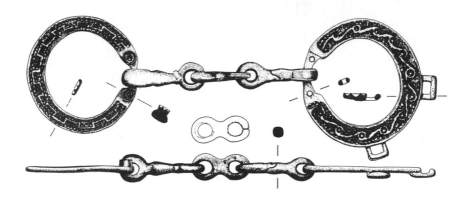

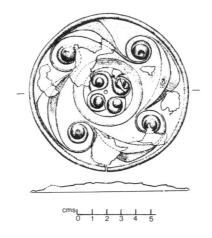

21 Bronze bit and disc, Killevan, Anlore,
Co. Monaghan. By courtesy of B. Raftery.

the bits with the Monasterevin Disc tradition also connect them
with Caledonian metalwork. One of the type E bits seems to have
been copied in Dacia, and Warner has suggested that as the II
Adiutrix from Pannonia was in Britain in the 70s and 80s, to return
to Dacia around 88, auxilliaries in the army might have been
responsible for the transmission of the type (1976, 281).

It is important to establish how late the bits continued in production, to establish whether they could provide any link with the
art of Dark Age Ireland. A bit from Killevan, Anlore, Co.
Monaghan was found associated with a bronze disc with running

192

scrolls which Lloyd-Morgan (1976, 217-222) has suggested came from the lower Rhine in the late first or second century AD (fig. 21). The bit however may be later. Enamelled in red, with running scrolls on one ring and a step pattern on the other, the style is reminiscent of a binding strip on a hanging bowl from Barlaston, Staffs, the product of a late Romano-British workshop (see p. 200). Where the rings are attached to the links they are fashioned into stylized birds' heads, recalling some penannular brooches or Anglo-Saxon ring brooches. A date in the fourth century seems quite possible for the Killevan bit, and this would be perhaps further supported by the discovery of a type E fragmentary horse-bit from Newgrange, Co. Meath, which has produced late Roman material (Carson & O'Kelly, 1977, 52).

A ring from a horse bit, without provenance, has ornament which Jope has compared with Romano-British bronzes (1955, 42-4) (fig. 22). Raftery has pointed out a closer analogy on a Roman openwork bracelet of the third century from Tunis (Raftery, 1984, 37; Higgins, 1961, pl. 60B). There is an even later comparison for the ornament, on a bracelet from Vermand, France, datable to the early fifth century (Evison, 1965, pl. 1c).

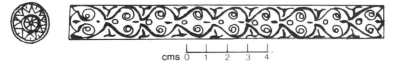

22 Decoration on an unprovenanced horse bit ring, Ireland.

One of the Irish bits from the River Bann (Raftery, 1984, fig. 24, no. 15) bears an elongated trellis and lentoid pattern that is also found on fragmentary silver mounts from the Norrie's Law hoard, Fife. The Norrie's Law mounts are likely to date from the fourth century.

ANIMAL MOTIFS

A feature of the Irish horse-bits discussed above is their use of a fillet just below the loop, producing the effect of a duck head, with the hole of the loop forming the 'eye'. A related animal head also appears on an unprovenanced bit ring illustrated by Raftery (1984, fig. 25, no. 1). The confronted animal heads on this ring (which recall those on the Killevan bit) are very close to the confronted heads on class F penannular brooches. The ring appears to be of type B or D — in view of its affinities D seems more likely.

193

cms|___|___|___|___|
  0   1   2   3   4

23 Ballymoney mirror
handle.

Warner, in noting the similarity between the ducks on the loops of horse bits and the terminals of penannular brooches, saw both in a relationship with the animal heads on a mirror handle from Ballymoney, Co. Antrim (fig. 23). It is Warner's contention that the terminals of the zoomorphic penannular brooches developed in southern Scotland out of Irish prototypes — the similarities between elements of the Caledonian School of metalwork and the penannulars lying in the common inheritance and interplay between Ireland and north-east Scotland (Warner, 1983, 174-5, and convincing diagram, Fig. 78).

Unlovely and stylized though they are, the zoomorphic terminals of penannular brooches are of importance in tracing threads though later Celtic art.

The tradition of bird heads has a long and accordingly complex evolution (fig. 24). The starting point perhaps lies in pre-Roman southern England, where bird heads appear on 'Birdlip' brooches. Such bird heads may have reached Ireland (along with spun bronze bowls) to give rise to products such as the Keshcarrigan bowl and the handle from the Somerset hoard. By the late first or early second century the bird head appears, crested and two-dimensional, on the Monasterevin Disc style metalwork. From here it may well have been transmitted to Scotland. In the South, it may have inspired penannular brooches, in Caledonia (among the proto-Picts and the Picts) it adorned a series of objects.

The mirror handle from Ballymoney, Co. Antrim should possibly be placed among these. Most scholars have followed Jope in assigning it to the first century AD (1955, 95). But despite its obvious links with certain of the horse bits (some of which could, as has been here suggested, be as late as the fourth century), the closest parallels are to be seen in a series of swivel rings from northern Scotland, studied by Stevenson and by Laing (Stevenson, 1976; Laing, 1972-4). The Ballymoney beasts are almost exactly paralleled on a swivel ring from A'Chrois, Tiree. They also share features in common with the form of the loops of some hanging-bowl escutcheons, for example one from Tummel Bridge, Perths (Kilbride-Jones, 1937).

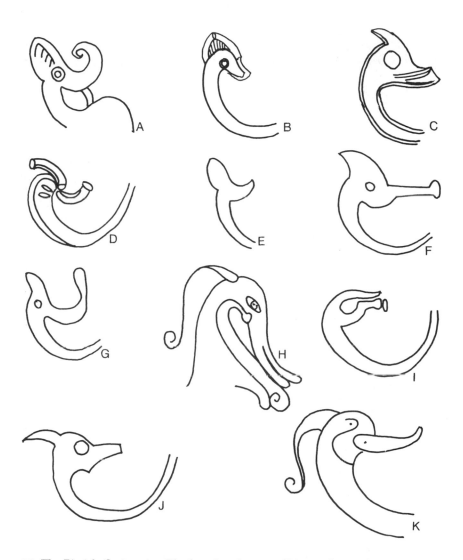

24 The Pictish 'Swimming Elephant' and some of his cousins: a, dragonesque fibular, Cirencester; b-c, the Petrie Crown; d, the Bann Disc; e, bronze ball from Walston, Lanarkshire; f, latchet, Ireland; g. hand-pin, Ireland; h, Pictish symbol stone; i, Sutton Hoo hanging bowl; j, the River Bann hanging bowl escutcheon; k, the Hunterston Brooch (scales various)

Closest in form to the Ballymoney mirror handle are two of bone, from Scotland. The first, from Bac Mhic Connain on N. Uist, has angle mouldings like duck beaks. The other is from Lochlee crannog, Ayrshire (Macgregor, 1976, nos. 271 and 272). Neither handle is paralleled by any known iron age mirror handle from Britain, and both sites have late occupation. Bac Mhic Connain has produced a Pictish knife handle (Beveridge & Callander, 1931-2), while Lochlee has finds of various dates including of the early Christian period (Munro, 1882).

In its two-dimensional form, the crested duck head appears as the terminal element in a spiral on the Bann Disc and on the Petrie Crown. With its crest it may owe something to dragonesque fibulae made in north Britain in the later first and second centuries (Feachem, 1951; Kilbride-Jones, 1980) but in this guise seems to be distinctively Irish. It first appears on one of the Somerset hoard mounts (Raftery, 1984, fig. 140, no. 6 — from Ballycastle, Co. Antrim, where it forms the centre of a triskele), and somewhat later perhaps on a coiled bronze armlet from Ballymahon, Co. Meath (Rynne, 1964). While sharing some elements of design with the Irish horse pendants, this armlet is probably best compared with the snake bracelets of the Caledonian School, such as that from Culbin, Moray.

The bird triskele is not a common feature of Scottish iron age metalwork, but it occurs on an openwork mount from Seamill, Ayrs (Macgregor, 1976, no. 40). Such 'triskele decorated fobs' have a long currency in Britain, from the pre-Roman iron age at Hunsbury, Northants, to possibly the fourth century — Macgregor assigned the Seamill stud to the mid-first century AD (1976, 37), in which case it is just possible that the motif was current in Britain before reaching Ireland. It was not however popular in Britain until the end of the Roman period, when it gained currency on enamelled hanging bowl escutcheons.

The development of the crested bird in Dark Age art has been traced by Laing & Laing (1987) and by Warner (1987). Warner has linked the birds of the Petrie Crown with those on the largest of the Sutton Hoo hanging bowls and the Book of Durrow (1987, 21 and fig. 1). His connections are surely right, as is his contention that the link with Ireland belongs to the pre-Christian iron age, rather than later.

Two objects of Scottish provenance perhaps point to channels of transmission — a bronze sphere from Walston, Lanarkshire (MacGregor, 1976, no. 350), and an ash wood block from Lochlee crannog, Ayrshire (fig. 25b). Both have crested bird heads, the former in a triquetra of spirals, the latter as a simple triskele. The Lochlee board also bears a swirled triskele and a simplified lyre loop between two trumpet coils. This motif is related to the 'hand pin eye peak' of later metalwork. But what date is the board? Lochlee has produced finds of various periods down to medieval.

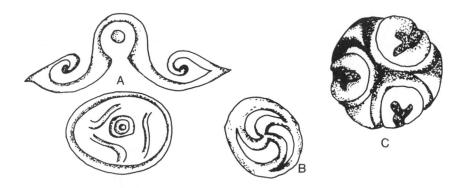

25 (a) and (b) Designs from wooden board, Lochlee Crannog, Ayrs.
(c) Bronze ball from Walston, Lanarkshire.
(Diam. of (a) 12.26 cm; diam. of (b) 4 cm; diam. of (c) 3.9 cm.)

The board however appears to have been found in a primary context, and the bulk of the finds can be dated by Roman brooches and pottery to the early second century AD. It is from such beginnings the art of the early Christian period developed.

The 'Dark Age' of Irish art

There is a hiatus in the flow of Roman artefacts into Ireland in the third century AD. If one can speak of an Irish 'Dark Age', then this is it. In all probability it was a period of internal strife in Ireland, when the country looked in on itself rather than to the outside world. Even so, some artefacts can perhaps be used to bridge the gap. One of these is a decorated strap-end from **Rathgall**, Co. Wicklow, with an openwork terminal composed of three inter-locking rings, and a raised triskele on the plate (Raftery, 1970) (fig. 26). As Raftery has argued, the affinities of this object are Roman, even though it is clearly a native product. The prototype are Roman strap tags of the second and third centuries AD, that appear to be associated with military equipment (Raftery, *op. cit.*, 208). The ornament is weak, and while of course it is unwise to draw any conclusions from one piece, it is stiff and unaccomplished compared with the art of the preceding and succeeding periods.

Still within the same period, a human-headed harness pendant from **Feltrim Hill**, Co. Dublin, is worthy of consideration (Raftery, 1970) (fig. 27). Its openwork pendant with three bosses suggests that it is modelled on a late Roman harness mount, though the interpretation is again purely Irish. In the Roman world such

197

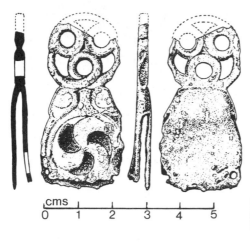
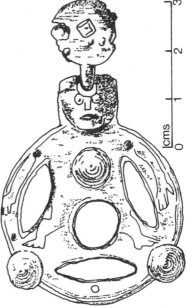

26 Bronze strap end, Rathgall, Co.
Wicklow. By courtesy of B. Raftery.
27 Bronze mount, Feltrim Hill, Co. Dublin

mounts are mostly found in the fourth century. The site produced (without a context) a Roman coin of Diocletian (AD 284-305), and this would probably be in keeping with the date of the Feltrim Hill mount. If the date and analogies can be accepted, it is of importance as providing a human representation in Ireland that is clearly the forerunner of the Celtic figures with amygdaloid eyes, down-turned mouths and rounded chins of the Early Christian period.

A tinned-bronze mount with openwork border, found at **Freestone Hill**, Co. Kilkenny, in an iron age hillfort, has close affinities to some late Roman metalwork, and also displays a design in its centre with a hatched curvilinear pattern of 'Dark Age' character (Raftery, 1969, 66-72). The object may be of later date than the fourth century, but if Raftery is correct in assigning it to this period, it points to influence from late Roman Britain.

Britain before 400

In contrast to Ireland of the same period, there was a flourishing insular school of art in Britain prior to the arrival of the Romans, which persisted through the first century AD, albeit in a less vigorous tradition. By the late first century the centre of Celtic artistic endeavour was no longer the south-east of England but in the less Romanized north, in Brigantia in the North of England and in Caledonian lands to the north of the Forth-Clyde line. Within Britannia as a whole, however, there were occasional manifestations of Celtic taste, most notably on a series of openwork mounts that seem to have been popular throughout the Empire and many of which may in fact have been produced by Celtic-inspired craftsmen working abroad. In the third and fourth centuries there was a minor revival of Celtic taste in Roman Britain, which manifests itself on a series of small objects, mostly brooches and pins, and which employ motifs of Roman provincial origin in a Celtic manner.

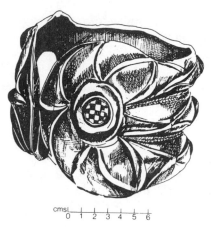

28 Caledonian bronze armlet, Castle Newe, Aberdeenshire

CALEDONIAN AND BRIGANTIAN ART

In Britain, the latest manifestations of native Celtic art are equally difficult to date. Morna Macgregor, in studying the northern British metalwork of the late first-second centuries AD, has suggested that some southern refugees from the lands of the Iceni fled north after the defeat of Boudicca's rebellion in AD 61, bringing with them such pieces as a mount from the Middlebie (Dumfries) hoard, which may have inspired native craftsmen to produce their own art in southern Scotland (1976, 180).

Similar refugees, she has argued, might have served as a warning to the hitherto dispersed Caledonian tribes, who may have rallied and in the process developed a uniform art style as part of their claim to corporate identity (1976, 181). It is some such tribal pride that she has seen as the inspiration behind a series of massive armlets with high relief modelling and trumpet patterns (Macgregor, 1968) (fig. 28). In these armlets, and a series of other examples of metalwork from Scotland, Macgregor has detected south-east British (Belgic)/Icenian influence. This extends to the use of die-stamping on foil, ('casket ornament') and use of colour, (e.g. the enamels on the armlet terminals). Along with this there are influences from traditional iron age 'B' art.

From these diverse origins emerged four 'schools' of art: (Macgregor, 1976, 184-5):

1 The 'South Brigantian' of the North of England
2 A 'School' without a clear focus, perhaps with one centre on the Eden Valley
3 A Lowland Scottish School
4 A North-East Scottish or 'Caledonian' School

There are certain elements in this northern Celtic art which have a contribution to make to the art of the succeeding 'Dark Ages'. These include the 'fleshy lips' or fillets that appear on certain types of terret (rein guide rings), the lathe-finishing of bowls, die-stamping on foil (though the use of this technique in the Dark Ages may be due to Anglo-Saxon influence), and certain decorative details such as berried rosettes, zoomorphic terminals (on spiral bracelets), or various polychrome patterns. The widespread use of engraved ornament (which was used for instance by the Picts) may also be a legacy to the Dark Ages from the North British iron age.

This northern art also drew upon a repertoire of Romano-British ornamental motifs to be found on a diversity of objects. From Gallic imported samian ware may have come leaf swags, petalled rosettes and coiled tendrils (Macgregor, 1976, 186).

TROMPETENMUSTER ORNAMENTS

Far more important than purely Roman artefacts in the subsequent development of Celtic art are the series of slender-trumpet pattern ornaments known as **trompetenmuster** (fig. 29). Although the inspiration behind these may well have been Celtic, they were produced from the first century AD on the continent, notably at Baden-Aargau in Switzerland. Here roundels, chapes and sword scabbard mounts were fashioned in openwork, using swollen jointed confronted mushroom shapes that are the forerunners of later 'confronted trumpet patterns' (Brogan, 1953, 152-3).

The makers were, to judge by one who signed his work 'Gemellianus', Roman in their affiliations if not origins. Their products were immensely popular, and were soon found in upper Germany, Gaul and also Italy (Berger, 1956). The signature of Gemellianus was copied, as was the style of his mounts, and local industries went into production. The Rhenish style was popular in

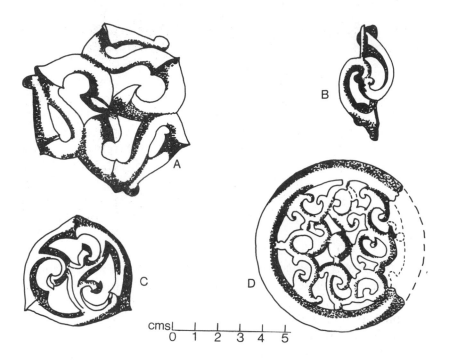

29 Trompetenmuster ornaments. (a) South Shields, Co. Durham;
(b) Corbridge, Northumberland; (c) Corbridge, Northumberland;
(d) Chesters, Northumberland. After Macgregor.

Britain, where almost certainly some mounts were made. They
even turn up at Dura-Europos in Syria (Rostovtzeff, Brown and
Welles, 1939, Pl. XXXIX).

Macgregor has discussed the dating of these pieces in Britain.
They may have arrived before the end of the first century, to judge
by finds from Corbridge, but finds from Volubilis in North Africa
that match British examples suggest that the key period for their
popularity was the last decade of the second century — too late, as
Macgregor has noted, to influence the development of the slender
trumpet pattern here (1976, 188-9). She has seen some as possibly
arriving as late as the third century; if this is so, they provide a data
base of motifs for Dark Age artists in which the ultimate inspiration
was Celtic, albeit filtered through a Roman mesh.

The range of motifs they offer comprises: triskeles, with or
without confronted trumpet patterns; leaf patterns; peltas; scrolls
and voids. They may have influenced the development of some of
the 'dragonesque' fibulae of north Britain: one object from
Corbridge figured by Macgregor (1976, fig. 9, no. 5), is a

201

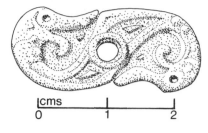

trompetenmuster ornament with crested bird head and other features of the dragonesque fibula series. It can be taken with a mount from Ronaldsway, Isle of Man (Neely, 1940, pl. XII, 2, no. 14) which dates from perhaps the seventh or eighth century (fig. 30) to provide a direct line into the Dark Ages.

30 Mount from Ronaldsway, Isle of Man.

cms

0   1   2

LATE ROMANO-BRITISH METALWORK

The 'northern' tradition of Celtic metalwork does not for the most part seem to outlive the late second or early third century AD, though some products of the Caledonian School, such as massive or 'Donside' terrets and knobbed spearbutts may have survived into the fourth century (see p. 187).

At this date there seems to have emerged a variety of different types of dress-fastener that are the prototypes for those current in the fifth to seventh centuries. Some of these bear ornament that can be seen as the beginnings of Celtic 'Dark Age' art.

Almost without exception the penannular brooches of the fourth century have no decoration other than the stylized zoomorphism of the terminals. The highly ornamented types appear to belong to the fifth century and later; though an F brooch from Bath (p. 76) and a newly-discovered G brooch with enamelled terminals from south Wales may belong to the fourth century. The most important series of objects artistically are a group of fasteners belonging to the family called 'hand-pins'.

HAND-PINS

In general terms, the development of hand-pins is clear enough, and the earlier stages have been traced by Stevenson (1955) and Fowler (1963); the sequence begins with projecting ring-headed pins in the first and second centuries AD (fig. 31). In the north, these developed in the second century AD into **rosette pins**, which had a ring head composed of small or large beads. In the north, **beaded-and corrugated-pins** were current perhaps in the fourth century, and are well-represented at Covesea, (Moray), which may have

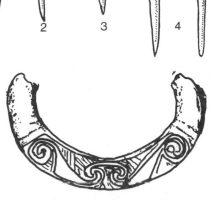

31 Development of the hand-pin. (1) rosette pin, Covesea, Moray (2) proto hand-pin, Covesea (3) beaded and corrugated pin, Covesea (4) ibex pin, Dundrum Sandhills. Slightly reduced. Pin (1) 6.1 cm long.

1   2   3   4

32 Base silver object, Atworth, Wilts. Actual size: 2 cms wide.

been a proto-Pictish cult centre. These have a corrugated upper portion to the ring and a beaded lower portion, and they are an 'evolutionary dead end' peculiar to Pictland.

The **ibex-headed pin** probably evolved in the third or fourth century. Ibex pins have projecting 'horns' and remained current into the Early Christian period (Laing, 1975, 323). Since they seem however to be ancestral to the proto-hand pins the date of their first appearance is quite important. They occur in Romano-British contexts, for example at Corbridge, Northumberland, Woodperry, Oxon, and Tingewick Villa, Bucks. as well as on the Jewry Wall site in Leicester. Of the starting date we cannot be certain; what we can be certain of was that they were in currency by the fourth century in Roman Britain.

It was probably in Roman Britain that the proto hand-pin emerged out of such antecedents. Despite claims for an earlier origin in Ireland or Scotland, there is no real evidence that they were to be found in either area before the end of the fourth or the beginning of the fifth century.

From purely Romano-British contexts have come four important finds. One from **Halton Chesters** in Northumberland has a smooth ring flattened into a plate at the bottom, decorated with two S-scrolls in reserve against a red enamel ground (Fowler, 1963, fig. 7, 5). From **Atworth villa** in Wiltshire has come a plate, keyed for enamel, which surely represents the bottom half of the head, decorated with a central pelta and flanking scrolls (Mellor & Goodchild, 1940, Pl. XIII) (fig. 32). The third comes from a hoard of fourth-century Roman coins from **Oldcroft**, Glos., deposited *c.* 360, where again the central pelta with flanking coils (this time dodo-heads) can be seen (Johns, 1974). Both the Atworth fragment and the Oldcroft pin are of silver. So too is the last of the Romano-British 'proto hand pins', from the Roman town at **Tripontium**, (Caves Inn), Warwickshire. The Tripontium pin has a slightly different pattern on the plate, consisting of three linked c-scrolls, and it was associated with Roman pottery — the latest finds from the site are two coins of Arcadius (AD 395-408) (site: Lucas, 1981, 31; pin Fowler, 1981, 47-8).

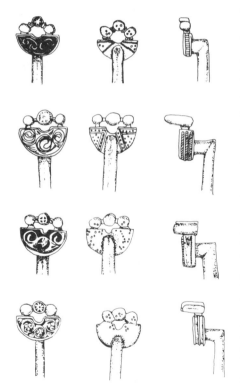

33 Proto hand-pins. (a) Tripontium, Warwicks (b) Long Sutton, Somerset (c) Norrie's Law, Fife (d) Gaulcross, Grampian; width of heads: (a) 1.4 cm, (b) 1.1 cm, (c) 0.9 cm, (d) 2.9 cm.

The importance of the Tripontium pin lies in a series of features it shares with other hand-pins of assumed 'Dark Age' date. These are the pins from the Pictish silver hoards from **Gaulcross**, Grampian (Stevenson & Emery, 1964), and **Norrie's Law**, Fife (Stevenson 1976), and a further pin from **Castletown, Kilberry**, Co. Meath (illus. Kilbride-Jones, 1980a, fig. 68, no. 6). The Gaulcross pin, the better of the two Norrie's Law pins and the Tripontium pin all have a beaded collar under the lateral fingers. All five pins have patterns on the edge of the crescentic plate. The Tripontium pin and Gaulcross pin both have a star in enamel on the central finger, which on the Norrie's Law pins is replaced by a cross and on the Castletown pin is replaced by confronted spherical triangles with central dot. On the back of one of the Norrie's Law pins is a pattern of punched rings which exactly matches that on the Tripontium pin, and similar punched ornament is also found on the other pins. A further unpublished silver pin, from **Long Sutton**, Somerset, is closely related to the group, having a star on the central finger, a pattern on the head similar to that on the Castletown pin, and the punched rings on the reverse (fig. 33 for all these pins). All in all, they constitute a group, and perhaps represent a late fourth-century stage in the development of the hand pin. In that they have fingers instead of beads the pins from Norrie's Law, Gaulcross and Castletown are typologically more evolved than the Tripontium pin, (in that the latter has projections that are transitional between beads and fingers), but such fine distinctions are probably meaningless chronologically. Similarly, the Norrie's Law and Gaulcross pins have sophisticated triskele patterns with (in the case of Gaulcross) dodo-heads, which are more complex, if not more evolved, that the Tripontium pin.

The dodo heads however also appear on a further series of fine-line ornamented objects, starting with the Oldcroft pin and continuing with a silver disc with ribbed metal frame with running peltas from near **Coventry**, Warwickshire (fig. 34). This disc is a mount which is clearly closely related to hanging bowl escutcheons. It links the Oldcroft pin with the escutcheons from a hanging bowl from **Faversham**, Kent (Henry, 1936, pl. XXVIII, 3-4) (fig. 35). The hanging bowls are discussed below, but here it may be noted that the Faversham mounts have the same triskele of dodo heads that are to be found on the Gaulcross pin, while the running scrolls are echoed on the pin from Tripontium.

We cannot assign these widely-dispersed objects to a workshop, though it is quite likely that the Oldcroft, Atworth and Tripontium

34 Bronze enamelled disc from Coventry, War., with milled frame (diam. 1.8 cms).

205

35 Enamelled hanging bowl escutcheon, Faversham, Kent.

36 Latchet brooch, Icklingham, Suffolk.

pins were products of some centre in the south-west Midlands, as surely was the Coventry mount — the Faversham hanging bowl may also emanate from there too. The Pictish symbol on the finer of the two Norrie's Law pins might suggest Pictish manufacture, though this may be a later addition.

In this context it is worth noting that the G1 penannular brooches may originate in the same sort of area (Dickinson, 1982, 53-4).

Still with the origin of Dark Age dress fasteners, a latchet brooch from **Icklingham**, Suffolk, with its stellate pattern and background of punched dots might suggest a Romano-British beginning for these characteristically Irish objects, too (fig. 36). Icklingham is a known late Roman site.

37 Roman enamelled patera handle, and 'Dark Age' design re-arranged from it, after Kendrick.

10

CELTIC ART, c. 400-700

C eltic art of the fifth and sixth centuries in Britain and Ireland
mostly comprises minimally-decorated penannular
brooches and pins, and a series of hanging bowls with
decorated mounts, the majority of which have been found in
Anglo-Saxon contexts. On present evidence the ornament on the
hanging bowls seems to suggest suggest that Britain was in
advance of Ireland in the development of Celtic art in the fifth and
earlier sixth centuries, and that developments in Ireland were
prompted through contact with Britain. From the later sixth
century however Ireland developed a distinctive tradition, which
reached its 'Golden Age' at the beginning of the eighth century.

Almost all the available evidence for Celtic art in the fifth and
sixth centuries comes from metalwork, and thus the first part of the
chapter discusses the general trends apparent in metalwork in
Britain and Ireland prior to the Golden Age. In the second section
there is a discussion of the different ornamental devices employed
by Dark Age Celtic metalsmiths, and the final section of the chapter
deals with manuscripts and sculpture.

Ireland

It has already been argued that penannular brooches reached
Ireland in the late fourth or early fifth centuries AD from Roman
Britain, and along with them probably came the hand-pins and
latchets also discussed above. If this is accepted, there is no conclusive evidence from Ireland of native ornamental metalworking
before the end of the fifth century or beginning of the sixth. To that
period belongs the workshop at the hillfort at **Clogher**, Co. Tyrone,
dated by finds of imported Mediterranean pottery and radiocarbon.

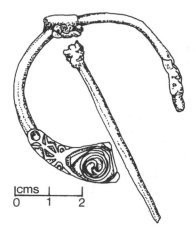

The Clogher chronology is crucial to understanding the beginnings of ornamental metalworking in Ireland. Layer (7) at Clogher produced evidence for a workshop manufacturing Irish-style penannulars (F2), one with yin-yang spirals (Warner, 1979, 37; Kilbride-Jones, 1980b, fig. 47, no. 124) (fig. 38). This was associated with 31 sherds of B-Ware, which thus dates the production to the period from the end of the fifth to the late sixth century. The presence of part of a Romano-British bracelet of the type found at Lydney, Glos., has led Warner to postulate that the occupants of Clogher originated perhaps in the Bristol Channel area (1979, 37). This possibility is of particular interest since it has already been suggested (p. 160) that this part of the West Midlands or South Wales might have been a centre for late Roman ornamental metal- working.

38 Penannular brooch, Clogher, Co. Tyrone (after Kilbride-Jones).

The end of this phase at Clogher is marked by the deposition of the 'Yellow Layer' which divides the early material from the ring-fort with its later metalwork (including hand-pins) and E ware. The deposition of this has been assigned to the horizon between AD 565 and 600 on the radiocarbon and documentary evidence (Warner, 1979, 38).

To judge by Clogher, it would appear likely that the type of ornament found on the developed Irish penannular brooches was current in the sixth century, and is ultimately of Romano-British derivation. On brooches of the type found at Clogher we see a variety of designs including spherical triangles, scrolls, yin-yangs and peltas, the repertoire, in fact, that is found on hanging bowl escutcheons in Britain.

Into the same sixth-century millieu as the Clogher workshop and the developed Irish penannular brooches can be fitted a few ornamented objects. The first is an antler 'motif piece' from a sandhills site at Dooey, Co. Donegal (fig. 39). This piece is decorated with running yin-yang scrolls, trellis and debased marigold patterns (Ó Riordáin & Rynne, 1961, 58). The Dooey piece was found under a midden in an occupation layer which also yielded a mould for a penannular brooch with baluster terminals. This is a type found at

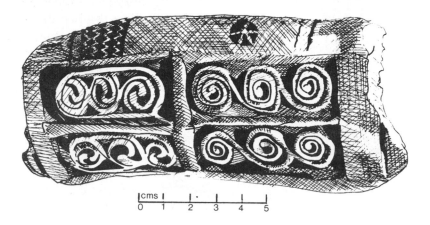

39 Motif piece, Dooey, Co. Donegal.

Dunadd, Argyll (unpublished, information from the excavator, Dr Alan Lane) where it cannot be earlier than the sixth century and is more probably of the seventh or eighth. The same layer that produced the trial piece also produced toilet articles of ultimately Romano-British derivation — all that can be said about their dating is that they are unlikely to be earlier than the fifth century. The Dooey piece on balance of evidence need not be earlier than the sixth century, and might even be later.

Perhaps earlier is a bronze latchet from Dowris, Co. Offaly, now in the British Museum (fig. 40). It has been argued above that latchets are possibly of Romano-British derivation. All elements on the Dowris latchet could fit in with a late Romano-British millieu: trellis, chevron and lentoid patterns make up the body of its latchet's ornament. Its head plate has a series of running scrolls with a central yin-yang scroll. On the 'foot' there is a 'dumbell' pattern. The ornament of the Dowris latchet is close in style to that on the 'Romanizing' hanging bowls discussed below, particularly in its use of trellis pattern after the manner of the Eastry escutcheon (p. 213). Unlike the other latchets the Dowris example has a solid plate with two slots into which,presumably, wire coils were fitted. In this respect it bears certain similarities to Roman buckle plates.

The group of latchets from Newry, Co. Down, clearly also belong to a late Romano-British millieu, though they are in a different tradition (fig. 41). The head has a hexafoil or marigold pattern

209

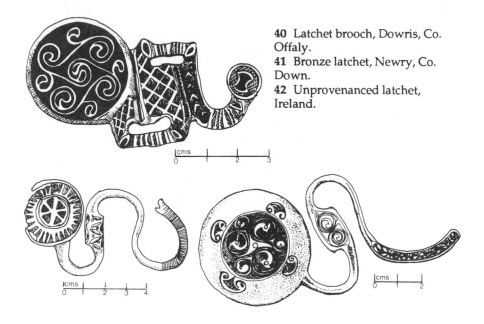

40 Latchet brooch, Dowris, Co. Offaly.
41 Bronze latchet, Newry, Co. Down.
42 Unprovenanced latchet, Ireland.

inside a starburst, while the expansion in the middle has confronted spherical triangles with central dot. The tail is ribbed. This ribbing shows the latchets to belong to the same tradition as the E and F penannular brooches, as do the confronted spherical triangles. Both elements appear on a penannular of Kilbride-Jones' A2 group from the River Greese in Co. Kildare (1980b, fig. 29, no. 54). Brooches of this type seem to have punched ring patterns on the back of the terminals, including an arrangement of three that is the same as that found on the Norrie's Law handpins. The marigold fits in with a Romano-British tradition, and thus the Newry latchets could belong to the fifth century.

Possibly of similar date is the latchet without provenance from Ireland with a triskele of crested bird's heads and dodo heads and with four peltas projecting from the central design (fig. 42). The fine-line work and the dodo-heads, as well as perhaps the crested bird's heads, link it to the Oldcroft pin and the Gaulcross pin, and, by extension, the Faversham escutcheon. Once again, a fifth century date is not impossible.

What little evidence there is, thus appears to suggest that traditions of ornamental metalworking, and possibly also certain types of Romano-British dress fastener, were introduced to Ireland from perhaps the Bristol Channel region in the late fourth or fifth centuries AD: the decorative elements including enamelling, peltas, yin-yang scrolls, marigolds or hexafoils and trellis pattern, as well

210

as perhaps chevrons. Some of the latchets and hand-pins as well as some of the penannular brooches may have been produced in Ireland in the fifth century. By the sixth traditions of ornamental metalworking were well established.

Britain

HANGING BOWLS

Hanging bowls have attracted more literature than almost any other aspect of Celtic archaeology. The first list was published by Romilly Allen in 1898, to be followed by Reginald Smith's fuller catalogue in 1909. Thereafter the bowls were set in perspective in two studies that are still of major importance, that of Thomas Kendrick (1932) and Françoise Henry (1936).

There are 95 finds of bowls or isolated bowl escutcheons, which taken together provide a 'source book' for 'Celtic' art of the early post-Roman centuries. As the name suggests, the assemblage comprises thin bronze bowls suspended by chains from three, sometimes four, escutcheons round the rim. On the base of the bowl is usually to be found a further mount or 'print'. The escutcheon hooks are usually zoomorphic, and turned in, so that the chains do not slide off, as would have been the case with some Roman hanging vessels on which the hooks turn outwards.

Nearly all the finds of bowls or escutcheons have been from Anglo-Saxon contexts, or as stray finds from areas settled by the Anglo-Saxons. Where the graves in which they have been found can be dated, they mostly belong to the seventh century. This however only tells us that the bowls were being produced by that date at the latest, and their absence from fifth and sixth century graves (with a couple of late sixth century exceptions) need only imply that they were fashionable as grave furniture among the Anglo-Saxons at that date, and not earlier.

Intensive study has clarified a number of problems, and has raised others, the latest statements (and lists) being those of Elizabeth Fowler (1968), David Longley (1975) and of Rupert Bruce-Mitford (1987).

A number of assumptions about hanging bowls have been made in much of the literature that are not necessarily valid. The first of these is that the surviving bowls are always contemporary with their mounts. It is clear from the way in which isolated escutcheons

211

appear to have been treasured, long after the bowl to which they had been attached had perished, that the escutcheons themselves had an importance for the sixth-seventh century Anglo-Saxons. It is therefore likely that old escutcheons could have been re-used on 'new' bowls. That seems to have been the case with the Badeley Bridge (Needham Market) bowl from Norfolk (White, forthcoming), and also appears to have been the case with the recently-discovered bowl from St Paul-in-the Bail, Lincoln (Gilmour, 1979).

Secondly, it is often assumed that the bowls have an 'ethnic' significance, and rival camps have argued that they are 'British', 'Irish' or 'Anglo-Saxon'. There is no reason to suppose that they are not all these — some bowls could have been made in a British millieu, some by Britons working for Anglo-Saxon patrons, some by Anglo-Saxons trying to imitate native British styles, some by Picts and some by Irish.

The view that the bowls were all of Irish origin was expounded by Henry (1936), and her case has been re-examined by Bruce-Mitford (1987), who summarized her arguments and pointed out that a mould for an openwork escutcheon has now been found in Pictland, strongly suggesting that not all bowls were produced in Ireland. He has also pointed out that although many more finds have come to light since 1936, they have simply reinforced the British distribution. There are still no hanging bowl escutcheons with enamelled 'developed trumpet pattern' ornament (i.e. with a triskele of confronted trumpets as the main device) in Ireland.

One of Henry's hypotheses was that as pre-Roman Celtic enamelling was in red (an assertion which of itself is not strictly true — Bateson, 1981, 70), and as polychrome enamel was current in Roman Britain, it was unlikely that the Britons reverted to single colour enamelling in red in the fifth century and later, whereas polychrome enamelling had never reached Ireland, and thus it was likely that all hanging bowl escutcheons in monochrome red were Irish. The fact is however, that 'simple' enamelling in one colour is quite common in Roman Britain, on seal box lids, head stud brooches and miniature stools (Bateson, 1981, 91). It is also now clear than enamelling was in fact employed in Roman Britain until the end of the fourth century, on oval and medallion plate brooches (Bateson, 1981, 120).

A detailed discussion of hanging bowls, their chronology and classification is to be published by L. Laing elsewhere. The conclusions argued should therefore only be summarized here.

Not only the form of the vessel, but also the ornament on hanging

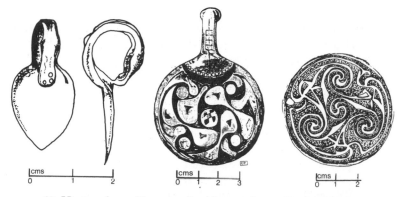

43 Heater-shaped hanging bowl escutcheon, Sleaford, Lincs.
44 Hanging bowl escutcheon with millefiori, Barlaston, Staffs.
(after Praetorius).
45 Enamelled basal print of hanging bowl, from 'near Oxford'.

bowls is firmly rooted in a Romano-British past. In the fourth-fifth century were probably made the decorated openwork escutcheons, the Eastry, Kent, pelta escutcheon and the earliest of the heater-shaped escutcheons. These were at first truly ornithomorphic, but with the passage of time became stylized under the influence of the hooks on other types of hanging bowl (fig. 43). These later heater escutcheons remained current probably to the end of the hanging bowl series. The plain openwork escutcheons similarly represent a later simplification of the original prototypes.

A few enamelled escutcheons with purely Roman-style ornament may belong too to the fifth century (fig. 44). These should probably be seen as products of a surviving Romano-British school of metalworking, perhaps mainly in the Midlands.

In the sixth century the 'developed trumpet pattern' bowls were produced, again perhaps in the Midlands. It is at this point that Anglo-Saxon workshops began manufacturing their own bowls, either with debased 'Romano-British' ornament or purely Germanic decoration, as on the Sutton Hoo 2 bowl (Bruce-Mitford, 1983, 244f) (fig. 45).

The bowls with millefiori ornament may constitute a survival from Roman Britain. The series may begin with products of Romano-British workshops such as Sutton Hoo 3 (Bruce-Mitford, 1983) and the 'Romanizing' escutcheons such as Barlaston (Ozanne, 1962). In the sixth century the Manton Common (Kendrick, 1941) and Sutton Hoo 1 bowls were produced, perhaps under the influence of the 'developed trumpet pattern' bowls, possibly in Lincolnshire.

The production of hanging bowls in Anglo-Saxon workshops probably coincides with their popularity as grave-goods from the late sixth century onwards. Once established, they became a feature of Anglo-Saxon metalworking until the coming of the Vikings.

Neither in Scotland nor Ireland were hanging bowls produced before the late sixth century, and they were never a particular feature of Scottish or Irish metalworking traditions.

Ornamental techniques in Britain and Ireland, c. 400-700

MILLEFIORI IN BRITAIN AND IRELAND

The millefiori decorated hanging bowls are virtually the only evidence for millefiori working in post-Roman Britain. Other millefiori decorated objects from pagan Saxon graves employ re-used Roman inlays, and we can only guess at the place of origin of the millefiori inlays used in the Sutton Hoo shoulder clasps, buttons and purse lid. They seem to be the products of the same workshop, but were probably imported ready-made for use, (as were garnets), in cloisonné settings. Perhaps they came from the same workshop that produced the Sutton Hoo 1 bowl.

There is no evidence that millefiori was worked in post-Roman Scotland. There is a millefiori rod from Glenluce Sands, Wigtown, decorated in a chequer pattern (Cramp, 1970, 333), but Luce Sands has produced a variety of objects not native to Scotland, and it could be derived from either Ireland or Northumbria. A millefiori decorated mount from Cramond, Midlothian, appears in fact to be a Roman brooch.

The same may be said for Wales, where the only evidence for millefiori takes the form of a rod from Dinas Powys, Glamorgan (Alcock, 1963, fig. 41, no. 12). Again this site has produced a lead casting of an Irish type of penannular brooch, so the rod could be an Irish import. The working of millefiori in Northumbrian monasteries could be either due to a local survival of a Romano-British technique, or due to Irish influence.

Apart from hanging bowls and the evidence from Monk-wear-mouth and Jarrow for Northumbrian millefiori working (Cramp, 1970), the only other millefiori decorated object is a shield-shaped mount from Bradwell-on-Sea, Essex, which has millefiori pieces floating in red enamel. Perhaps from a reliquary, it should be seen as a product of the same workshops as the 'Romanizing' bowls.

Millefiori, on the other hand, is common enough on Irish metal-work. But how early? What little evidence there is suggests it was not fashionable before the sixth century. A millefiori rod and holder was found at Garranes, Co. Cork. There was no stratigraphy at Garranes, all the finds coming from a midden which had clearly accumulated over a long period of time (Ó Riordáin, 1942). Although the finds included imported pottery of classes A and B, this need not indicate an occupation commencing earlier than c.500, and the presence of E ware shows the site was still occupied in the late sixth century or more probably even the seventh. The finds are in keeping with a sixth-seventh century date for the site as a whole. Millefiori is not found on the pennanular brooches of Kilbride-Jones' groups A or B brooches, which were certainly current in the sixth century. It occurs on the C and D brooches, one of which (without millefiori) was associated with B ware at Clogher, Co. Tyrone (Kilbride-Jones, 1980b, 63). Perhaps a date in the late fifth century is likely for the introduction of millefiori to Ireland, though it is just possible it was introduced earlier in the late fourth or early fifth century from Roman Britain.

INTERLACE

One element not encountered in Celtic Dark Age art before the sixth century is interlace. It is important stylistically to distinguish between zoomorphic and non-zoomorphic interlace. In zoomorphic interlace the ribbon patterns terminate in a head and tail, however stylized. In non-zoomorphic interlace there are no animal features, and the ribbons simply form an abstract patttern.

Interlace can be single strand or multiple strand. It can be built up into plaits of two, three or four ribbons, sometimes more (fig. 46). Romilly Allen discussed the construction of interlace and discussed the geometric principles underlying it (1904), and more recently some of the features have been discussed by Haseloff in connection with the Continental material (1981, 591-2).

Non-zoomorphic geometric interlace is a phenomenon of the Roman world. Here it can be of single, double or triple strand composition, but is always geometric (fig. 46). The simplest is a two-strand cable pattern, such as appears on one of the Ilchester bowls (Kendrick, 1932, pl. 1, no. 2 for a convenient illustration). In

46 4-, 3- and 2-strand interlace.

Romano-British mosaics two-strand interlace is found in a variety of symmetrical arrangements: a good series of patterns can be seen in the fourth-century floors at Lydney, Glos. (Wheeler & Wheeler, 1932, pl. XXII B) (fig. 47). Directly relevant to metal-work, interlace composed of filigree can be seen on a gold armlet from Rhayader, South Wales (BM, *Antiquities of Roman Britain*, (1958), pl. III).

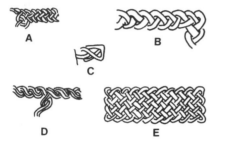

47 Romano-British interlace.
A, Brading, Isle of Wight, mosaic;
B, Eccles, Kent, mosaic;
C, ornament on penannular
  brooch, Newstead, Roxburgh;
D, mosaic, Rudston, Humberside;
E, mosaic, Winterton, Humberside.

That such ornament survived in Italy is shown by the church of San Clemente in Rome, where a ciborium panel and a capital were both ornamented with multi-strand interlace in a symmetrical plait, combined with two other motifs that occur in later Celtic art — bead-and-reel and egg-and-dart. It is here datable to AD 533-5 (Haseloff, 1981, 596).

Interlace is also found in Coptic Egypt, but there is some dispute about the dating, though it certainly seems to have been current there in the sixth century.

In Germanic Europe it is possible to trace the gradual development of Style II, a Germanic interlace style, out of the earlier animal Style I. The extent to which late Antique interlace of the kind found at San Clemente influenced the development of Germanic Style II is disputed — in the Lombard cemeteries of Northern Italy it is certainly conceivable that this was a strong source of influence.

It is possible to trace the development of interlace on a series of Lombard radiate brooches, of which one from Grave 22 at Castel Trosino is a classic example (fig. 48). Here can be seen both zoomorphic and non-zoomorphic double and triple strand interlace (Haseloff, 1981, fig. 433), and similar interlace is apparent on a brooch from Heilbronn II in Freidenskirche, Germany, both of the

47 Germanic interlace, before about 600: (a) from a brooch head, Freiweinheim, Germany, grave 10; (b) from a radiate brooch, Castel Trosino, Italy; (c) from a brooch, grave 56, Szentendre, Hungary; (d) from a disc brooch, Hockwold, Norfolk; (e) from a basal disc of a hanging bowl, Ipswich, Suffolk; (f) from a sword pommel, Coombe, Kent; (g) from a square-headed brooch, Ruskington, Lincolnshire; (h) from a square-headed brooch, Thornborough, North Yorkshire (a-c after Haseloff, d-e after Scull, f after Davidson and Webster, g-h after Hinds).

sixth century. Somewhat related in style is another radiate brooch from Grave 1803 from the large cemetery at Krefeld-Gellep (Haseloff, 1981, 644 and fig. 450). Haseloff has seen Lombard interlace beginning around the middle of the sixth century through Byzantine (Roman) influence, and to be introduced on Lombard brooches into Central Europe, where it was taken up by the Franks and Alamanni (Haseloff, 1981, 709). For Haseloff, such interlace is a component of Style II.

Other scholars believe the Lombards has already developed their ornament, both the Style I and Style II, before their migration to Italy out of Pannonia.

In Frankish lands Style II had possibly evolved by the time of the presumed burial of Queen Arnegunde at St Denis, whose grave-goods included strap ends and buckles with Style II ornament (Werner, 1964). Arnegunde was buried around 565-70, and the

217

importance of the discovery lies in the demonstration that Style II was current among the Franks by the third quarter of the sixth century. Somewhat earlier, simple interlace was being used on gold strap mounts at Cologne in a princess' grave dated to the second quarter of the sixth century. The same grave contained Mediterranean imports, suggesting one avenue of transmission of interlace patterns into the Frankish world (Doppelfield, 1960; Werner, 1964). As Hawkes (1964, 253) has pointed out, Queen Arnegunde was step-grandmother and great-aunt to Bertha, queen of Kent, and '. . . Style II animals, then, will have flourished at the Kentish court at latest by the century's fourth quarter'. Recently, however, some doubt has been cast on the dating of the grave finds of St Denis, since the ring does not necessarily identify the body as that of the queen.

Leslie Webster, in discussing a sword pommel with zoomorphic interlace from Coombe, Kent, felt confident that the pommel belonged to shortly after the mid-sixth century (Davidson & Webster, 1967, 36) (fig. 48). Because she saw, with Hawkes, that it was unlikely that Style II was apparent in England before the time of Bertha and Ethelbert, it seemed to her likely that the pommel was therefore later than the grave of Queen Arnegunde. As George Speake has commented, 'Implicit in the reasoning of both Professor Hawkes and Mrs Webster are three assumptions: first, Style II ornament must have come to England, more specifically to Kent, from the Franks. Secondly, Style II in England has to be later than the date of Queen Arnegunde's grave. Thirdly, Style II originated among the Franks. No other source is considered' (Speake, 1980, 28).

The important feature of the Coombe pommel interlace is the fact that it lies in the transitional stage between Styles I and II. Mrs Webster has also pointed to non-zoomorphic interlace on a belt mount from Bifrons, Kent, a cemetery which, as she has emphasised, has produced no material later than the sixth century. In the same context she has drawn attention to a set of mounts from Eastry, Kent, with non-zoomorphic interlace which she dates to c.550, on fairly strong evidence (Davidson & Webster, 1980, 30), and to some some other Style I pieces in which simple zoomorphic interlace is apparent, such as a saucer brooch from Long Wittenham, Berks. Non-zoomorphic interlace is also apparent on a saucer brooch of the late sixth century from Fairford, Berks (Davidson & Webster, 1980, 31 and fig. 10h).

Alongside these examples may now be set others. Hines has

drawn attention to two square-headed brooches from Ruskington, Lincs and Thornborough, Yorks., with triple-band interlace ornament (1984, 173-5). The Ruskington brooch has non-zoomorphic interlace, on the Thornborough brooch the interlace is part of a scheme of zoomorphic decoration, without actually being a Style II product (fig. 48). Hines assigns the brooches to his phase 3 (c.530-570), probably towards its end (1984, 197).

Interlace is also found on a brooch from Market Overton, Rutland. Leeds identified the brooch, which is silver, as an early piece of Continental derivation (1911, 491). Holmqvist suggested that the brooch was imported from southern Germanic areas and decorated in England (1955, 42). There can be no doubt however that the brooch was decorated on the Continent, since its ornament is cast. It must have been imported in the sixth century, as Speake has

49 Interlace-decorated Anglian square-headed brooch, Nettleton Thorpe, Lincs. Sixth century. From a photograph.

pointed out (1980, 36). Speake has also noted that the type of ornament is also found on pieces from Sutton Hoo, from Vendel, Sweden and on two objects from Cambridge (*loc. cit.*). The importance of the find, and of the two square-headed brooches discussed above, lies in the fact that they show that interlace ornament was reaching the Anglian areas as well as the Kentish from the Continent in the sixth century.

A recent discovery has been of a square-headed brooch from a cemetery at Nettleton Thorpe, Lincs., which has extensive use of non-zoomorphic interlace (fig. 49). It is unstratified, but is a sixth century type of brooch (Information from Mr Kevin Leahy, Scunthorpe Borough Museum).

Scull has drawn attention to some further interlace-decorated pieces from East Anglia, notably a disc from Hockwold cum Wilton in Norfolk, which has triple-strand interlace in chip carving, of a type which was current on the Continent in the sixth century, prior to the development of Style II (Haseloff, 1980, 594-7). Scull has argued that the Hockwold piece can be linked with the similar mounts from Caenby, Lincs., and with the interlace on the base of the Hadleigh Road, Ipswich, hanging bowl (1986). He sees all as the products of an East Anglian tradition, with connections with Sutton Hoo.

The same type of non-zoomorphic triple strand interlace appears on the foils of the openwork mount from the Sutton Hoo 2 hanging bowl. The style of the foils on the escutcheons of this bowl are closer to Style I than to Style II, and in view of its condition it is likely that it was a product of the second half of the sixth century.

Style II and simpler forms of interlace are a key element in the decoration of the products of the Sutton Hoo workshop.

Sutton Hoo is clearly of utmost importance in determining the chronology of Style II in England. The helmet and shield from the burial are recognized as Swedish products, closely related to finds from the graves at Vendel. Other objects, of East Anglian manufacture, such as the buckle and purse lid, have Vendel affinities. Although the date of deposition (c. 625) is not now in dispute, the relative age of the individual objects is open to question. The shield and helmet were probably heirlooms. As long ago as 1948 Lindqvist suggested the Sutton Hoo shield was made 'about AD 600; but with reservations in favour of a possibly still earlier date' (1948, 136). Lindqvist also postulated that the helmet was older still — 'not much later than the Anastasius dish' (1948, 136), which has been dated to 491-518. In discussing the various arguments for the date of the shield and the helmet, Speake has favoured a date around 550 for the importing of both into East Anglia from Sweden, when the Wuffinga dynasty was introduced.

Multi-strand interlace also appears on a buckle from Melton, Suffolk (Speake, 1980, fig. 15, f), on a disc from Spelsbury, Oxon. (Speake, 1980, fig. 10, c) and on a girdle-hanger from Painsthorpe Wold, Gr. 6a, Yorks. (Speake, 1980, fig. 9, m). For Speake, pieces such as these, along with the Faversham, Kent 'Phalerae', the Hardingstone Down, Northants., mount, and an annular brooch from Castle Bytham, Lincs., represent the last fling of Style II in England, and display residual zoomorphic elements: this is particularly noteworthy on the Caenby disc, where the zoomorphism had not previously been noted (Speake, 1980, 64-5). In the same tradition is a mount formerly in the Crossthwaite Museum, Kendal, now in the British Museum on which this tight, all-over multi-strand interlace is apparent.

It has been noted above that multi-strand interlace seems to be a feature of the sixth century on the Continent, and there is some evidence for it appearing in the sixth-century in England, attested by the objects discussed above. The Spelsbury mount is very close in many respects to the Hockwold disc, and its inner zone of interlace matches that on the Hadleigh Road, Ipswich, hanging bowl. If these two pieces are sixth-century, then so is the Spelsbury mount.

The same type of tight interlace that is found on the Faversham phalerae, the Hardingstone mount, the Caenby discs and the Kendal disc is found on a mount from Sutton Hoo mound 2, now in Ipswich Museum (Speake, 1980, pl. 16f). There are reasons for thinking that Sutton Hoo mound 2 is earlier than the great ship-barrow, and thus a date in the late sixth century is not impossible for the disc.

Uta Roth has drawn attention to a Lombard brooch from Torino-Ligotto in Italy, datable to the late sixth century, that has looped multi-strand interlace ornament. This type of ornament is characterized by usually assymetrical loops filled with animal ornament of different density, and is known as *Schlaufenornamentik*. Occasionally, a measure of symmetry is apparent. On the Continent it is found during the second half of the sixth century, reaching a peak around 600, and being fashionable roughly contemporarily with Style I in its latest phases and with early Style II. The Torino-Ligotto brooch has Style I ornament on its headplate (Roth, 1973; Roth, 1987, 26). It is found in Scandinavia, Italy and England, both at Sutton Hoo and Faversham.

From the foregoing, certain points seem to emerge. Symmetrical, non-zoomorphic interlace is apparent in the Mediterranean where it represents a survival in the fifth and sixth centuries from the Classical world. This may have had an effect on barbarian art styles from the beginning of the sixth century, but independently Germanic art was developing interlace, both zoomorphic and non-zoomorphic, from the early part of the century. In Scandinavia the beginnings of interlace are discernible perhaps in the series of bracteates: loose assymetrical interlace is apparent on the D-bracteates which Hawkes and Pollard have shown in Kent to begin around the 520s (Finglesham grave D3 Hawkes & Pollard, 1981, 342-50), with the bracteates from Sarre, gr. IV in the second quarter of the sixth.

221

A considerable body of evidence now suggests that interlace was developed in England from the middle of the sixth century under stimulus from the Continent. In East Anglia the stimulus may have come from Sweden as well as other Scandinavian sources; in Kent we should probably be looking to Scandinavia as well as to the Frankish world. The interlace represented in the grave of Queen Arnegunde is hardly mainstream Style II, nor is it necessarily typologically early: the artist of the buckle only partially understood his models. Interlace, either Style II or non-zoomorphic, could easily have reached the Frankish areas before 550, from a northern origin.

This long discussion of the possible date of Style II and interlace in England has been necessary to provide the background for dating the appearance of interlace in the Celtic areas.

All the early interlace from the Celtic world belongs to the *Schlaufenornamentik* type. It is found in Ireland on a bone mould for a sword mount, from Rathtinaun, Lough Gara, Co. Sligo (unpublished, information from Dr J. Raftery) (fig. 50), where the associated finds are in keeping with a late sixth century date, at the Mote of Mark, Kirkcudbright, on a series of clay moulds, (figs. 51-2) and on a sword pommel from Culbin Sands, Moray (fig. 51). Roth has seen as falling into the *Schaufenornamentik* category a scutiform pendant from Lagore, Co. Meath, on which a sea-serpent with long jaws and fish tail bites it convoluted body. The body is composed of a hatched-infill ribbon, similar stylistically to those on the great buckle at Sutton Hoo (Roth, 1987, 26). The Lagore pendant is almost

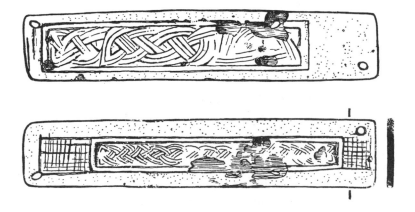

50 Mould for a sword mount, late sixth century, Rathinaun, Lough Gara, Co. Sligo, courtesy of Dr J. Raftery (length 5.2 cms).

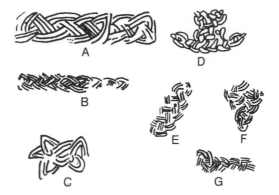

51 Celtic interlace before *c.* AD 600. A and B, Rathtinaun, Lough Gara; C, Culbin Sands, Grampian; D-G, Mote of Mark Kilcudbright.

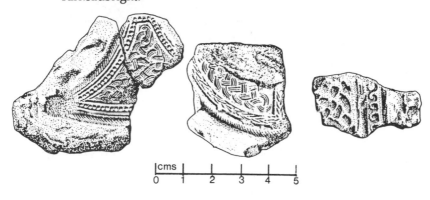

52 Clay moulds with interlace, Mote of Mark, Kirkcudbright.

certainly an import from Anglo-Saxon England, and dates probably from around 600. It shows that imports from Anglo-Saxon England were possibly one source of inspiration for Celtic artists.

The other instances of interlace are much more uniform in style. The Culbin pommel has multi-strand sharp-angled bends in its two panels of interlace. The form of the pommel is close to that from Coombe, and from other finds of the mid-sixth century from Kent. Its empty settings for inlays are however in a different tradition, and its interlace points towards the Continent. It could be an import, but it is equally likely to be a Pictish product of the later sixth century (Laing, 1975d, 48-9, Callendar; 1932-3, 33-4).

The interlace decorated moulds from the Mote of Mark have aroused considerable controversy (fig. 52). Radiocarbon dating, and material associated with them including E ware and imported Germanic glass, suggest they should be dated to the late sixth century or the early years of the seventh at the latest (Laing, 1975;

223

Longley, 1980 and above, p. 58). The Mote of Mark interlace is non-zoomorphic (unless the 'tail' apparent in the corner of one of the circular mount moulds (Curle, 1914, fig. 12, no. 2) is seen as a zoomorphic feature) and has two types of band, multi-strand and coarser, single strand. All the interlace would be quite at home on the Continent or in England in the late sixth century, and could have reached south-west Scotland from either source.

FILIGREE AND GRANULAR WORK

This account has taken us, thus far, into the opening years of the seventh century (and later in the case of the story of hanging bowls). The seventh century saw the acquisition of some further techniques and ornamental devices in metalwork, of which the use of filigree (twisted gold wire) and granular work (gold beading) were two of the most important.

Celtic filigree has recently been studied by Niamh Whitfield (1987), and her conclusions need only be summarized here. The origins of both filigree and granular work are undoubtedly Classical, and were certainly well-established in Anglo-Saxon England before the end of the sixth century. That the Celts learned the techniques from their Germanic neighbours cannot be disputed, but from which of their Germanic counterparts and when are more difficult questions.

53 Gold filigree bird, Garryduff, Co. Cork (maximum width 14 mm).

As far as date is concerned, Whitfield is of the view that a mount in the form of a tiny gold bird from Garryduff, Co. Cork (fig. 53), and an elliptical gold mount from Lagore should both be dated to the seventh century. Both sites produced E ware, which simply provides a context from the end of the sixth to the eighth century for the pieces (1987, 83).

One item of Pictish filigree craftsmanship may however be more readily dated. This is the terminal for a penannular brooch from the Pictish hoard from Croy, Inverness (fig. 54). The hoard was deposited in the ninth century, but the Croy penannular may be very much earlier. A unique feature of it is a setting in the terminal of garnet cloisonné work, of a type fashionable in south-east England in the last years of the sixth century and the early years of the seventh. Although apparently regarding the Croy brooch as a later (eighth century) piece, Whitfield has drawn attention to the fact that the back plate for the filigree work is set into the terminal of the brooch using rivets collared with a little ring of ornamental wire. The technique is used on the Hunterston brooch from Ayrshire, which general agreement places c. AD 700 (Stevenson, 1983, 469) and on a sword pommel from Cumberland, in the British Museum.

54 Filigree and garnet decoration brooch terminal, Croy, Inverness.

A feature of Celtic metalwork is its use of amber instead of garnet for its stone settings. While the garnet setting on the Croy brooch may be cannibalized from an Anglo-Saxon import of some antiquity, there is no real reason to believe a great time-lag separates it from the Anglo-Saxon work: by the later seventh century garnet was less popular in Anglo-Saxon jewellery.

Certain techniques used by the Celts seem to be derived from Anglo-Saxon England rather than any other part of the Germanic world. One technique of triple-band filigree using a central beaded wire between two finer beaded wires is found on the Hunterston, Tara and Breadalbane brooches, but on the Hunterston brooch and at one point on the Tara brooch the central strand is cut and pressed forward to close the gap where the interlace crosses: this is not found on the Continent but occurs on a buckle from Taplow, Bucks (not Kent, as Whitfield suggests, 1987, 80).

The main repertoire of Celtic filigree and granular working techniques can be matched in Anglo-Saxon work of the late sixth-early seventh centuries, and it seems absurd to suggest there was nearly a century's time lag before it was taken up by the Celts. Whitfield has pointed out that the Hunterston Brooch, usually regarded as the 'earliest' of the series of richly decorated penannulars, shows that already the Celts had developed techniques of their own — flattened beaded wire, a beaded wire soldered on top of another, and a beaded wire on a ribbon on edge. The Hunterston brooch is far too sophisticated a piece to have been produced by a craftsman who had just mastered a new skill, and we should see it as the product of perhaps a century of filigree and granular working, if indeed it is quite as late as AD 700.

That Celtic craftsmen were experimenting with gold wire (perhaps at the beginning of the seventh century) is shown by a fragment from the Mote of Mark, Kirkcudbright, and it is important to remember the imported pieces of filigree and granular work in Scotland, on the Dalmeny, Midlothian, harness pyramid, the Tynron Doon, Dumfries bracteate (Laing, 1975c) and the disc brooch centrepiece from Dunadd, Argyll, all of which were manufactured, if not imported to Scotland, at a date not far removed from 600.

Before leaving granular and filigree work, however, it should be noted that some techniques found on Celtic metalwork are matched on the Continent but not in Anglo-Saxon work, e.g. twisted gold ribbons and wires inserted into stud matrices (Whitfield, 1987,83). Byzantine and Merovingian parallels can be found for these.

PRESSBLECH AND GRILLES

Two further techniques of seventh-eighth century Celtic metalwork are of Germanic derivation. The first is the use of thin foils stamped with a die from the back. Such foils appear for instance on the Moylough belt shrine, and on the paten from the Derrynavlan hoard.

Although this technique was known in later iron age Britain (for the production of 'casket ornament' mounts), it is not found in later Roman Britain or in Scotland or Ireland before the seventh century. **Pressblech** plates were used to decorate helmets of the type known as **spangenhelmen** that are found in Migration Period Europe — such as the famous example from Morken in Germany. The same technique is also used on some bindings for vessels in the fifth century. Dies and die stamped foils in Europe have been studied by Capelle and Vierck. Anglo-Saxon examples occur in the sixth and seventh centuries, for instance from Salisbury and Suffolk (Capelle & Vierck, 1971, figs. 8 & 14).

Such foils appear on the base of hanging bowl 3 at Sutton Hoo. More significantly, foils decorated in 'Celtic' style appear on a similar style of openwork mount to that on the base of the Sutton Hoo hanging bowl from a later seventh century grave at Swallowcliffe Down, Wilts (Speake, 1980, pl. 16i). The foils comprise interlace-decorated axe-shaped panels, in a style not unlike Sutton Hoo, and similarly-shaped panels with pelta ornament and scrolls. The central round foil has C-scrolls not unlike those found on the Tara brooch. Such objects are unknown in the Celtic world, and the

226

Swallowcliffe mount should be seen as a Saxon piece showing Celtic influence, perhaps produced by a 'Briton' working for a Saxon patron around the middle of the seventh century, or possibly slightly earlier. It is a clear indication how such **pressblech** work reached Ireland during the seventh century.

The remaining technique in Celtic metalwork may be termed 'pseudo cloisonné' work, and involved setting enamel in grilles to produce ornamental studs. The cells have step-pattern ornament, which reflects that used in Anglo-Saxon cloisonne work, notably on the Kentish disc brooches of the later sixth and seventh centuries and at Sutton Hoo. As Henry showed (1956), the designs on such products as the Kingston Brooch are closely comparable to the studs found on the Ardagh chalice or Roscrea brooch from Ireland. The reflux of this two-way artistic trade can be seen in a set of linked pins from Roundway Down, Wilts, with a glass setting similar to the glass stud (Meaney & Hawkes, 1970, pl.V) and stud mould from Lagore, Co. Meath (Hencken, 1950, fig. 62).

Manuscripts and sculpture

MANUSCRIPTS

The earliest surviving manuscript is the so-called **Cathach of St Columba**, of which 58 folios survive out of an original presumed 110 (Henry, 1965, 59) (fig. 55). The Cathach is decorated with only initials. It is said to be a copy made by St Columba of a book borrowed without his permission from St Finnian, and would thus have been written around 560 (Haseloff, 1987, 45). Palaeographically this is considered possible (Alexander, 1978, 29), but many would assign it to the early seventh century, because they see Continental influence being the result of the foundation of Bobbio by Columbanus in 615. However, the initials are different from those in late Antique manuscripts (in that they are not breaking out of the main body of the text, and the letters following the initial are diminished till they merge with the rest). Imported pottery shows links between Ireland and the Continent before the foundation of Bobbio, and there is no real reason for not dating the Cathach to the late sixth century. The ornamental devices used in the initials include confronted trumpet patterns, peltas, S-scrolls and open-mouthed animal heads. Some of the ornamental detail is in keeping with that on sixth-century penannular brooches, and the animal

227

55 Initials from the
Cathach of St
Columba.

56 Detail from
Durham Cathedral
A II 10.

57 Page from Book
of Durrow, after
Stokes.

heads are not totally unlike the hippocamps on the Faversham hanging bowl.

To Bobbio have been assigned two Irish-influenced manuscripts of the early seventh century, the **Milan Orosius** and the **Ambrosian Ms SS. 45 sup.** (Alexander, 1978, 27-8).The latter is particularly interesting, since it has an inscription attributing it to the time of Atalanus, who followed Columbanus as abbot c.615 and died in 622 (Alexander, 1978, 27; Haseloff, 1987, 45). As a later forger would probably have assigned the book to Columbanus, the ascription is probably correct. The ornament is more sophisticated than in the Cathach, and has an initial N in the form of a pair of fish, a device also used in the **Durham Cathedral A II 10**.

The Durham A II 10 comprises twelve pages of a Gospel Book (fig. 56). The A II 10 has interlace and an N composed of two lacertines. Palaeographers assign the A II 10 to Northumbria (Wilson, 1984, 33). Haseloff sees it linked to, but later than, the Ambrosian Ms S 45 Sup. (1987, 45). Despite claims by Henry that the A II 10 is Irish (1965, 165),the confronted fish have heads with distinctive lower lip lappets, which are best matched in Anglo-Saxon metalwork. We see the feature on some sixth-century Anglian square headed brooches, for example on two brooches from Kenninghall and one from Ipswich (Leeds, 1949, nos. 49-51). There is no intrinsic reason why the A II 10 is any later than the early seventh century, but presumably must be later than 635 when Aidan founded Lindisfarne, the first Northumbrian monastery.

Stylistically later than these manuscripts is the **Book of Durrow** (fig. 57). Durrow is a fascinating museum of ornament. It comprises 248 folios decorated throughout. There are six 'carpet pages' of all-over ornament, including one primarily based on animal patterns, an evangelist symbol page at the start of each gospel, five pages of canon tables and a page with four symbols arranged round a cross.

There are two main reasons for believing the Book of Durrow was produced in Britain and not in Ireland. The first is that the text is the same as that used in two other Northumbrian manuscripts, the Codex Amiatinus and the Lindisfarne Gosepls, and the palaeography points to a Northumbrian scriptorium (Bruce-Mitford, 1960, 255; Wilson, 1984, 33). The colophon in the book attributing the manuscript to St Columba is clearly a later fabrication, from a time when the book reached Ireland: it was certainly taken to Ireland by the late eleventh or twelfth century, since a document about Durrow is added on the last page (Wilson, 1984, 33). It could however easily have reached Ireland at any stage from the seventh to the eleventh century.

The second factor for suggesting Durrow was produced in Britain lies in the fact that the type of animal ornament found in the interlaced-animal patterns are without parallel in Ireland, but are readily matched in the treasures from Sutton Hoo and in other Anglo-Saxon metalwork. There is in fact no element in the decoration of the Book of Durrow that is exclusively Irish in character: even the patterns that have been compared to the bosses on the Ardagh Chalice have in fact their counterparts in Anglo-Saxon England, for example on the central stud of the Roundway Down pin set (even if it were an Irish import, its re-use in an Anglo-Saxon object shows the currency of the design in England). There are however some features of the Durrow creatures that are more closely related to later Anglo-Saxon metalwork than Sutton Hoo. The Crundale Down sword pommel (dated to c.650) which was found with a buckle with similar animal scratched on its back is a good example (Speake, 1980, 56n).

Attention has been drawn to the 'ankle bracelets' that appear on the Durrow animals, which also appear on some Sutton Hoo animals and which Speake has seen as the remains of an extended toe looped round the back of the hind leg of some Swedish creatures. It is apparent on some of the Sutton Hoo shield mounts. In Durrow, the bracelets are more degenerate, suggesting they are later than Sutton Hoo, which might imply a context for it around 650.

PICTISH SYMBOL ART

Thus far we have looked at metalwork and manuscripts. Sculpture however is also relevant to this study.

It is extremely likely that the emergence of Pictish leaders in the fourth-fifth centuries was contemporary with the appearance on stone of the Pictish symbols.

These comprise a series of animal motifs such as wolf, stag, salmon, boar and bull (as well as two fantastic creatures, the 's-dragon' and 'swimming elephant'), and a series of abstract patterns named descriptively, for example 'double disc', 'z-rod and crescent', 'notched rectangle', and so on (fig. 58).

Controversy over Pictish symbol stones has been long and fierce. In 1903 Joseph Andserson and Romilly Allen made a catalogue of

58 Some Pictish symbols.

the early Christian stones of Scotland, defining three main classes, I comprising undressed slabs with incised symbols, II relief-carved dressed slabs with a Christian cross as the main element on one face and III relief sculptures without the symbols.

Subsequent controversy has focussed on three problems (1) the date of the stones (2) the function of the stones and (3) the meaning of the symbols. Clearly, an understanding of the date and purpose of the symbols would cast a great deal of light on Pictish society.

The Date Two main schools of thought dominate discussions of the date of the symbol stones. The traditional school favours the view that the class I stones do not much predate the seventh century, and support the idea that they were invented at one time, possibly under the sponsorship of Bridei mac Maelchon or Bridei mac Bili, in the late seventh century (Henderson, 1967, 112). This view suggests that the origin-centre was the inner Moray Firth, since there is a concentration of stones there with the 'earliest' characteristics (Henderson, 1958). This school of thought argues that the symbols, particularly the animal types, are closely matched in Hiberno-Saxon manuscripts — it is summed up by Stevenson who saw 'the whole system as devised . . . under the influence of the Evangelists' animal symbols and other Christian manuscript sources' (Appendix 2 in re-issue of Wainwright, 1955, 167). Henderson has not gone as far as that, for while supporting a 'late' date for the start of the symbols, she has seen the Pictish beasts as being contributors to the Hiberno-Saxon manuscript beasts, rather than the other way round (1967, 126-7).

In further support of the idea that the symbols were produced at a particular point in time then copied, is the suggestion of the 'declining symbol' first advanced by Stevenson (1955, 104) and developed by Henderson (1958; 1967). Recently, the idea was further developed by Murray (1988) in a more detailed analysis than had hitherto been attempted. The 'declining symbol' approach is concerned with defining a 'true' form for each symbol, something which has built-in problems when the meaning of the symbols is not understood. It is argued that by arranging the symbols in a sequence of degeneration, a chronological scheme can be provided for the symbol series as a whole.

Murray's survey was based on exhaustive study of the stones, and demonstrates fairly clearly that different symbols seem to originate in different areas. Thus the typical Z-rod is found in Aberdeenshire, the 'swimming elephant' is found in its 'classic' form in Angus and Eastern Perthshire. His conclusion was that 'the various symbols are seen as having originated and developed in different areas of Pictland, with the practice of cutting them on stone probably having a unique origin centre' (1988, 251).

Most of the evidence for 'decline' is apparent on the class II stones. As the designs were originally conceived of as essentially linear, not three-dimensional, once the Picts turned to relief carving the problems of rendering two-dimensional figures in relief would have led to various experiments and solutions. If the majority of the class II stones date from the eighth century (which the supporters of a 'late origin' would support) then we must envisage symbols being first modelled on Hiberno-Saxon manuscript art in the period around 680, then developing very rapidly till they were carved on class II stones around 710 (for this date, Henderson, 1967, 133). If it is argued that class I stones are mostly contemporary with class II, i.e. continue through the eighth century, this would allow time for the symbols to 'decline' and for the large number of extant class I stones to be carved. It would raise however the question of why the simple incised stones continued to be erected alongside more sophisticated monuments.

The case for an earlier date has been set out by us (Laing & Laing, 1984), and need only be briefly summarized here. The arguments rest on the facts that

(1) Broken down into its constituent elements, the art of the class I stones is firmly rooted in Romano-Celtic art of the fourth-fifth centuries, and does not have many of the key elements to be found in even the earliest of the Hiberno-Saxon manuscripts.

(2) The Norrie's Law hoard which has symbol-decorated silverwork was probably deposited in the early fifth century (see above), and the same arguments apply to the Gaulcross silver and the massive chains.

(3) Some of the symbols are representations of objects current in the fourth-fifth centuries.

(4) The animal symbols owe a strong debt to Eurasiatic art, which reached the West at the time of the migrations in the fourth-fifth centuries.

(5) Some of the symbols appear to be stylized versions of Roman motifs.

(6) The general absence of symbol stones from Dalriada does not mean that they post-date the Scottish colonization there — they could have been current in eastern Scotland for some time before they were more widely adopted following the Pictish expansion of power. The boar symbol at Dunadd could pre-date the Dalriadic occupation there.

(7) There is no reason to argue that the stones are 'Christian' in significance simply because they are used on cross-slabs. Definite pagan subject matter appears on Christian stones, such as the pagan Celtic god Cernunos on a class II slab from Meigle.

Recently some confirmation for the dating of Pictish symbols to the fifth century has come to light at Pool, Orkney. A pin-like bone object has a double disc and z-rod, and comes from a context which radiocarbon suggests may be as early as the fourth century AD. A cattle phalange has a crescent and V-rod and was found in a building dated to between the fifth and seventh centuries. There is also a stone with a symbol, which again radiocarbon dating suggests predates the seventh century (*Archaeology Extra*, 5, Bradford, 1988).

All the evidence seems to point to an origin for the system of symbols in the late Roman or early post-Roman period. Despite the arguments of Charles Thomas (1961; 1963) there is no reason to suppose all the symbols go back to a pre-Roman iron age, and indeed some of the symbols, such as the combs, cannot be earlier than the third or fourth centuries.

Murray's analysis might argue that the symbols were in fact developed in different parts of Pictland and possibly at differing times: the 'Pictish beast' (a hippocamp) does not in fact appear on class I stones at all, suggesting it is a late addition to the series. in short, the symbols could have been devised at various times from (say) the third century AD onwards, probably in different parts of Pictland. Originally perhaps executed in other media, their transfer to stone could have happened sometime between the late fourth and late sixth centuries, possibly, but not necessarily, at one time.

The long life of class I stones is also suggested by their re-use, in the case of the Inchyra stone, at least twice (Stevenson, 1959, 36).

The function of the stones and the meaning of the symbols are actually two interconnected problems. The most widely held view is that they are tombstones, modelled perhaps on Roman grave-slabs. While we still cannot prove that any symbol stone was directly associated with a burial, there is a sufficient body of circumstantial evidence to suggest that in some cases at least there is a funerary connection. Tombstones are not however the only possible explanation, and most recently an anthropologist, Anthony Jackson, has attempted to demonstrate that the stones are not funerary but commemorate dynastic alliances and that their symbols stem from the matrilineal kinship structure of Pictish society.

Jackson has made a very detailed analysis of all the stones, and has argued, quite convincingly, that Pictish symbols are in pairs, and that where a single symbol appears on a stone usually the stone is broken or the design is not in fact a symbol, and does not recur in pair groups. By studying pairs, he has reduced the number of symbols to twenty-eight (1984, 18-19). The only exception to the two-symbol ruling on class I stones is the mirror-and-comb symbol, which is a 'special symbol' providing information about the pair of symbols above it.

Using anthropological parallels, he has argued that the symbols are dynastic, and record marriage alliances between dynasties. A somewhat different situation prevails on the class II stones, when, Jackson argues, the Picts abandoned matriarchy for patriarchy and there was a break with symbol pairing, marriage rules and inheritance patterns (1984, 213).

He has shown that there is a significance in the regional distribution of symbol pairs.

This is not the place to discuss in detail the mass of detailed analysis put forward by Jackson. What can be said is that his interpretation, based as it is on very detailed study, is difficult to question, though it presupposes matrilinear succession among the Picts. Despite his conviction that the stones are not funerary, there is nothing incompatible in his interpretation with the idea that stones were erected over graves to announce the lineage of the deceased, even though the stones were not primarly devised as gravestones. In his interpretation he comes close to Henderson's suggestion that the stones were territorial boundaries (1971).

Against the view that Pictish society was matrilinear is the case advanced recently by Smyth (1984, 68f). His arguments, though detailed and thorough, have not convinced all historians (Anderson, 1987, 10). Until a better explanation for the symbol stones is advanced, Jackson's seems the most plausible.

SCULPTURE IN IRELAND

There is no relief sculpture in Ireland that certainly pre-dates the eighth century. The pillar at Kilnasaggart, south Co. Armagh, carries an inscription and incised crosses. It has been dated to the beginning of the eighth century since it names someone called Ternoc, who has been identified from the Irish Annals as one who died in 714 or 716 (Henry, 1965, 119).

There are a few other incised slabs which have been claimed to belong to the early eighth century. The Killaghtee slab, Co. Donegal, which Henry saw as probably contemporary with Kilnasaggart has relief decoration, and shows features in common with tenth-century sculptures at Whithorn, Wigtowns, and some sculptures in Wales, notably Nash-Williams' 'panelled cartwheel' group

(1950, pls. LVI-LVIII) which he dated to the late tenth-eleventh centuries. It also carries a triquetra knot, which was not fashionable until the later eighth century.

The cross-slabs on Inishkea North are more problematical, as the main 'monastic' site excavated by Henry (1945) produced no closely datable finds (though a bone comb was of 'Early Christian' type). However, a hut excavated subsequently on the island produced an object identified as a mirror handle and a penannular brooch. The brooch is in fact a ring-brooch, possibly of the eighth century, and the 'mirror handle' could be from a Roman patera. As Raftery has noted, there can be no certain date for the house site on Inishkea North (1981, 85-6), and there is certainly no reason to date the stone buildings any earlier than the late eighth century or even ninth. The slabs of course could have been survivors from an earlier phase of use with timber buildings not detected by Henry, but there is no good case to be made for dating them earlier than the eighth century.

Similarly no earlier than the eighth century are some slabs from Inishmurray with interlace-decorated low relief crosses. The interlace has triquetra-knot ends, and they compare quite closely with certain Welsh crosses, notably one of the Crux Xri group from Margam, Glamorgan, dated by Nash-Williams to the tenth century (1950, no. 232).

To the seventh century have been ascribed the group of cross slabs in Donegal which include the examples from Fahan Mura and Carndonagh. This group has been discussed by Harbison (for his conclusions see p. 46), and need be no earlier than the ninth century.

In sum, apart from the possibility that some stones with engraved decoration may pre-date 700, there is no evidence for relief sculpture in Ireland before the eighth century.

The development of incised ornament on pre-eighth century stones has been discussed by Thomas (1987), whose chronology however remains suspect.

BIBLIOGRAPHY

ADDYMAN, P.V. & LEIGH, D. 1973, 'The Anglo-Saxon village at Chalton, Hampshire: second interim report', *Medieval Archaeol* XVII (1973), 1-25.

ADDYMAN, P.V., LEIGH, D. & HUGHES, M.J. 1972, 'Anglo-Saxon houses at Chalton, Hampshire', *Medieval Archaeol* XVI (1972), 13-32.

AGER, B. 1985, 'The smaller variants of the Anglo-Saxon quoit brooch', in Hawkes, S.C., Brown, D. and Campbell, J. (eds.), *Anglo-Saxon Studies in History and Archaeology*, 4 Oxford, 1-58.

ALCOCK, L. 1960, 'Roman sherds from Castle Ditches, Llancarfan (Glam.)', *Bulletin Board Celtic Studies* 18, (1958-60), 221-7.

_____ 1960b, 'Dark Age objects from Lesser Garth Cave, Glamorgan', *Bulletin Board Celtic Studies* 18 (1958), 221-7.

_____ 1963, *Dinas Powys, an iron age, dark age and early medieval settlement in Glamorgan*, Cardiff.

_____ 1967, 'Excavations at Degannwy Castle, Caernarvonshire, 1961-6', *Archaeol J* 124 (1967), 190-201.

_____ 1970, 'Was there an Irish Sea culture-province in the dark ages?' in Moore, D. (ed.), *The Irish Sea Province in Archaeology and History*, Cardiff, 55-65.

_____ 1971, *Arthur's Britain*, London.

_____ 1972, *By South Cadbury is that Camelot . . .*, London.

_____ 1972b, 'Excavations at Cadbury-Camelot, 1966-70' *Antiquity* 46 (1972), 29-38.

_____ 1979, 'The north Britons, the Picts and the Saxons', in Casey, P.J. (ed.), *The End of Roman Britain*, Oxford (BAR 71), 134-42.

_____ 1982, 'Cadbury-Camelot; a fifteen-year perspective', *Proc. Brit. Acad.* 68 (1982), 355-88.

_____ 1983, 'Gwyr y Gogledd: an archaeological appraisal', *Arch. Cambrensis* 132, 1-18.

_____ 1980, 'Refortified or newly fortified? The chronology of Dinas Powys', *Antiquity* 54 (1980), 231-2.

_____ 1987, *Economy, Society and Warfare among the Britons and Saxons*, Cardiff.

_____ 1987b, 'Pictish Studies: Present and Future', in Small, A. (ed.), *The Picts, a New Look at Old Problems*, Dundee, 80-92.

ALLEN, J.R. 1898, 'Metal bowls of the late-Celtic and Anglo-Saxon periods', *Archaeologia* 56 (1898), 39-56.

_____ 1904, *Celtic Art in Pagan and Christian Times*, London.

ANDERSON, J. 1876, 'Notes on the survival of pagan customs in Christian burial . . .' *Proc. Soc. Antiq. Scot.* 11 (1874-6), 363-406.

_____ 1881, *Scotland in Early Christian Times*, 2 vols, Edinburgh.

_____ 1987, 'Picts — the Name and the People', in Small, A. (ed.) *The Picts, a New Look at Old Problems*, Dundee, 7-14.

ALEXANDER, J.J.G. 1978, *A Survey of Manuscript Illumination in the British Isles, Vol 1 — Insular Manuscripts of the Sixth to Ninth Century*, London.

ANTHONY, I.E. 1958, *The Iron Age Camp at Poston, Herefordshire*, Hereford.

ANON., 1977, Note on Ravenglass, *Britannia*, 8, (1977), 378.

ARCHER, S. 1979, 'Late Roman gold and silver coin hoards in Britain: a gazetteer', in Casey, P.J. (ed.), *The End of Roman Britain*, Oxford, (BAR 71), 29-64.

ARNOLD, C.J. 1984, *Roman Britain to Saxon England*, London.

ARNOLD, C.J. & WARDLE, P. 1981, 'Early Medieval Settlement Patterns in England', *Medieval Archaeol XXV* (1981),145-9.

BANNERMAN, J. 1966, 'The Convention of Druim Cett', *Scottish Gaelic Studies* 11, 1 (1966), 3-25.

_____ 1968, 'The Dal Riata and Northern Ireland in the sixth and seventh centuries', in Carney, J. & Greene, D. (eds.), *Celtic Studies: Essays in memory of Angus Matheson*, Edinburgh, 1-11.

_____ 1974, *Studies in the History of Dalriada*, Edinburgh.

BARBER, J.W. 1981, 'Excavations on Iona, 1979', *Proc. Soc. Antiq. Scot.* 111 (1981), 282-380.

BARBER, K. 1981 'The Stratigraphy and Palynology of Recent Ombotrophic Peat', in Smith, C.D. & Parry, M. (eds.), *Consequences of Climatic Change*, Nottingham, 129-34.

BARBOUR, J. 1907, 'Notice of a stone fort near Kirkandrews, in the parish of Borgue, Kirkcudbright . . .', *Proc. Soc. Antiq. Scot.* XLI (1906-7), 68-80.

BARING-GOULD, S. & BURNARD, R. 1904, 'An exploration of some of the Cytiau in Tr'er Ceiri', *Arch Cambrensis* 6, 4 (1904), 1-16.

BATESON, J.D. 1973, 'Roman material from Ireland: a re-consideration', *Proc. Royal Irish Academy* 73, 21-97.

_____ 1976, 'Further finds of Roman material from Ireland', *Proc. Royal Irish Academy*, 76 (1976), 171-80.

_____ 1981, *Enamel-working in Iron Age, Roman and Sub-Roman Britain*, Oxford (BAR, Brit Ser. 93).

BARKER, P.A. & LAWSON, J. 1971, 'A pre-Roman field system at Hen Domen, Montgomeryshire', *Medieval Archaeol XV* (1971) 58-72.

BENTON, S. 1931, 'The Excavation of the Sculptor's Cave, Covesea, Morayshire', *Proc. Soc. Antiq. Scot.* LXV (1930-31), 177-216.

BERGER, L. 1956, 'Die Thekenbeschlage des Gemellianus von Baden-Aquae Helveticae', *Fünfundvierzigstes Jahrbuch der Schweizerischen Gesellschaft für Urgeschichte* 1956, 24-39.

BEVERIDGE, E. & CALLANDER, J.G. 1932 , 'Earth-houses at Garry Iochdrach and Bac Mhic Connain, in North Uist', *Proc. Soc. Antiq. Scot.* LXVI (1931-2), 32-66.

BIDDLE, M. 1975, 'Excavations at Winchester, 1971: Tenth and Final report, Part I', *Antiq J* LV (1975), 96-126.

_____ 1976, 'Towns' in Wilson, D.M. (ed.), *The Archaeology of Anglo-Saxon England*, London, 99-15.

BINCHY, D.A. 1954, 'Secular Institutions' in Dillon, M. (ed.), *Early Irish Society*, Dublin, 52-65.

_____ 1962, 'Patrick and his biographers: ancient and modern', *Studia Hibernica* 2 (1962), 7-173.

BLAIR, P.H. 1947, 'The Origins of Northumbria', *Archaeol Aeliana* 4th Ser 25 (1947), 1-51.

_____ 1956, *An Introduction to Anglo-Saxon England*, Cambridge.

BONNEY, D.J. 1960, 'Pagan Saxon boundaries in Wilts', *Wiltshire Archaeol Magazine* 61 (1960), 25-30.

_____ 1972, 'Early Boundaries in Wessex', in Fowler, P.J. (ed.), *Archaeology and the Landscape*, London, 168-86.

_____ 1976, 'Early Boundaries and Estates in southern England', in Sawyer, P. (ed.), *Medieval Settlement: Continuity and Change*, London, 72-82.

BOON, G.C. 1958, 'Notes on the Byzantine AE coins said to have been found at Caerwent', *Bull of the Board of Celtic Studies*, XVII (1958), 316.

_____ 1959, 'The Latest Objects from Silchester, Hants', *Medieval Archaeol* III (1959), 79-88.

_____ 1972, *Isca. The Roman Legionary Fortress at Caerleon, Mon*, Cardiff.

_____ 1974, *Calleva. The Roman Town of Silchester*, Newton Abbot.

BRANIGAN, K. 1976, 'Villa settlement in the West Country', in Branigan, K. and Fowler, P.J. (eds.), *The Roman West Country*, Newton Abbot, 120-41.

BREESE, C.E. 1930, 'The fort at Dinas Emrys', *Archaeologia Cambrensis* 85 (1930), 342-54.

BREEZE, D. 1982, *The Northern Frontiers of Roman Britain*, London.

BREEZE, D. & DOBSON, B. 1976, *Hadrian's Wall*, Harmondsworth.

BROGAN, O. 1953, *Roman Gaul*, London.

BROWN, A.E. 1965, 'Records of surface finds made in Herefordshire', *Transactions Woolhope Naturalists Field Club* 37 (1961-3), 77-91.

BROWN, P.D.C. 1972, 'The Ironwork' in Brodribb, A.C., Hands, A.R. and Walker, D.R., *Excavations at Shakenoak*, III, Oxford, 109.

_____ 1976, 'Archaeological evidence for the Saxon period' in McWhirr, A. (ed.), *Studies in the History of Cirencester*, Oxford (BAR 30), 19-46.

_____ 1977, 'The significance of the Londesborough Ring Brooch', *Antiq J* 57 (1977), 95-7.

_____ 1981, 'Swastika patterns', in Evison, V. (ed.), *Angles, Saxons and Jutes*, Oxford, 227-40.

BRUCE-MITFORD, R.L.S. 1956, 'A Dark-Age settlement at Mawgan Porth, Cornwall,' in Bruce-Mitford, (ed.), *Recent Archaeological Excavations in the British Isles*, London, 167-96.

_____ 1983, *The Sutton Hoo Ship Burial, Vol 3 — Late Roman and Byzantine Silver, hanging bowls, drinking vessels . . . and other items*, London.

_____ 1960, 'Decoration and Miniatures', in Kendrick, T.D., Brown, T.J. and Bruce-Mitford, R.L.S., et. al., *Evangeliorum Quattuor Codex Lindisfarnensis*, 2 vols, Olten & Lausanne.

BRUCE-MITFORD, R.L.S. 1987, 'Ireland and the hanging bowls: a review' in Ryan, M. (ed.), *Ireland and Insular Art, AD 500-1200*, Dublin, 30-9.

BUIST, G. 1838, *Report by Mr George Buist on the silver fragments in the Possession of General Durham, Largo . . .*, Cupar.

BU'LOCK, J.D. 1960, 'The Celtic, Saxon, and Scandinavian Settlement at Meols in Wirral', *Trans Historical Soc Lancs and Cheshire* 112 (1960), 1-28 ,

_____ 1972, *Pre-Conquest Cheshire, 383-1066*, Chester.

BURROW, I.G. 1974, 'Tintagel — some Problems' *Scot Archaeol Forum* 5 (1974), 99-103.

_____ 1979, 'Roman Material from Hillforts', in Casey, P.J. (ed.) *The End of Roman Britain*, Oxford (BAR 71), 212-29.

_____ 1981, *Hillfort and Hill-top Settlement in Somerset in the First to Eighth Centuries AD*, Oxford, (BAR 91).

BUSHE-FOX, J.P. 1949, *Fourth report on the Excavations of the Roman Fort at Richborough, Kent*, London, Soc. Ant. Res. Rep. XVI.

BYRNE, F.J. 1973, *Irish Kings and High Kings*, London.

CALLANDER, J.G. 1929, 'Land movements in Scotland in Prehistoric Times', *Proc. Soc. Antiq. Scot.* LXIII (1928-9), 314-22.

_____ 1933, 'A Collection of prehistoric relics from the Stevenston Sands, Ayrshire, and other Objects in the National Museum of Antiquities', *Proc. Soc. Antiq. Scot.* LXVII (1932-3), 26-34.

CAMDEN, W. 1590, *Britannia*, London.

CAMERON, K. 1968, 'Eccles in English Place-Names' in Barley, M.W. & Hanson, R.P.C., *Christianity in Britain, 300- 700*, Leicester, 87-92.

CAMPBELL, E. 1984, 'E Ware and Aquitaine: a reappraisal of the petrological evidence', *Scot. Archaeol. Rev.*, 3, (i), 35-41.

_____ 1987, 'Dark Age Pottery: E Ware', in Close-Brooks, J. 'Excavations at Clatchard Craig, Fife' *Proc. Soc. Antiq. Scot.* 116 (1986), 117-84.

CANT, R.G. 1981, 'David Steuart Erskine, 11th Earl of Buchan: Founder of the Society of Antiquaries of Scotland', in Bell, A.S. (ed.), *The Scottish Antiquarian Tradition*, Edinburgh, 1-30.

CAPELLE, T. & VIERCK, H. 1971, 'Modeln der Merowinger- und Wikingerzeit', *Frümitterlalterliche Studien* 5 (1971), 42-100.

CARNEY, J. 1971, 'Three Old Irish accentual poems', *Ériu* 22 (1971), 23-80.

CARSON, R.A.G. & O'KELLY, C. 1977, 'A Catalogue of the Roman Coins from Newgrange, Co. Meath and Notes on the Coins and Related Finds', *Proc. Royal Irish Academy* 77C (1977), 35-55.

CARTER, S.P., HAIGH, D., NEIL, N.J.R. & SMITH, B. 1984, 'Interim report on the structures at Howe, Stromness, Orkney', *Glasgow Archaeol Journal* 11 (1984), 61-73.

CASEY, J. 1980, *Roman Coinage in Britain*, Aylesbury.

CAULFIELD, S. 1981, 'Some Celtic problems in the Irish Iron Age', in Ó Corráin, D. (ed.), *Irish Antiquity, Cork* , 205-15.

CHADWICK, H.M. 1949, *Early Scotland*, Cambridge.

CHADWICK, N.K. 1958, 'Intellectual Contacts between Britain and Gaul in the Fifth Century', in Chadwick, N.K. (ed.), *Studies in Early British History*, Cambridge, 189-263.

CHAMPION, T. 1982, 'The Myth of Iron Age Invasions in Ireland', in Scott, B.G. (ed.), *Studies on Early Ireland*, Essays in honour of M.V. Duignan, n.d. 51-73.

CHILDE, V.G. 1935, *The Prehistory of Scotland*, London.

CLARKE, D.V. 1971, 'Small Finds in the Atlantic Province: Problems of Approach', *Scottish Archaeol Forum* 3, Edinburgh, 55-72.

CLARKE, G.N. 1979, *Pre-Roman and Roman Winchester, Part 2: The Roman Cemetery at Lankhills*, Oxford.

CLOSE-BROOKS, J. 1988 'Excavations at Clatchard Craig, Fife', *Proc. Soc. Antiq. Scot.* 116 (1986), 117-184.

240

COLES, J. 1960, 'Scottish Late Bronze Age Metalwork: typology, distribution and chronology', *Proc. Soc. Antiq. Scot.* 93 (1959-60), 16-134.

COOMBS, D. 1970, 'Mam Tor, a bronze age hillfort?', *Current Archaeology* 27 (July 1971), 100-2.

COWIE, T.G. 1980, 'Excavations at the Catstane, Midlothian, 1977', *Proc. Soc. Antiq. Scot.* 109 (1980), 166-201.

CRAMP, R. 1970, 'Decorated Window-Glass and Millefiori from Monkwearmouth', *Antiq. J* 50 (1970), 327-335.

CRAW, J.H. 1930, 'Excavations at Dunadd and at other sites on the Poltalloch Estates, Argyll', *Proc. Soc. Antiq. Scot.* LXIV (1929-30), 111-46.

CRAWFORD, I. 1972, *Excavations at Coileaghan an Udail (The Udal), N. Uist — 9th Interim Report*, Cambridge.

CRAWFORD, I.A. & SWITSUR, R. 1977, 'Sandscaping and C14: The Udal, N. Uist', *Antiquity* LI (1977), 124-36.

CROWE, C. 1987, 'An Excavation at Kirkmirran, Dalbeattie, 1985', *Trans Dumfries & Galloway Nat History & Antiquarian Soc.* LXI (1986), 55-62.

CUNLIFFE, B. 1975, *Excavations at Portchester Castle, Vol II Saxon*, London, Soc. Ant. Res. Rep. XXXIII.

_____ 1980, 'The Excavation of the Roman Spring at Bath, 1979', *Antiq. J* LX (1980), 187-206.

CUNLIFFE, B. & PHILLIPSON, J. 1968, 'Excavations at Eldon's Seat, Encombe, Dorset', *Proc Prehist. Soc.* 34 (1968), 191-237.

CURLE, A.O. 1914, 'Report on the Excavation, in September 1913, of a vitrified fort at Rockcliffe, Dalbeattie, known as the Mote of Mark', *Proc. Soc. Antiq. Scot.* XII (1913-14), 125-68.

_____ 1923, *The Treasure of Traprain*, Glasgow.

CURLE, C.M. 1982, *Pictish and Norse Finds from the Brough of Birsay, 1934-74*, Edinburgh, Soc. Ant. Scot. Monographs, 1.

CURLE, J. 1932, 'An Inventory of Objects of Roman and Provincial Roman Origin found on sites in Scotland not definitely associated with Roman constructions', *Proc. Soc. Antiq. Scot.* LXVI (1931-2), 277-397.

CURWEN, E.C. 1929, *Prehistoric Susex*, London.

DAVIDSON, H.R.E. & WEBSTER, L. 1967, 'The Anglo-Saxon burial at Coombe (Woodnesborough), Kent', *Medieval Archaeol* XI (1967), 1-41.

DAVIES, G. & TURNER, J. 1979, 'Pollen diagrams from Northumberland', *New Phytol.* 82 (1979), 783-804.

DAVIES, J.L. 1967, 'Excavations at Caer Dynnaf, Llanblethian, Glamorgan, 1965-6', *Morgannwg*, 11 (1976), 77-8.

DAVIES, W. 1978, *An Early Welsh Microcosm. Studies in the Llandaff Charters*, London.

_____ 1979, 'Roman Settlements and Post-Roman Estates in South-East Wales', in Casey, P. (ed.), *The End of Roman Britain*, Oxford (BAR 71), 153-73.

_____ 1982, *Wales in the Early Middle Ages*, Leicester.

DAVIS, K.R. 1982, *Britons and Saxons: The Chiltern Region 400-700*, Chichester.

DE PAOR, M. 1979, *Early Irish Art*, New York.

DICKINSON, T.M. 1979, 'On the origin and chronology of the Early Anglo-Saxon disc brooch', in Hawkes, S.C., Brown, D. and Campbell, J. (eds.), *Anglo-Saxon Studies in History and Archaeology*, 1, Oxford (BAR 72), 39-80.

_____ 1982, 'Fowler's Type G Penannular Brooches Reconsidered', *Medieval Archaeol* 26 (1982), 41-68.

241

DILLON, M. 1954, 'The Irish Language', in Dillon, M. (ed.), *Early Irish Society*, Dublin, 7-21.

DIXON, N. 1984, 'Oakbank Crannog', *Current Archaeology* 90 (Jan, 1984), 217-20.

DIXON, P. 1982, 'How Saxon is a Saxon House?' in Drury, P.J. (ed.), *Structural Reconstruction*, Oxford (BAR),275-88.

_____ 1988, 'Crickley Hill', *Current Archaeology* 110 (July, 1988), 73-8.

DODGSON, J. McN. 1966, 'The significance of the distribution of the English place-name in -ingas, -inga- in south-east England', *Medieval Archaeol* X (1966), 1-29.

_____ 1973. 'Placenames from '-ham' and the settlement of Kent, Surrey and Sussex', *Anglo-Saxon England*, 2 (1973), 1-50.

DOLLEY, M. 1976 'Roman coins from Ireland and the date of St Patrick', *Proc. Royal Irish Academy* 76 (1976), 181-90.

_____ 1976b, 'The Coins', in Wilson, D.M. (ed.), *The Archaeology of Anglo-Saxon England*, London, (1976), 349-372.

DONALDSON, A. & TURNER, J. 1977, 'A pollen diagram from Hallowell Moss, near Durham City', *Biogeography* 4 (1977), 25-33.

DOPPELFELD, O. 1960, 'Das Frankische Frauengrab unter dem Chor des Kolner Doms', *Germania* XXXVIII (1960), 89-113.

DOUCH, H.C. & BEARD, S.W. 1970, 'Excavations at Carvossa, Probus, 1968-70, Preliminary Report', *Cornish Archaeol* 9 (1970), 93-98.

DRURY, P.J. & WICKENDEN, N.P. 1982, 'An Early Saxon Settlement within the Romano-British Small Town at Heybridge, Essex', *Medieval Archaeol* XXVI (1982), 1-40.

DUIGNAN, M.V. 1976 'The Turoe Stone. Its place in insular La Téne art', in Duval, P.M. & Hawkes, C. (eds.), *Celtic Art in Ancient Europe: Five Protohistoric Centuries*, London (1976), 201-17.

DUMVILLE, D. 1977, 'Sub-Roman Britain: History and Legend', *History*, 62, (1977), 173-92.

DUNCAN, A.A.M. 1975, *Scotland, the Making of a Kingdom*, Edinburgh.

DUNNETT, R. 1975, *The Trinovantes*, London.

EAGLES, B.N. 1979, *The Anglo-Saxon Settlement of Humberside*, Oxford (BAR 68).

EDWARDS, A.J.H. 1939, 'A massive double-linked Silver Chain', *Proc. Soc. Antiq. Scot.* 73 (1938-9), 326-7.

EDWARDS, K.J. & RALSTON, I. 1978, 'New dating and environmental evidence from Burghead fort, Moray', *Proc. Soc. Antiq. Scot.* 109 (1977-8), 202-10.

EDWARDS, N. & LANE, A. (eds.), 1988, *Early Medieval Settlements in Wales, AD 400-1100*, Cardiff.

ENRIGHT, M.J. 1983, 'The Sutton Hoo whetstone sceptre: a study of iconography and cultural millieu', *Anglo-Saxon England*, 11, (1983), 119-34.

EOGAN, G. 1964, 'The Later Bronze Age in Ireland in the light of recent research', *Proc. Prehistoric Soc.* XXX (1964), 268-351.

EVANS, A.J. 1897, 'On a votive deposit of gold objects found on the North-West Coast of Ireland', *Archaeologia* 55 (1897), 391-408.

EVANS, E.M. 1986, '1986 Caerleon Mill Street suburb', *Archaeol. Wales* 26 (1986), 46-7.

EVANS, J.G. 1976, *The Environment of Early Man in the British Isles*, London.

EVISON, V. 1965, *Fifth Century Invasions South of the Thames*, London.

_____ 1975, 'Pagan Saxon Whetstones', *Antiq. J* LV (1975), 70-85.

_____ 1977, 'An Enamelled Disc from Great Saxham', *Proc. Suffolk Institute of Archaeol & Hist*, XXXIV (1977), 1-13.

FANNING, T., 'Excavation of an Early Christian Cemetery and Settlement at Reask, Co. Kerry', *Proc. Royal Irish Academy*, 81 (1981), 67-72.

FAULL, M.L. 1975, 'The semantic development of Old English wealh', *Leeds Studies in English* VII (1975), 20-44.

_____ 1977, 'British Survival in Anglo-Saxon Northumbria', in Laing, L. (ed.), *Studies in Celtic Survival*, Oxford (BAR 37), 1-55.

FEACHEM, R.W. 1951, 'Dragonesque Fibulae', *Antiq. J* XXXI (1951), 32-44.

_____ 1967, 'The Hill-forts of Northern Britain', in Rivet, A.L.F. (ed.), *The Iron Age in Northern Britain* (1967), Edinburgh, 59-87.

FORD, W.J. 1971, 'Stretton-on-Fosse, Warks (SP 2182 3831)', in *West Midlands Archaeol Newsletter*, 14 (1971), 22.

FOWLER, E. 1960, 'The origins and development of the Penannular Brooch in Europe', *Proc. Prehist Soc.* XXVI (1960), 149-177.

_____ 1963, 'Celtic Metalwork of the Fifth and Sixth Centuries AD', *Archaeol J* CXX (1963),98-160.

_____ 1968, 'Hanging Bowls' in Coles, J. & Simpson, D.D.A. (eds.), *Studies in Ancient Europe*, Leicester, 287-310.

_____ 1981, 'A fragment of an enamelled bronze bowl from Bradley Hill, Somerton, Somerset', in O'Connor, A. & Clarke, D., *From the Stone Age to the Forty-Five*, Edinburgh, 237-42.

_____ 1984, 'Silver proto hand-pin', in *Lucas*, 1984, 47-8.

FOWLER, P. 1960, 'Excavations at Madmarston Camp, Swalcliffe, 1957-8', *Oxoniensia* 25 (1960), 3-48.

_____ 1971, 'Hill-forts AD 400-700', in Jesson, M. & Hill, D. (eds.), *The Iron Age and its Hillforts, Southampton*, 203-13.

FOWLER, P. & THOMAS, C. 1962, 'Arable fields of the pre-Norman period at Gwithian', *Cornish Archaeol* I (1962), 61-84.

FOWLER, P.J. *et. al.* 1970, *Cadbury-Congresbury, Somerset, 1968* (Dept. of Extra-Mural Studies, Bristol).

FOX, A. 1946, 'Settlements and other Remains', in Nash-Williams, J. (ed.), *A Hundred Years of Welsh Archaeology*, Cardiff, 105-122.

FOX, C. 1923, *The Archaeology of the Cambridge Region*, Cambridge.

FRERE, S.S. 1962, 'Excavations at Dorchester-on-Thames, 1962', *Archaeol J* CXIX (1962), 114-149.

_____ 1966, 'The end of towns in Roman Britain', in Wacher, J.S. (ed.), *The Civitas Capitals of Roman Britain*, Leicester, 87-100.

_____ 1972, *Verulamium Excavations, Vol 1*, London, Soc. Ant. Res. Rep. no. 28.

_____ 1974, *Britannia*, London, 2nd (paperback) ed.

_____ 1975, 'Verulamium and the towns of Britannia', *Aufstieg und Niedergang der Romischen Welt*, II, 290-327.

FULFORD, M. 1979, 'Pottery production and trade at the end of Roman Britain: the case against continuity', in Casey, P.J. (ed.), *The End of Roman Britain*, Oxford (BAR Brit Ser. 71), 120-32.

_____ 1982, *Guide to the Silchester Excavations 1979-81*, Reading.

_____ 1982b, 'Silchester', *Current Archaeology* 82 (1982), 326-31.

GARDNER, W. & SAVORY, H.N. 1964, *Dinorben: a Hillfort occupied in Early Iron Age and Roman Times*, Cardiff.

GELLING, M. 1967, 'English place-names derived from the compound wicham', *Medieval Archaeol* XI (1967), 87-104.

_____ 1977, 'Latin loan-words in Old English place-names', *Anglo-Saxon England*, 6, (1977), 1-13.

_____ 1978, *Signposts to the Past*, London.

GELLING, P.S. 1969, 'A metalworking site at Kiondroghad, Kirk Andreas, Isle of Man', *Medieval Archaeol* XIII (1969), 67-83.

GELLING, P. & STANFORD, S.C. 1967, 'Dark Age Pottery or Iron Age Ovens?' *Trans. Proc. Birmingham Archaeol Soc.* 82 (1967), 77-91.

GILLAM, J. 1979, 'Romano-Saxon Pottery: an alternative interpretation', in Casey, P. (ed.), *The End of Roman Britain*, Oxford (BAR 71), 103-18.

GILMOUR, B. 1979, 'The Anglo-Saxon church at St Paul-in-the-Bail', *Medieval Archaeol* XXIII (1979), 214-17.

GRAHAM, A. 1973, 'Records and Opinions: 1780-1930', *Proc. Soc. Antiq. Scot.* 102 (1973), 241-84.

_____ 1978, 'The Archaeology of Joseph Anderson', *Proc. Soc. Antiq. Scot.* 107 (1975-6), 279-98.

_____ 1981, 'In Piam Veterum Memoriam', in Bell, A.S. (ed.), *The Scottish Antiquarian Tradition*, Edinburgh, 212-26.

GRAHAM-CAMPBELL, J., CLOSE-BROOKS, J., & LAING, L. 1976, 'The Mote of Mark and Celtic Interlace', *Antiquity* 50 (1976), 48-53.

GRESHAM, A.C. 1965, *Review of Dinas Powys, Antiq. J* XLV, 127-8.

GRIEG, J.C. 1972, 'Cullykhan', *Current Archaeology* 32 (1972), 227-31.

GRIEG, S. 1940 Scotland, in Shetelig, H., *Viking Antiquities in Great Britain and Ireland, II*, Oslo.

GRIFFITHS, W.E. 1951, 'The Development of Native Homesteads in North Wales', *Antiquity* 25 (1951), 174-86.

_____ 1952, 'Decorated Rotary Querns from Wales and Ireland', *Ulster J. Archaeol* 14 (1951), 49-61.

_____ 1959, 'A Pre-Roman Vessel from Pen Llystyn, Caernarvonshire', *Arch Cambrensis* 108 (1959), 114-25.

_____ 1959b, 'The excavation of an enclosed hut-group at Cae'r Mynydd in Caernarvonshire', *Antiq J*. IXL, (1959), 33-60.

GRIMES, W.F. 1931 'Romano-British pottery from Crocksydam Camp, Warren, Pemb.', *Bulletin Board Celtic Studies* 5 (1929- 31), 392.

GUIDO, M. 1974, 'A Scottish Crannog Re-Dated', *Antiquity* 48 (1974), 54-6.

GUILBERT, G.C. 1979, 'Dinorben, 1977-8' *Current Archaeology* 65 (1979), 182-8.

HAMILTON, J.R.C. 1956, *Excavations at Jarlshof, Shetland*, Edinburgh.

_____ 1966, 'Forts, brochs and wheelhouses in Northern Scotland', in Rivet, A.L.F. (ed.), *The Iron Age in North Britain*, Edinburgh, 111-30.

_____ 1968, *Excavations at Clickhimin, Shetland*, Edinburgh.

HAMLIN, A. 1982, 'A Chi-Rho carved stone at Drumqueran, Co. Antrim', *Ulster J Archaeol* 35 (1982), 22-8.

HARBISON, P. 1970, 'How old is Gallarus oratory? A reappraisal of its role in early Irish architecture', *Medieval Archaeol* XIV (1970), 34-59.

_____ 1981, 'The Date of the Moylough belt shrine', in Ó Corráin, D. (ed.), *Irish Antiquity*, Cork, 231-40.

_____ 1985, 'Three Miniatures in the Book of Kells', *Proc. Royal Irish Academy* 85 (1985), 181-94.

_____ 1986, 'A group of Early Christian Carved Stone Monuments in County Donegal', in Higgitt, J. (ed.), *Early Medieval Sculpture in Britain and Ireland*, Oxford, BAR 152, 49-68.

HARDEN, D.B. 1956, 'Glass vessels in Britain and Ireland, AD 400-1000', in Harden, D.B. (ed.), *Dark Age Britain*, London, 132-67.

HARVEY, A. 1987, 'Early Literacy in Ireland — the Evidence from Ogham', *Cambridge Medieval Celtic Studies* 14 (1987), 1-15.

HASELOFF, G. 1978, 'Der Einband des Ragundrugis — Codex in Fulda, Codex Bonifatianus 2' in Brall, A. (ed.), *Von der Klosterhbibliothek zur Landesbibliothek. Beiträge zum Zweihunderljähringen Beshen der Hessisihen Landesbibliothek Fulda*, 1-46, Stuttgart.

_____ 1979, 'Irland', in Roth, H. (ed.), *Kunst der Völkerwanderungszeit*, Propylaen Kunstgeschichte, Supp. IV, Berlin, 223-43.

_____ 1981, *Die germanische Tierornamentik der Völkerwanderungszeit. Studien zu Salin's Stil I*, 3 vols, Berlin.

_____ 1988, 'Insular animal styles with special reference to Irish art in the early medieval period', in Ryan, M. (ed.), *Ireland and Insular Art, AD 500-1200*, Dublin, 44-55.

HAWKES, C.F.C. 1935, 'The pottery from the sites on Plumpton Plain', *Proc. Prehist. Soc.* 1 (1935), 39-59.

_____ 1964, 'Sutton Hoo Twenty-Five Years After', *Antiquity* XXXVIII (1964), 252-57.

_____ 1982, 'The Wearing of the Brooch in Early Iron Age Dress among the Irish' in Scott, B.G. (ed.), *Studies on Early Ireland*, n.d. , 51-73.

HAWKES, S.C. 1961, 'The Jutish Style A. A Study of Germanic Animal Art in Southern England', *Archaeologia* XCVIII (1961), 29-74.

HAWKES, S.C. & POLLARD, M. 1981, 'The gold bracteates from sixth century Anglo-Saxon graves in Kent in the light of a new find from Finglesham', *Frümitttelalteriche Studien* 15 (1981), 316-70.

HAWORTH, R. 1971, 'The horse harness of the Irish Early Iron Age', *Ulster J Archaeol* 34 (1971), 26-49.

HAYES, J.W. 1972, *Late Roman Pottery*, London (British School in Rome).

_____ 1977, 'North African flanged bowls: a problem in fifth-century chronology', in Dore, J. & Green, K. (eds.), *Roman Pottery Studies in Britain and Beyond*, Oxford (BAR Supp. Ser. 30), 279-88.

_____ 1980, *A Supplement to Late Roman Pottery*, Rome.

HEDGES, J.W. 1987, *Bu, Gurness and the Brochs of Orkney*, 3 vols, Oxford (BAR 163-5).

HEIGHWAY, C.M., GARROD, A.P. & VINCE, A.G. 1979 'Excavations at 1 Westgate St, Gloucester, 1975', *Medieval Archaeol* 23 (1979), 159-213.

HEMP, W.J. & GRESHAM, C. 1944, 'Hut-circles in North-West Wales', *Antiquity* 18 (1944), 183-96.

HENCKEN, H. O'N. 1936, 'Ballinderry 1 Crannog', *Proc. Royal Irish Academy* XLIII (1936), 103-226.

_____ 1938, *Cahercommaun, a stone fort in Co. Clare*, Dublin.

_____ 1942 'Ballinderry 2 Crannog', *Proc. Royal Irish Academy* 47 (1942),1-75.

_____ 1950, 'Lagore Crannog: An Irish Royal Residence of the 7th to 10th Centuries AD', *Proc. Royal Irish Academy* 53 (1950), 1-247.

HENDERSON, I. 1958 'The origin centre of the Pictish symbol stones', *Proc. Soc. Antiq. Scot.* XCI (1957-8), 44-60.

____ 1967, *The Picts*, London.

____ 1971, 'The meaning of the Pictish symbol stones', in Meldrum, P. (ed.), *The Dark Ages in the Highlands*, Inverness, 53-68.

____ 1979, 'The Silver Chain from Whitecleugh, Shieldholm, Crawfordjohn, Lanarkshire', *Trans Dumfries & Galloway Nat. Hist. Antiq. Soc.* 54 (1979), 20-8.

HENIG, M. 1984, *Religion in Roman Britain*, Oxford.

HENRY, F. 1930, 'Les Origines de l'Iconographie Irlandaises', *Revue Archéologique*, 5 Ser, 32 (1933), 89-109.

____ 1933, *Les Sculptures irlandaises pendant les douze premiers siècles de l'ère chrétienne*, Paris.

____ 1934, 'Finds of Prehistoric Pottery at Knocknaholet, Co. Antrim', *J. Roy. Soc. Antiq. Ireland* 64 (1934), 264-5.

____ 1936, 'Hanging bowls', *J. Roy. Soc. Antiq. Ireland* 66 (1936), 209-46.

____ 1945, 'Remains of the Early Christian period on Inishkea North', *J. Royal Soc. Antiq. Ireland*, LXXV (1945), 127-55.

____ 1952, 'A wooden hut as Inishkea North, Co. Mayo', *J. Roy. Soc. Antiq. Ireland*, LXXXII (1952), 163-78.

____ 1956, 'Irish enamels of the Dark Ages and the cloisonne technique', in Harden, D.B. (ed.), *Dark Age Britain*, London, 71-87.

____ 1957, 'Early Monasteries, Beehive Huts and Drystone Houses in the neighbourhood of Caherciveen and Waterville (Co. Kerry), *Proc. Royal Irish Academy* 57 (1957),45-166.

____ 1965, *Irish Art in the Early Christian Period to AD 800*, London.

HIGGINS, R.A. 1961, *Greek and Roman Jewellery*, London.

HIGHAM, N. 1986, *The Northern Counties to AD 1000*, London.

HILLGARTH, J.N. 1963 'Visigothic Spain and Early Christian Ireland', *Proc. Royal Irish Academy* LXII (1962), 167-94.

HINES, J. 1984, *The Scandinavian Character of Anglian England in the pre-Viking period*, Oxford, (BAR 124).

HIRST, S. 1985, *An Anglo-Saxon inhumation cemetery at Sewerby, E Yorks*, York Univ. Pubs. 4 (Leeds).

HOBLEY, B. & SCHOFIELD, J. 1977, 'Excavations in the City of London: first interim report, 1974-5', *Antiq. J* LVII (1977), 31-66.

HOGG, A.H.A. 1948, 'The date of Cunedda', *Antiquity*, XXII (1948), 201-5.

____ 1951, 'The Votadini', in Grimes, W.F. (ed.), *Aspects of Archaeology*, Essays for O.G.S. Crawford, London, 200-20.

____ 1957, 'A Fortified Round Hut at Carreg-y- llam near Nevin', *Arch Cambrensis* 106, (1957), 46-55.

____ 1966, 'Native Settlement in Wales', in Thomas, A.C. (ed.), *Rural Settlement in Roman Britain*, London (CBA Res Rep 7), 28-38.

____ 1977, 'Castle Ditches, Llancarfan, Glamorgan', *Arch Cambrensis* 125 (1976), 13-39.

____ 1979, 'Invasion and Response: the problem in Wales' in Burnham, B.C. and Johnson, H.B. (eds.), *Invasion and Response*, Oxford (BAR 73), 285-95.

HOLMQVIST, W. 1955, *Germanic Art*, Stockholm.

HOPE-TAYLOR, B. 1977, *Yeavering: an Anglo-British centre of early Northumbria*, London.

HUGHES, H.H. 1906, 'Tr'er Ceiri', *Archaeologia Cambrensis*, 6 Ser VI (1906), 38-62.

HUGHES, K. 1966, *The Church in Early Irish Society*, London.

____ 1972, *Early Christian Ireland: Introduction to the Sources*, London.

____ 1980, *Celtic Britain in the Early Middle Ages*, Woodbridge.

____ 1981, 'The Celtic Church — is this a valid concept?' *Cambridge Medieval Celtic Studies* 1 (1981), 1-20.

HULL, V. 1957, 'The Later Version of the Expulsion of the Dessi', *Zeitschrift für Celtische Philologie* 27 (1958), 14-63.

HUME, C.R. & JONES, G.W. 1961, 'Excavations on Nesscliff Hill', *Trans Shropshire Archaeol Soc.* 56 (1957-60), 129-32.

HUNTER, M. 1974, 'Germanic and Roman Antiquity and the sense of the past', *Anglo-Saxon England*, 3 (1974), 29-50.

HURST, H. 1972, 'Excavations at Gloucester, 1968-71', *Antiq J* 52 (1972), 24-69.

____, 1974, 'Excavations at Gloucester, 1971-3, Second Interim report, Part II', *Antiq J* 54 (1974), 8-52 .

____, 1975, 'Excavations at Gloucester: Third Interim Report: Kingsholm, 1965-75', *Antiq J.* CV (1975), 267-94.

IRELAND, A. 1982, 'The Royal Society of Antiquaries of Ireland, 1849-1900', *J. Roy. Soc. Antiq. Ireland* 112 (1982) 72-92.

ISAAC, P. 1976, 'Coin Hoards and History in the West', in Branigan, K. & Fowler, P. (eds.), *The Roman West Country*, Newton Abbot, 52-62.

IVENS, R.J., SIMPSON, D.D.A., BROWN, D., 'Excavations at Ireland Island MacHugh 1985, interim report', *Ulster J Archaeol* 49 (1986), 99-102.

JACKSON, A. 1984, *The Symbol Stones of Scotland*, Stromness.

JACKSON, K.H. 1953, *Language and History in Early Britain*, Edinburgh.

____ 1964, *The Oldest Irish Tradition: A Window on the Iron Age*, Cambridge.

____ 1969, *The Gododdin*, Edinburgh.

JAMES, E. 1977, *Merovingian Archaeology of South-West Gaul*, Oxford, (BAR Internat. Ser. 27).

____ 1982, 'Ireland and Western Gaul in the Merovingian Period', in Whitelock, D., McKitterick, R. & Dumville, D.N. (eds.), *Ireland in early medieval Europe*, Cambridge, 362-86.

JAMES, S., MARSHALL, H. & MILLETT, M. 1984, 'An early medieval building tradition', *Archaeol J* 141 (1984), 182-215.

JOBEY, G. 1959, 'Excavations at the native settlement at Huckhoe', *Archaeol Aeliana* 4th Ser XXXVII (1959), 217-78.

JOHNS, C., 1974, 'A Roman silver pin from Oldcroft, Gloucestershire', *Antiq. J* LIX (1974), 295-7.

JOHNSON, S. 1979, *Late Roman Fortification*, London.

____ 1980, *Later Roman Britain*, London.

JONES, A.H.M. 1966, *The Decline of the Ancient World*, London.

JONES, G.D.B. 1976, 'Roman Lancashire', *Archaeol J* 127 (1976), 240-5.

JONES, G.R.J. 1960 'The Pattern of Settlement on the Welsh Border', *Agricultural History Rev.* 8, (1960), 66-81.

JONES, M.E. 1979, 'Climate, Nutrition and Disease: an Hypothesis of Romano-British Population' in Casey, P. (ed.), *The End of Roman Britain*, Oxford, (BAR 71), 231-51.

JOPE, E.M. 1954, 'The Keshcarrigan Bowl and a Bronze Mirror Handle from Ballymoney', *Ulster J Archaeol* 17 (1954), 92-6.

____ 1955, 'Chariotry and Paired-Draught in Ireland during the Early Iron Age: the Evidence of some Horse-Bridle-Bits', *Ulster J Archaeol* 18 (1955), 37-44.

____ 1972, 'Models in Medieval Studies', in Clarke, D.L. (ed.), *Models in Archaeology*, London, 963-90.

JOPE, E.M. & WILSON, B. 1957, 'The decorated cast bronze disc from the river Bann near Coleraine', *Ulster J Archaeol* 20 (1957), 95-102.

KELLEHER, J.V. 1963, 'Early Irish History and pseudo-history', *Studia Hibernica* 3 (1963), 113-27.

KELLY, 1974, 'The stone forts at Aughinish', *Excavations* 1974, Belfast, 21.

KENDRICK, J. 1980, *Douglasmuir: the excavation of an early settlement and Neolithic enclosure 1979-80: Preliminary Report*, Edinburgh, S.D.D.

_____ 1982, 'Excavations at Douglasmuir, 1979-80', in Harding, D.W. (ed.), *Later Prehistoric Settlement in the South East of Scotland*, Edinburgh University occasional paper.

KENDRICK, T. 1932, 'British Hanging Bowls', *Antiquity* VI (1932), 161-84.

_____ 1941, 'The Scunthorpe Bowl', *Antiq J* 21 (1941), 236-8.

KENNEY, J.F. 1929, *Sources for the early history of Ireland, Vol. I Ecclesiastical*, New York.

KENT, J.P.C. 1961, 'From Roman Britain to Saxon England', in Dolley, M. (ed.), *Anglo-Saxon Coins London* (1961), 1-22.

_____ 1979, 'The end of Roman Britain: the literary and numismatic evidence reviewed' in Casey, P.J. (ed.), *The End of Roman Britain*, Oxford (BAR 71),15-27.

KENYON, K.M. 1954, 'Excavations at Sutton Walls, Herefordshire, 1948-1951', *Archaeol J* 110 (1953), 1-87.

KERMODE, P.C.M. 1907, *Manx Crosses*, London.

KILBRIDE-JONES, H.E. 1936, 'Scots Zoomorphic Penannular Brooches' *Proc. Soc. Antiq. Scot.* LXX (1935-6), 124-38.

_____ 1937, 'The Evolution of Penannular Brooches with Zoomorphic Terminals in Great Britain and Ireland', *Proc. Royal Irish Academy* 43 (1935-7),379-455.

_____ 1937b, 'A bronze hanging-bowl from Castle Tioram, Moidart: and a suggested Absolute Chronology for British Hanging Bowls', *Proc. Soc. Antiq. Scot.* LXXI (1936-7), 206-47.

_____ 1980, *Celtic Craftsmanship in Bronze*, London.

_____ 1980b, *Zoomorphic Penannular Brooches*, London, Soc Ant Res Rep XXXIX.

LAING, L. 1969, 'Timber Halls in Dark Age Britain: Some Problems', *Trans Dumfries & Galloway Nat. Hist. Antiq. Soc.* XLVI (1969), 110-27.

_____ 1969b, 'Medieval Settlement Archaeology in Scotland', *Scottish Archaeol Forum* 1 (1969), 69-79.

_____ 1969c, *Coins and Archaeology*, London.

_____ 1975, *The Archaeology of Late Celtic Britain and Ireland, c.* 400-1200, London.

_____ 1975b, *Settlement Types in Post-Roman Scotland*, Oxford (BAR).

_____ 1975c, 'People and Pins in Dark Age Scotland', *Trans Dumfries & Galloway Nat. Hist. & Antiq. Soc.* L. (1973), 53-71.

_____ 1975d, 'The Angles in Scotland and the Mote of Mark', *Trans Dumfries & Galloway Nat. Hist. & Antiq. Soc.* L. (1973), 37-52.

_____ 1975e, 'Picts, Saxons and Celtic metalwork', *Proc. Soc. Antiq. Scot.* 105 (1972-4), 189-99.

_____ 1976, 'Some Scottish and Irish Penannular Brooches', *Ulster J Archaeol* 39 (1976), 15-19.

_____ 1977, 'Segontium and the post-Roman occupation of Wales', in Laing, L. (ed.), *Studies in Celtic Survival*, Oxford (BAR 37), 57-60.

_____ 1979, *Celtic Britain*, London.

_____ 1988, 'The Romanization of Ireland in the Fifth Century', *Peritia* 4 (1985), 261-78.

_____ 1988b, 'Celts, Romans and the Great Divide', in Jones, R.F.J., Bloemers, J.H.F., Dyson, S.L. and Biddle, M. (eds.), *First Millennium Papers, Western Europe in the First Millennium AD*, Oxford, (BAR Internat Ser. 401), 303-7.

LAING, L. & LAING, J. 1984, *The Dark Ages of West Cheshire*, Chester (Council Monograph Series 6).

_____ 1985, 'The Date and Origin of the Pictish Symbols', *Proc. Soc. Antiq. Scot.* 114 (1984), 261-76.

_____ 1985b, 'Archaeological Notes on some Scottish Early Christian Sculptures', *Proc. Soc. Antiq. Scot.* 114 (1984), 277-87.

_____ 1988, 'Scottish and Irish metalwork and the 'conspiratio barbarica', *Proc. Soc. Antiq. Scot.* 116 (1986), 211-21.

LAMB, H.H. 1977, *Climate Present Past and Future*, Vol 2, London.

_____ 1981, 'Climate from 1,000 BC to 1,000 AD', in Jones, M. & Dimbleby, G. (eds.), *Environment of Man: the Iron Age to the Anglo-Saxon Period*, Oxford (BAR Brit Ser. 87), 53-65.

LANE, A. 1980, *The Excavations at Dunadd, Mid Argyll, 1980 An Interim Report*, Cardiff, Dept. of Archaeology.

_____ 1981, *The Excavations at Dunadd, Mid-Argyll, 1981 An Interim Report*, Cardiff, Dept. of Archaeology.

_____ 1984, 'Some Pictish problems at Dunadd', in Friell, J.G.P. & Watson, W.G. (eds.), *Pictish Studies*, Oxford, (BAR 125), 43-62.

LASKO, P. 1971, *The Kingdom of the Franks*, London.

LEASK, H.G. 1955, *Irish Churches and Monastic Buildings, Vol I — The First Phases and the Romanesque*, Dundalk.

LEEDS, E.T. 1911, 'Supplementary note on a gold bracteate and silver brooch from Market Overton,', *Archaeologia* 62 (1911), 491-6.

_____ 1912, 'The distribution of the Anglo-Saxon saucer brooch in relation to the battle of Bedford, AD 571', *Archaeologia* LXIII (1911), 159-202.

_____ 1945, 'The Distribution of the Angles and Saxons Archaeologically Considered', *Archaeologia* 91 (1945), 1-106.

_____ 1949, *Great Anglo-Saxon Square-headed Brooches*, Oxford.

LETHBRIDGE, T.C. & DAVID, H.E. 1930, 'Excavation of a house-site on Gateholm, Pembrokeshire', *Arch Cambrensis*, 85 (1930), 366-74.

LEWIS, J.M. 1982 'Recent finds of penannular brooches from Wales', *Medieval Archaeol 26* (1982), 151-4.

LINDSAY, J. 1860, *A View of the Coinage of Ireland*, Cork.

LINDQVIST, S. 1948, 'Sutton Hoo and Beowulf', *Antiquity* XXII (1948), 131-40.

LLOYD, J. 1946, 'Introduction' in Nash-Williams, V.E. (ed.), *A Hundred Years of Welsh Archaeology*, Cardiff, 11-23.

LLOYD-MORGAN, G. 1976, 'A note on some Celtic discs from Ireland and the province of Lower Germany', *Proc. Royal Irish Academy* 76 C (1976), 217-22.

LLOYD JONES, M. 1984, *Society and Settlement in Wales and the Marches, 500 BC to AD 1100*, Oxford (BAR 121).

LONGLEY, D. 1975, *Hanging bowls, penannular brooches and the Anglo-Saxon Connexion*, Oxford (BAR 22).

_____ 1982, 'The date of the Mote of Mark', *Antiquity* 56 (1982), 132-4.

LOSCO-BRADLEY, S. 1977, 'Catholme', *Current Archaeology* 59 (1977), 358-64.

LOWE, E.A. 1934, *Codices Latini Antiquiores*, Oxford.

LUCAS, A.T. 1975, 'Irish Ploughing Practices', *Tools & Tillage* 2 (1972-75), Pt 1, 52-62, Pt 2 67-83.

LUCAS, J. 1984, 'Tripontium, third interim report', *Trans Birmingham & Warwick-shire Archaeol Soc.*, 91 (1981), 25-54.

LYNCH, A. 1981, *Man and Environment in Sout-West Ireland 4,000 BC - AD 800*, Oxford, BAR 85.

LYNN, C.J. 1975, 'The medieval ring-fort — an archaeological chimaera?' *Irish Archaeol Research Forum*, 11 (i),(1975), 29-36.

_____ 1977, 'The Dating of Raths: an Orthodox View', *Ulster J Archaeol* 38 (1975), 45-7 .

LYNN, C.J. 1983, 'Some "Early" Ring-forts and Crannogs', *Journal of Irish Archaeology* 1 (1983), 47-58.

MACALISTER, R.A.S. 1928, *The Archaeology of Ireland*, London.

_____ 1945, *Corpus Inscriptionum Insularum Celticarum*, I, Dublin.

_____ 1946, 'Inscribed and Sculptured stones' in Nash-Williams, V.E. (ed.), *A Hundred Years of Welsh Archaeology*, Cardiff, 123-8.

MACALISTER, R.A.S. & PRAEGER, R.L., 'Report on the Excavation of Uisneach', *Proc. Royal Irish Academy* XXXVIII, (1928), 69-127.

McCARTHY, M. 1982, 'Thomas, Chadwick and post-Roman Carlisle', in Pearce, S. (ed.), *The early church in western Britain and Ireland*, Oxford (BAR 102), 241-56.

MacDONALD, A.D.S. 1981, 'Notes on monastic archaeology and the Annals of Ulster, 650-1050', in Ó Corráin, D. (ed.), *Irish Antiquity*, Cork, 304-319.

MacGREGOR, M. 1968, 'Massive armlets in the North British Iron Age', in Coles, J. & Simpson, D.D.A. (eds.), *Studies in Ancient Europe*, Leicester, 233-54.

_____ 1976, *Early Celtic Art in North Britain*, Leicester.

MACKIE, E. 1964, 'A dwelling site of the Earlier Iron Age at Balevullin, Tiree', *Proc. Soc. Antiq. Scot.* 96 (1962-3), 155-83.

_____ 1965 'The Origin and Development of the Broch and Wheelhouse building cultures of the Scottish iron age', *Proc. Prehist. Soc.* XXXI (1965), 93-146.

_____ 1965b, 'Brochs and the Hebridean Iron Age', *Antiquity* XXIX (1965), 266-78.

_____ 1970, 'The Scottish iron age: a review', *SHR* XLIX (1970), 1-32.

_____ 1971, 'Some Aspects of the Transition from the Bronze- to Iron-using Periods in Scotland', *Scottish Archaeol Forum* 3, Edinburgh, 55-72.

MACKRETH, D.F. 1978, 'Orton Hall Farm, Peterborough: a Roman and Saxon Settlement' in Todd, M. (ed.), *Studies in the Romano-British Villa*, Leicester, 209-28.

MacNEILL, E. 1933, 'The Pretannic Background in Britain and Ireland', *J. Roy. Soc. Antiq. Ireland* 63 (1933), 1-28.

McPEAKE, J. 1978, 'The End of the Affair', in Strickland, T.J. & Davey, P.J. (eds.), *New Evidence for Roman Chester*, Liverpool, 41-4.

MacPHAIL, R.I. 1981, 'Soil and Botanical Studies of the "Dark Earth"', in Jones, M. & Dimbleby, G. (eds.), *The Environment of Man*, Oxford (BAR 87), 309-31.

MacSWEENEY, P.M. 1913, *A Group of Nation Builders, O'Donovan, O'Curry, Petrie*, Dublin.

MAQUEEN, J. 1956, 'Kirk- and Kil- in Galloway Place-Names', *Archivum Linguisticum* (Glasgow), 8 (1956), 135-49.

MANN, J.C. 1974, 'The Northern Frontier of AD 369', *Glasgow Archaeol J.* 3 (1974), 34-42.

MARSDEN, P.V.R. 1975, 'Excavations on the Site of St Mildred's Church, Bread Street, London, 1973-1974', *Trans. London Middx Archaeol Soc.* 26 (1975), 171-208.

MASSON PHILLIPS, E.W. 1965, 'Excavation of a Romano-British site at Wells Farm, Stoke Gabriel, Devon', *Devon Archaeol Soc. Trans.* 23 (1966), 3-34.

MATTINGLY, H. & PEARCE, J.N E. 1937, 'The Coleraine Hoard', *Antiquity* XI (1937), 39-45.

MAXFIELD, V. 1981, *The Military Decorations of the Roman Army*, London.

MAXWELL, G.S. 1987, 'Settlements in Southern Pictland — a New Overview', in Small, A. (ed.), *The Picts, a New Look at Old Problems*, Dundee, 31-44.

MAYR-HARTING, H. 1972, *The Coming of Christianity to Anglo-Saxon England*, London.

MEANEY, A. 1964, *Gazetteer of Early Anglo-Saxon Burial Sites*, London.

_____ 1981, *Anglo-Saxon Amulets and Curing Stones*, Oxford (BAR 96).

MEANEY, A. & HAWKES, S.C. 1970, *The Anglo-Saxon Cemeteries at Winnal*, London (Soc. Medieval Archaeol Monograph 4).

MEGAW, J.V.S. & MEGAW, R. 1986, *Early Celtic Art in Britain and Ireland*, Aylesbury.

MELLOR, A.S. & GOODCHILD, R. 1940 'The Roman Villa at Atworth, Wilts', *Wiltshire Archaeol Mag* XLIX (1940), 46-95.

MILES, T. & MILES, H. 1973, 'Trethurgy', *Current Archaeology* 40, 142-7.

MILLER, M. 1976, 'Historicity and the pedigrees of the Northcountrymen', *Bulletin Board Celtic Studies* 26 (1972- 5), 255-80.

_____ 1978, 'Foundation-legend of Gwynedd in Latin texts', *Bulletin Board Celtic Studies* XXVII (1976-8), 515-32.

_____ 1981, 'Hiberni reversuri', *Proc. Soc. Antiq. Scot.* 110 (1978-80), 305-27.

MITCHELL, F. 1965, 'Littleton Bog, Tipperary: an Irish agricultural record', *J. Roy. Soc. Antiq. Ireland* 95 (1965), 12-32.

_____ 1976, *The Irish Landscape*, London.

MORRIS, J. 1965, 'Dark Age Dates' in Dobson, B. & Jarrett M. (eds.), *Britain and Rome*, Kendal, 145-85.

_____ 1973, *The Age of Arthur*, London.

MORRISON, A. 1977, 'Question of Celtic Survival or Continuity in Some Elements of Rural Settlement in the Scottish Highlands', in Laing, L. (ed.), *Studies in Celtic Survival*, Oxford (BAR 37), 67-76.

MORRISON, I. 1985, *Landscape with Lake Dwellings*, Edinburgh.

MUNRO, R. 1882, *Ancient Scottish Lake-Dwellings*, Edinburgh.

_____ 1899, 'Notes on a crannog at Hyndford, near Lanark . . .' *Proc. Soc. Antiq. Scot.* IX (1898-99), 373-87.

MURRAY, G. 1986, 'The declining Pictish Symbol — a reappraisal', *Proc. Soc. Antiq. Scot.* 116 (1986), 223-254.

MUSSON, C.R. 1976, 'Excavations at the Breiddin 1969-1973' in Harding, D.W. (ed.), *Hill-forts, later prehistoric earthworks in Britain and Ireland*, London, 293-302.

MYRES, J.N.L. 1956, 'Romano-Saxon Pottery', in Harden, D.B. (ed.), *Dark Age Britain*, London, 16-39.

_____ 1969, *Anglo-Saxon Pottery and the Settlement of England*, Oxford.

_____ 1986, *The English Settlements*, Oxford.

NASH-WILLIAMS, V.E. 1950, *Early Christian Monuments of Wales*, Cardiff.

NEELY, G.J.H. 1940, 'Excavations at Ronaldsway, Isle of Man', *Antiq J.* XX (1940), 72-86.

NICHOLSON, E.W. 1908, 'The dynasty of Cunedag', *Y Cymmrodor*, XXL (1908), 61-104.

NICOLAISEN, W. 1965, 'Scottish place-names: 24, Slew- and sliabh', *Scottish Studies* 9 (1965), 91-106.

___ 1976, *Scottish Place-names*, London.

NORDENFALK, K. 1947, 'Before the Book of Durrow', *Acta Archaeologica* 18 (1947), 141-74.

___ 1968, 'An Illustrated Diatessaron', *Art Bulletin* 50 (1968), 119-40.

___ 1987 '150 years of varying views on the Early Insular Gospel Books', in Ryan, M. (ed.), *Ireland and Insular Art, AD 500-1200*, Dublin, 1-6.

NORTH, J.J. 1963, *English Hammered Coinage*, I, London.

O'KELLY, M.J. 1958, 'Church Island, near Valencia, Co. Kerry', *Proc. Royal Irish Academy* LIX (1958), 57-136.

___ 1961, 'The Cork Horns, the Petrie Crown and the Bann Disc', *J Cork Hist Archaeol Soc.* 66 (1961), 1-12.

___ 1962, 'Two Ring-forts at Garryduff, Co. Cork', *Proc. Royal Irish Academy* 63 (1962), 17-125.

O'NEIL, B.H. St J. 1937, 'Excavations at Breiddin Hill Camp, Montgomeryshire, 1933-35', *Archaeologia Cambrensis* 92 (1937), 86-128.

___ 1943, 'Grim's Bank, Padworth, Berks', *Antiquity* XVII (1943), 188-195.

___ 1944 'The Silchester region in the 5th and 6th Centuries AD', *Antiquity* XVIII (1944), 113-122.

O'RAHILLY, 1946, *Early Irish History and Mythology*, Dublin.

Ó RIORDÁIN, S.P. 1940, 'The excavation of conjoined ringforts at Cush', *Proc. Royal Irish Academy* 45 (1940), 83-181.

___ 1942, 'The excavation of a large earthen ring-fort at Garranes, Co. Cork', *Proc. Royal Irish Academy* LXVII (1942), 77-150.

___ 1947, 'Roman material in Ireland', *Proc Royal Irish Academy* 51 (1947), 35-82.

___ 1949, 'Lough Gur excavations: Carraig Aille and the "Spectacles"', *Proc Royal Irish Academy* LII (1949), 39-110.

___ 1968, *Tara, the Monuments on the Hill*, Dundalk.

Ó RÍORDÁIN, S.P. & RYNNE, E. 1961, 'A Settlement in the Sandhills at Dooey, Co. Donegal', *J. Roy. Soc. Antiq. Ireland* 91 (1961), 58-64.

OZANNE, A. 1963, 'The Peak Dwellers', *Medieval Archaeol* VI-VII (1962-3), 15-52.

PADEL, O. 1981, 'Tintagel — an alternative view', in Thomas, A.C. (ed.), *A provisional list of imported pottery in post-Roman western Britain and Ireland*, Redruth, 28-9.

PAINTER, K.S. 1970, 'A Late Roman Silver Ingot from Kent', *Antiq J.* 52 (1972), 84-92.

___ 1977, *The Water Newton Early Christian Silver*, London.

PALMER, L. 1955, *Achaeans and Indo-Europeans*, London.

PAULSEN, P. 1953, 'Koptische und irische Kunst und ihre Aussbrahlungen auf altgermanische Kulturen', *Tribus (Jahrbuch des Linden-Museums)*, Stuttgart, (1952-3), 149-87.

PEACOCK, D. 1977, 'Roman Amphorae: Typology, Fabric and Origins' in Methodes Classiques et Methodes Formelles dans l'etude des Amphores', *Collection de l'Ecole de Rome* 32, Rome, 261-78.

___ 1977b, 'Late Roman amphorae from Chalk, near Gravesend, Kent' in Dore, J. & Greene, K. (eds.), *Roman Pottery Studies in Britain and Beyond*, Oxford (BAR Supp Ser 30), 295-300.

PEACOCK, D. & THOMAS, C. 1967 'Class E Imported post-Roman Pottery; a suggested origin', *Cornish Archaeol* 6 (1967), 35-56.

PEARCE, S.M. 1978 *The Kingdom of Dumnonia*, Padstow.

PENDER, S. 1947, 'Two unpublished versions of the Expulsion of the Dessi' in Pender, S. (ed.), *Feilscribhinn Torna*, Cork, 209-17.

PHILIPS, C.W. 1934 'The excavation of a hut-group at Pant-y-Saer in the parish of Llanfair-Mathafarn-Eithaf, Anglesey', *Arch Cambrensis* 89 (1934), 1-36.

PIGGOTT, C.M. 1950, 'The excavations at Hownam Rings, Roxburghshire, 1948', *Proc. Soc. Antiq. Scot.* 82 (1947-8), 193-224.

_____ 1954 ,'Milton Loch Crannog I. A native house of the 2nd century AD in Kircudbrightshire', *Proc. Soc. Antiq. Scot.* 87 (1952-3), 134-52.

_____ 1959 'The carnyx in Early Iron Age Britain', *Antiq J.* XXXIX (1959), 19-32.

_____ 1965, *Ancient Europe*, Edinburgh.

_____ 1976, *Ruins in a Landscape*, Edinburgh.

PRETTY, K. 1975, Note on spiral headed pins in Cunliffe, B., *Excavations at Portchester Castle, II*, London, 211-14.

PROUDFOOT, V.B. 1954, 'Excavations at Cathedral Hill, Downpatrick, Co. Down, 1953', *Ulster J Archaeol*, 17 (1954), 97-102.

_____ 1956 'Excavations at the Cathedral Hill, Downpatrick, Co. Down: Preliminary note on Excavations in 1954', *Ulster J Archaeol* 19 (1956), 57-72.

_____ 1970, 'Irish raths and cashels: some notes on Chronology, Origins and Survivals', *Ulster J Archaeol* 33 (1970), 37-48.

_____ 1977, 'Economy and Settlement in Rural Ireland', in Laing, L. (ed.), *Studies in Celtic Survival*, Oxford (BAR Brit Ser. 37), 83-106.

RADFORD, C.A.R. 1935, 'Tintagel: the Castle and Celtic Monastery', *Antiq J* 15 (1935), 401-19.

_____ 1951, 'Report on the Excavations at Castle Dore', *J Roy. Inst. Cornwall*, ns 1, appendix.

_____ 1956, 'Imported Pottery found at Tintagel, Cornwall' in Harden, D.B. (ed.), *Dark Age Britain*, London, 59-70.

_____ 1975, *The Inscriptions of Dumnonia*, Truro.

RAFTERY, B. 1969, 'Freestone Hill, Co. Kilkenny: an Iron Age Hillfort and Bronze Age Cairn', *Proc. Royal Irish Academy* 68, (1969), 1-108.

_____ 1970, 'A Decorated Strap-end from Rathgall, Co. Wicklow', *J. Roy. Soc. Antiq. Ireland* 100 (1970), 200-11.

_____ 1972, 'Irish Hillforts', in Thomas, C. (ed.), *The Iron Age in the Irish Sea Province*, London, CBA Res Rep 9, 37-58.

_____ 1970, 'The Rathgall Hillfort, County Wicklow', *Antiquity* XLIV (1970), 51-4.

_____ 1976, 'Rathgall and Irish Hillfort Problems', Chapter 16 of Harding, D.W. (ed.), *Hillforts*, London, 339-57.

_____ 1982, 'Knobbed spearbutts of the Irish iron age' in Scott, B.G. (ed.), *Studies on Early Ireland*, Belfast, 75-92.

_____ 1984, *La Tène in Ireland*, Marburg.

_____ 1987, 'La Tène art in Ireland', in Ryan, M. (ed.), *Ireland and Insular Art, AD 500-1200*, Dublin, 12-18.

RAFTERY, J. 1941, 'A bronze zoomorphic brooch from Toomullin, Co. Clare', *J Roy. Soc. Antiq. Ireland* LXXI (1941), 56-60.

_____ 1944, 'The Turoe Stone and the Rath of Feerwore', *J Roy. Soc. Antiq. Ireland* 74 (1944), 23-52.

_____ 1951, *Prehistoric Ireland*, London.

_____ 1960, 'A hoard of the Early Iron Age', *J Roy. Soc. Antiq. Ireland* 90 (1960), 2-5.

_____ 1965, 'Ex oriente . . .' *J Roy. Soc. Antiq. Ireland* 95 (1965), 193-204.

_____ 1970 'Iron Age and Irish Sea: Problems for research', in Thomas, A. C.(ed.), *The Iron Age in the Irish Sea Province*, London, CBA Res Rep. 9, 1-10.

_____ 1970b, 'Bronze Mount from Feltrim Hill, Co. Dublin', *J Roy. Soc. Antiq. Ireland*, 100 (1970), 175-9.

_____ 1981, 'Concerning Chronology', in Ó Corráin, D., *Irish Antiquity*, Cork, 82-90.

RAHTZ, P.A. 1971 'Castle Dore, a reappraisal of the post-Roman structures', *Cornish Archaeol* 10 (1971), 49-54.

RAHTZ, P.A. & WATTS, L. 1979, 'The end of Roman temples in the west of Britain', in Casey, P. (ed.), *The End of Roman Britain*, Oxford (BAR 71), 183-201.

RALSTON, I. 1982, 'A timber hall at Balbridie Farm', *Aberdeen Univ Rev*, no. 168, (1982), 238-49.

RALSTON, I. & INGLIS, J. 1985, *Foul Hordes: the Picts in the North-East and their Background*, Aberdeen.

REECE, R. 1973, 'Recent work on Iona', *Scottish Archaeol Forum* 5 (1973), 36-46.

_____ 1980, 'Town and Country: the end of Roman Britain', *World Archaeol* 12 (1980), 77-92.

REES, S.I. 1979, *Agricultural Implements in Prehistoric and Roman Britain*, Oxford (BAR 69).

RENFREW, C. 1987, *Archaeology and Language: The Puzzle of Indo-European Origins*, London.

REYNOLDS, N.M. 1980, 'Dark Age Timber Halls and the Background to Excavation at Balbridie', *Scottish Archaeol Forum* 10 (1980), 41-60.

RICHARDS, M. 1960, 'The Irish Settlements in South-West Wales', *J Roy. Soc. Antiq. Ireland* XC (1960), 133-62.

_____ 1962, 'Welsh Meidiír, Moydir, Irish Bothar, "Lane, Road"', *Lochlann* 2 (1962), 128-34.

RICHMOND, I.A. 1932, 'Irish Analogies for the Romano-British Barn Dwelling', *Journal of Roman Studies* XXII (1932), 96-106.

_____ 1965, 'Roman Wales', in Daniel, G. & Foster, I.Ll. (eds.), *Prehistoric and Early Wales*, London, 151-76.

RIGOIR, J. 1968, 'Les sigillées paléochrétiennes grises et orangees', *Gallia* 26 (1968), 177-244.

RILEY, J.A 1975, 'Pottery from the 1st session of excavation in the Caesarea Hippodrome', *Bulletin American School Oriental Research*, 218 (1975).

RITCHIE, A. 1987, 'The Picto-Scottish Interface in material culture' in Small, A. (ed.), *The Picts: A New Look at Old Problems*, Dundee, 59-67.

RITCHIE, G. & RITCHIE, A. 1981, *Scotland: an Archaeology and Early History*, London.

RIVET, A.L.F. 1969, *The Roman Villa in Britain*, London.

RIVET, A.L.F & SMITH, C. 1979, *The Place-names of Roman Britain*, London.

ROBERTS, W.I. 1982, *Romano-Saxon Pottery*, Oxford (BAR 106).

ROBERTSON, A.S. 1970, 'Roman Finds from Non-Roman sites in Scotland', *Britannia* 1 (1970), 198-226.

_____ 1975, *Birrens (Blatobulgium)*, Edinburgh.

RODWELL, W. & RODWELL, K. 1973, 'Excavations at Rivenhall Church, Essex: an Interim Report', *Antiq J* 53 (1973), 219-31.

ROSTOVTZEFF, M.I, BROWN, F.E. & WELLES, C.B. 1939, *The Excavations at Dura Europos 1933-35*, New Haven.

ROTH, U. 1973, 'Die Ornamentik der Langobarden in Italien', *Antiquitas Reihe* 3 (1973), 15.

_____ 1987, 'Early Insular manuscripts: Ornament and Archaeology, with sepcial reference to the dating of the Book of Durrow', in Ryan, M. (ed.), *Ireland and Insular Art, AD 500-1200*, Dublin, 23-29.

RYAN, M. 1973, 'Native Pottery in Early Historic Ireland', *Proc. Royal Irish Academy* 73 (1973),619-45.

RYAN, M. (ed.), 1983, *Treasures of Ireland*, Dublin.

RYAN, M. 1987, 'Some aspects of Sequence and Style in the metalwork of eighth- and ninth-century Ireland', in Ryan, M. (ed.), *Ireland and Insular Art AD 500-1200*, Dublin, 66-74.

RYNNE, E. 1961, 'The Introduction of La Tène into Ireland', in *Bericht uber swn V Internationalen Kongress für Vor- und Frügeschichte*, Hamburg 1958, 705-709.

_____ 1965, 'A bronze ring-brooch from Luce Sands, Wigtowns, its affinities and significance', *Trans. Dumfries & Galloway Nat. Hist. & Antiq. Soc.* XLII (1965), 99-113.

_____ 1964, 'The Coiled bronze armlet from Ballymahon, Co. Meath', *J Roy. Soc. Antiq. Ireland* 94 (1964), 69-72.

_____ 1976 'The La Tène and Roman Finds from Lambay, Co Dublin: a re-assessment', *Proc. Royal Irish Academy* 76C (1976), 231-244.

_____ 1987 'The Date of the Ardagh Chalice', in Ryan, M. (ed.), *Ireland and Insular Art AD 500-1200*, Dublin, 85-89.

SALWAY, P. 1981, *Roman Britain*, Oxford.

SAUNDERS, C. 1972, 'The Excavation at Grambla, Wendron, 1972: Interim Report', *Cornish Archaeology* 11 (1972), 50-2.

SAVORY, H.N. 1960, 'Excavations at Dinas Emrys, Beddgelert, Caernarvonshire, 1954-6', *Archaeol Cambrensis*, 109 (1960), 13-77.

_____ 1971, *Excavations at Dinorben 1965-9*, Cardiff.

SCULL, C. 1985, 'Further evidence from East Anglia for enamelling on early Anglo-Saxon metalwork', in Hawkes, S.C., Brown, D & Campbell, J. (eds) *Anglo-Saxon Studies* 4 (1985), 117-24.

SELKIRK, A. 1971, 'Isle of Man (IV) The Archaeologists', *Current Archaeology* 27 (July 1971), 98-9.

_____ 1988, 'Dorchester', *Current Archaeology* 112 (1988), 169-73.

_____ 1988b, 'Round Up: The Summer of '88', *Current Archaeology* 112 (1988), 156-8.

_____ 1981, 'Lydney Park', *Current Archaeology* 76 (1981), 149.

SELKIRK, A. & WATERMAN, D. 1970, 'Navan Fort' *Current Archaeology* 22 (Sept 1970), 304-8.

SHEPHERD, I.G. & SHEPHERD, A.N. 1980, 'An incised Pictish figure and a new symbol stone from Barflat, Rhynie, Gordon District', *Proc. Soc. Antiq. Scot.* 109 (1977-8), 211-22.

SILVESTER, R.J. 1980, 'Forts and Farms: the Iron Age in Devon', in *Archaeology of the Devon Landscape*, Exeter, 63-70.

SIMPSON, G. 1964, *Britons and the Roman Army*, London.

SMALL, A. 1969, 'Burghead', *Scottish Archaeol Forum*, 1, Edinburgh, 61-8.

SMITH, C.A. 1978, 'Late Prehistoric and Romano-British Enclosed Homesteads in North-West Wales', *Archaeologia Cambrensis* 126 (1977), 38-52 .

SMITH, J. 1919, 'Excavation of the forts of Castlehill, Aitnock and Coalhill, Ayrs', *Proc. Soc. Antiq. Scot.* LIII (1918-19), 137-52.

SMITH, R.A. 1909, 'Note on hanging bowls', *Proc. Soc. Antiq.* Lond 2nd Ser. 22 (1909), 67-86.

_____ 1913, 'Irish brooches through five centuries', *Archaeologia* LXV (1913-14), 223-50.

SMYTH, A.P. 1982, *Celtic Leinster*, Dublin.

_____ 1984, *Warlords and Holy Men*, London.

SPEAKE, G. 1980, *Anglo-Saxon Animal Art*, Oxford.

STANFORD, S C. 1974, *Croft Ambrey*, Hereford.

_____ 1974b, 'Native and Roman in the Central Welsh Borderland', in Birley, E., Dobson, B. & Jarrett, M. (eds), *Roman Frontier Studies*, 1969, Cardiff, 44-60.

STENBERGER, M. 1966, 'A ringfort at Raheennamadra, Knocklong, Co. Limerick', *Proc. Royal Irish Academy* 65, (1966), 37-54.

STEVENSON, R.B.K. 1955, 'Pins and the Chronology of Brochs', *Proc. Prehist Soc.* XXI (1955), 282-294.

_____ 1955b, 'Pictish Art', in Wainwright, F.T., *Problem of the Picts*, London, 97-128.

_____ 1956, 'Pictish Chain, Roman silver and Bauxite Beads', *Proc. Soc. Antiq. Scot.* LXXXVIII (1954-6), 228-9.

_____ 1956b, 'The chronology and relationship of some Irish and Scottish crosses', *J .Roy. Soc. Antiq. Ireland* 86 (1956), 84-96.

_____ 1961, 'The Inchyra Stone and other unpublished Early Christian monuments', *Proc. Soc. Antiq. Scot.* XCII (1958-9), 33-55.

_____ 1974, 'The Hunterston brooch and its significance', *Medieval Archaeol* XVIII (1974), 16-42.

_____ 1976 'The earlier metalwork of Pictland', in Megaw, J.V.S. (ed.), *To Illustrate the Monuments*, London, 246-51.

_____ 1981 'The Museum, its Beginnings and its Development', in Bell, A.S. (ed.), *The Scottish Antiquarian Tradition*, Edinburgh, Part I, 131-85; Part II, 142-211

STOKES, W. 1868, *The Life and Labours in Art and Archaeology of George Petrie*, London.

SUTHERLAND, C.H.V. 1948, *Anglo-Saxon Gold Coinage*, Oxford.

TAYLOR, C.C. 1983, *Village and Farmstead*, London.

THOMAS, C. 1956, 'Evidence for post-Roman occupation of Chun Castle, Cornwall', *Antiq J.* 36 (1956), 75-8.

_____ 1958, *Gwithian: Ten Years' Digging*, Truro.

_____ 1959, 'Imported Pottery in Dark-Age Western Britain', *Medieval Archaeol* 3 (1959), 89-111.

_____ 1961, 'Animal art of the Scottish iron age', *Archaeol J* 118 (1961), 14-64.

_____ 1963, 'The Interpretation of the Pictish Symbols', *Archaeol J* 120 (1963), 14-64.

_____ 1966, 'The Character and Origins of Roman Dumnonia', in Thomas, C. (ed.), *Rural Settlement in Roman Britain*, London (CBA Res Rep 7), 74-98.

_____ 1966b, 'Ardwall Isle: the Excavation of an Early Christian Site of Irish Type 1964-5', *Trans Dumfries & Galloway Nat. Hist. and Antiq. Soc.* XLIII (1966), 84-116.

_____ 1967, 'An Early Christian Cemetery and Chapel of Ardwall Isle, Kirkcudbright', *Medieval Archaeol* 11 (1967), 177-83.

_____ 1968, 'Grass-marked pottery in Cornwall', in Coles, J. & Simpson, D. (eds.), *Studies in Ancient Europe*, Edinburgh, 311-32.

_____ 1968b, 'The Evidence from North Britain', in Barley, M.W. & Hanson, R.P.C. (eds.), *Christianity in Britain, 300- 700*, Leicester, 93-122.

____ 1970, 'Souterrains in the Irish Sea Province: a note', in Thomas, C. (ed.), *The Iron Age in the Irish Sea Province*, London, CBA Res Rep.9, 75-8.

____ 1972, *The Early Christian Archaeology of North Britain*, Oxford.

____ 1972b, 'The Irish Settlements in Post-Roman Western Britain: A Survey of the Evidence', *Journal Royal Institution of Cornwall*, ns VI (1972), 251-74.

____ 1973, 'Irish Colonists in South-West Britain', *World Archaeol* 5 (1973), 5-12.

____ 1976 'The end of the Roman South-West', in Branigan, K. & Fowler, P. (eds.), *The Roman West Country*, Newton Abbot, 198-213.

____ 1979 'St Patrick and Fifth Century Britain: an historical model explored', in Casey, P.J. (ed.), *The End of Roman Britain*, Oxford (BAR Br Ser 71), 81-101.

____ 1981, *A Provisional List of Imported Pottery in Post Roman Western Britain and Ireland*, Redruth.

____ 1981b, *Christianity in Roman Britain to AD 500*, London.

____ 1982, 'East and West: Tintagel, Mediterranean imports and the Early Insular Church', in Pearce, S. (ed.), *The early Church in western Britain and Ireland*, Oxford (BAR 102), 17-34.

____ 1987, 'The earliest Christian art in Ireland and Britain', in Ryan, M. (ed.), *Ireland and Insular Art, AD 500-1200*, Dublin, 7-11.

THOMPSON, E.A. 1968, 'Britonia', in Barley, M. & Hanson, R.P.C., *Christianity in Britain 300-700*, Leicester, 201-6.

TODD, M. 1978, 'Villas and Romano-British Society', in Todd, M. (ed.), *Studies in the Romano-British Villa*, Leicester, 197-208.

____ 1987, 'The Falkirk Hoard of denarii: trade or subsidy?' *Proc. Soc. Antiq. Scot.* 115 (1985), 229-32.

WACHER, J. 1974 *The Towns of Roman Britain*, London.

____ 1976 'Late Roman Developments' in McWhirr, A. (ed.), *Studies in the History of Cirencester*, Oxford, (BAR 30), 15-19.

WAILES, B. 1982, 'The Irish "Royal Sites" in History and Archaeology', *Cambridge Medieval Celtic Studies* 3 (1982), 1-23.

WAINWRIGHT, F.T. 1963, *The Souterrains of Southern Pictland*, London.

WAINWRIGHT, G J. 1967, *Coygan Camp*, Cardiff.

____ 1971, 'The Excavation of a fortified settlement at Walesland Rath, Pembrokeshire', *Britannia* 2 (1971), 48-108.

WALTERS, H.B. 1921, *Catalogue of the Silver Plate* (Greek, Etruscan, Roman) in the British Museum, London.

WARNER, R.B. 1976, 'Some observations on the context and importation of exotic material in Ireland, from the first century BC to the second century AD', *Proc. Royal Irish Academy* 76C (1976), 267-292.

____ 1979, 'The Clogher Yellow Layer', *Medieval Ceramics* 3 (1979), 37-40.

____ 1983, 'Ireland, Ulster and Scotland in the earlier Iron Age', in O'Connor, A. and Clarke, D. (eds.), *From the Stone Age to the Forty-Five*, Edinburgh, 161-87.

____ 1987, 'Ireland and the Origins of Excutcheon Art', in Ryan, M. (ed.), *Ireland and Insular Art, AD 500-1200*, Dublin, 19-22.

____ 1986, 'The Date of the Start of Lagore', *Journal of Irish Archaeology* III (1985-6), 75-7.

WATKIN, T. 1981, 'Excavation of an Iron Age open settlement at Dalladies, Kinkardineshire', *Proc. Soc. Antiq. Scot.* 110 (1978-80), 122-64.

____ 1981b, 'Excavation of a settlement and souterrain at Newmill, near Bankfoot, Perthshire', *Proc. Soc. Antiq. Scot.* 110 (1978-80), 165-208.

____ 1984, 'Where were the Picts?' in Friell, J.G.P. & Watson, W.G. (eds.), *Pictish studies: Settlement, Burial and Art in Dark Age Northern Britain*, Oxford (BAR 125), 63-86.

WEBSTER, G. 1958 *The Roman Site at Wall*, Staffordshire, London, MPBW.

_____ 1969, 'The Future of Villa Studies', in Rivet, A.L.F. (ed.), *The Roman Villa in Britain*, London, 217-49.

WELCH, M.G. 1971 'Late Romans and Saxons in Sussex', *Britannia* 2 (1971), 232-7.

_____ 1983, *Early Anglo-Saxon Sussex*, Oxford (BAR 112).

WELLER, S.G.P., WESTLEY, B & MYRES, J.N.L. 1974, 'A late fourth-century cremation from Billericay, Essex', *Antiq J.* 54 (1974), 282-5.

WERNER, J. 1964, 'Frankish royal tombs in the cathedrals of Cologne and St Denis', *Antiquity* XXXVIII (1964),.

WEST, S.E. 1985, *West Stow The Anglo-Saxon Village*, Ipswich (East Anglian Archaeology 24).

WHEELER, R.E.M. 1935, 'The Topography of Roman London', *Antiquity* VIII (1935), 290-302.

_____ 1935b, *London and the Saxons*, London Mus Cat.

_____ 1954, *The Stanwick Fortifications*, London, Soc Ant Res Rep No 17.

_____ 1958, *Still Digging*, London (paperback ed).

WHEELER, R.E.M. & WHEELER, T.V. 1932, *Report on the Excavation of the Prehistoric, Roman and Post-Roman site of Lyndey Park, Gloucestershire*, London, Soc Ant Res. Rep. IX.

_____ 1936, *Verulamium, a Belgic and two Roman Cities*, London, Soc Ant Res. Rep. XI.

WHITE, R.B. 1973, 'Aberffraw', *Archaeology in Wales*, 13 (1973), 36-7.

_____ 1977, 'Cefn Graeanog', in Goodburn, R (ed.), 'Roman Britain in 1977', *Britannia* 9 (1977), 406-7.

_____ 1980, 'Excavations at Aberffraw, Anglesey, 1973 and 1974', *Bulletin Board Celtic Studies* 28 (1978-80), 319-42.

WHITE, R.H. 1988, *Roman and Celtic Objects from Anglo-Saxon Graves*, Oxford, (BAR 191).

_____ forthcoming, 'The Hanging bowl from Badleybridge (Needham Market), Suffolk: a reappraisal', *Anglo-Saxon Studies*.

WHITFIELD, N. 1987, 'Motifs and techniques of Celtic filigree: are they original?' in Ryan, M. (ed.), *Ireland and Insular Art, AD 500-1200*, Dublin, 75-84.

WHITTING, P.D. 1961, 'The Byzantine empire and the coinage of the Anglo-Saxons', in Dolley, M. (ed.), *Anglo-Saxon Coins*, London (1961), 23-38.

WHITTOCK, M.J. 1986, *The Origins of England, 410-600*, London.

WILLIAMS, J.E.C. 1966, 'Mallaen, Dinllaen, Lleyn', *Bulletin Board Celtic Studies* 22, 1 (1966), 37-41.

WILSON, D.M. 1968, 'An Early Christian Cemetery at Ancaster', in Barley, M.W. & Hanson, R.P.C. (eds.), *Christianity in Britain 300-700*, Leicester, 197-200.

_____ 1984, *Anglo-Saxon Art*, London.

WILSON, D., SMALL, A. & THOMAS, A.C. 1973, *St Ninian's Isle and its Treasure*, Aberdeen.

WOOD-MARTIN, 1886, *Lake Dwellings of Ireland*, Dublin.

_____ 1895, *Pagan Ireland*, London.

WRIGHT, M.D. 1985, 'Excavations at Peel Castle, 1947', *Isle of Man. Nat. Hist. and Antiq. Soc.* 9, no. 1 (April 1980-March 1982), 21-57.

YOUNG, A. 1956, 'Excavations at Dun Cuier, Isle of Barra', *Proc. Soc. Antiq. Scot.* 89 (1955-6), 290-328

INDEX